TAKE MY WORD FOR IT

Self-Portrait: oil on hardboard

RALPH THOMPSON

TAKE MY WORD FOR IT

A JAMAICAN MEMOIR

PEEPAL TREE

First published in Great Britain in 2016
Peepal Tree Press Ltd
17 King's Avenue
Leeds LS6 1QS
England

ISBN13:9781845233181

Supported using public funding by
ARTS COUNCIL
ENGLAND

CONTENTS

Foreword   7

Chapter One: Roots   9

Chapter Two: St George's College   31

Chapter Three: Fordham University   41

Chapter Four: Hollywood   50

Chapter Five: Law School   53

Chapter Six: Law and the Japanese Adventure   59

Chapter Seven: The Pilocarpine Case   68

Chapter Eight: Flight to Arabia   73

Chapter Nine: A Close Escape   77

Chapter Ten: Love and Marriage   82

Chapter Eleven: Abe Issa   88

Chapter Twelve: Investment Consortium   96

Chapter Thirteen: Wherry Wharf   105

Chapter Fourteen: Selling Wherry Wharf   112

Chapter Fifteen: Family   120

Chapter Sixteen: San San   124

Chapter Seventeen: Jamaica's First Contested Takeover   128

Chapter Eighteen: Put on Trial   134

Chapter Nineteen: Departure   137

Chapter Twenty: Starting Over in America   146

Chapter Twenty-one: Business Adventures in Florida   153

Chapter Twenty-two: Agro 21   159

Chapter Twenty-three: Financial Crisis   166

Chapter Twenty-four: Seprod   175

Chapter Twenty-five: Selling Brands   180

Chapter Twenty-six: Goodbye Seprod   183

Chapter Twenty-seven: Education in Jamaica   186

Chapter Twenty-eight: The Consolations of Poetry   191

Chapter Twenty-nine: Walcott   200

Chapter Thirty: A Reading with the Laureates   207

Chapter Thirty-one: The Weaning and the Winnowing   213

ILLUSTRATIONS

Self-Portrait: frontispiece

The Young Poet   30

Audrey, my mother & me   37

Laurence Thompson, Ralph's Father   48

Lieutenant Ralph Thompson in the US Airforce   61

Ermyn Lyons   83

The Lyons Family   83

Pan-Jamaican – Wherry Wharf Merger   118

Pavilion: San San   126

San San Beach   126

Lovers   127

Port Antonio   127

John Hearne   140

National Award   165

Kingston North   172

The Thompson Clan   185

Ralph as Educationist: *The Gleaner* Cartoon   188

Cycling   195

Derek Walcott and Ralph Thompson on Reduit Beach   201

FOREWORD

We who write poems know
How grudgingly our true emotions flow,
Insisting that the stress of line and living
Leave little time for ritual thanksgiving

I composed those words a long time ago in celebration of my eldest daughter's birthday, little knowing they would return to confront me, as guide and conscience, in trying to write this memoir. Coming from an eccentric family as I did, tainted by the times with racial prejudices and false pride, the "stress of line and living" has been relatively easy to record. But how to deal with "true emotions" and "ritual thanksgivings"?

Any venture into autobiography runs the danger of self-laceration or vaingloriousness – two extremes I have tried to avoid. Looking back over my career as a Jamaican businessman and "company doctor", I calculate that it has probably absorbed most of my time and energy, followed closely by Public Service. But in the context of Jamaica as an emerging modern economy I have felt obliged to record some of the business adventures in which I played a critical part.

However in terms of satisfaction it has been painting and poetry that have been the ordering passions of my life. The ubiquitous camera has made realistic painting virtually passé, especially landscapes and portraiture so the challenge for me from the beginning was how to stamp my personality on the scene or sitter in front of me. This bent me under the influence of the Impressionists, especially Matisse who wisely proclaimed *L'exactitude n'est pas la verité* (exactitude is not truth)" . This could also be a fitting personal motto.

I am sure that my limping prose has not been able to convey my abiding love for the island of Jamaica and its warm and friendly people. Yes, we have crime but we also have the tradition of "share pot", "Saturday soup", music, dance and laughter, symbols of a caritas that somehow seems able to overcome all tribulations.

The obligation of "ritual thanksgivings" includes Jeremy Poynting of Peepal Tree Press, which has published five collections of my poems. My gratitude also to dear friends and fellow poets, Eddie Baugh and Mervyn Morris, who have been kind enough to read the manuscript and make many invaluable suggestions.

Over the years that I have worked on the memoir, my wife Doreen has been patient in accepting my solitary sojourns in the study where the research filing cabinets are stored. She has been my proof reader, my editor and my conscience.

To my children and Doreen, my wife of sixty-two years, I dedicate this memoir.

CHAPTER ONE

ROOTS

My mother, Stephanie (God rest her soul), was one of three daughters in a family of seven, the offspring of Ralph Henry Isaacs, Managing Commissioner of the Kingston and St. Andrew Corporation, and his wife Hannah, née Fielding. The Isaacs family passed as white Jamaicans at a time when colour was the most important factor in determining identity and social status. To a large extent, it still is. Nor, despite the name, was the Isaacs tribe Jewish in faith; in fact it was almost fanatically Roman Catholic, closely allied with the American Jesuit priests who ran the church in Jamaica and especially with Bishop Emmet who everyone in the family referred to as "Uncle Bishop".

Grandfather Isaacs, after whom I am named, had an illustrious career at the Kingston and St. Andrew Corporation, a colonial administrative centre of great importance to the efficient functioning of local government. He rose through the ranks and although his remuneration was relatively small the perquisites of office allowed the family to live in comparative splendour. He was entitled to rent free residence at Cavaliers Great House which came with a battery of servants including cooks, gardeners, coachmen and parlour maids. He was also entitled to generous travel, entertainment and education allowances. Grandfather was well-read and possessed a phenomenal memory. When the earthquake and subsequent fire of 1907 destroyed the accounts receivable ledger of the Corporation, he was able to reconstitute 1400 accounts from memory and collected all outstanding moneys due. Grandfather Ralph was an avid reader and wrote learned articles, under the sobriquet "Julian", for a section of *The Gleaner* printed on pink stock and dubbed the "pink pages".

About education, Grandpa Ralph was a fanatic. Influenced by the American Jesuits who ran St. George's College, he decided on an American education for his children, a choice considered gauche by other prominent families of the time, who automatically sent their bright sons to Oxford or Cambridge in England. Daughters were seldom educated beyond high school. Three of my uncles, Vincent, Tony and Michael, attended Fordham University in New York where they all excelled academically and obtained their baccalaureate degrees *cum laude*. Vincent went on to Oxford where he read law at Exeter College.

It may be apocryphal, but one account has it that Vincent, while at Oxford, applied for a commission in the British army during World War I but was turned down because he was a Jew and Jews were not allowed to serve in the officer ranks. He pleaded in vain that the family had been Catholic for generations, but it was only when the army was running desperately short of officer candidates that, with typical British compromise, a Jewish regiment was formed in which he was offered a commission as a second lieutenant. There is a family photograph of him in uniform wearing a Sam Brown belt and boasting a swagger stick. Three days before the Armistice, leading his men in battle at Ypres, he was killed by German machine gun fire. He is buried in France but his field binoculars were sent back to Jamaica by the War Office in a small wooden casket.

It was into this tragic, mysterious, secretive family that my sister Audrey and I were born in far away Poughkeepsie, New York; me on April 19, 1928 and Audrey on October 13, 1930. Mother and her younger sister, Antoinette, were both attractive young ladies and suitable suitors being scarce in Jamaica, Grandfather Ralph, fearing that they might fall in love with men of colour, sent them to school in America. Mother did succeed in keeping pure the racial stream by marrying a handsome white man who had served honourably in World War I and now worked as a conductor in the New York Central railroad system.

There were ironies aplenty. Mother was a chronic asthmatic and it was only her iron will that saw her through the ordeal of giving birth to two healthy children. She, who was brought up with servants and hardly knew how to boil water, was now obliged, while taking care of her family, to do all the cooking, cleaning and shopping under the watchful eye of a husband who loved her, but whose social status took it for granted that these chores were women's work. The marriage faltered and mother felt obliged to return with her children to the class comforts of Jamaica.

Exacerbated by Catholic guilt at not being able to hold the marriage together, Mother's asthma reached crisis proportions. Hardly a day passed without her having an attack or two, mostly at night. For routine attacks she resorted to Kellogg's Asthma Remedy imported from India in an orange box which contained a mixture of tiny granules and assorted dried twigs and leaves. This trash was sprinkled into a saucer, lit with a match and covered with the shade of a Home Sweet Home lamp which soon filled up with aromatic smoke. Bent over this miniature chimney, mother's asthmatic gasps facilitated the inhaling of lungs full of whatever fumes the concoction was giving off. After about ten minutes the asthma attack would subside, whether as a result of the healing properties of the potion or because it had run its natural course, no one could tell.

Upon her return to Jamaica from America my mother was so ill it was impossible for her to care for two children. Under the auspices of Bishop Emmet, a new order of local nuns had been formed and they agreed to take me in as a boarder for a year. It was a standing joke that I spent the first few nights at the convent sleeping in the Mother Superior's bed. The Blue Sisters, as they were affectionately known, showered me with love. My favourite was Sister Rita with whom I remained in love until her peaceful death at ninety-one.

In 1922, five years after Vincent's death, Grandpa Ralph, fifty-six years old, distraught by the tragic loss of a life so full of promise, suddenly died of a heart attack and the family was plunged almost immediately into marginal poverty. But Ralph Isaacs was generously honoured in death. His funeral at the Cathedral was a grand affair reported in detail in *The Gleaner* that featured an editorial on his public service. It highlighted his conception and implementation of the Ferry irrigation scheme for Kingston and the construction of the Mona reservoir, the financing for which he was able to marshal with interest at four percent and with a repayment period of forty years. A hundred and fifty motorcars and buggies formed a procession to the Cathedral that was packed with fifteen hundred mourners for the funeral Mass.

Now, with no status, the family's official residency at Cavaliers was terminated and Grandpa Ralph's meagre savings were used to purchase Camperdown, a three-storey wooden house of no architectural integrity, located off Windward Road. All family members returned to Jamaica and huddled at Camperdown in survival mode. Uncle Mike had to abandon his plans to become a barrister like Vincent, his brother, and Tony dropped out of medical school in England without completing his final year.

The backyard at Camperdown was a magical kingdom for Audrey and me. The ground was compacted dirt, clean as concrete, bounded by a line of mango trees on one side, a dim row of servants' quarters on the other. It was there that Audrey and I romped with the servants' children who were allowed day visits. It was there, under the open sky, that I was bathed in a yellow portable tub. Lorna, the nubile daughter of our laundress, performed the ablutions and I remember the lather of red carbolic soap, the linger of her nimble fingers high between my thighs, the occasional caress of my genitals. I mentioned this to Mother who flew into a rage, threatening to call the police if the laundress and Lorna did not immediately pack up their belongings and leave the house, never to return. The ensuing commotion upset me. I felt sorry for Lorna and, truth to tell, found her ministrations quite pleasant. Mother accepted without reservation my account of what had transpired but did not explain to me its significance – the matter left hanging like a dangling participle. Whatever, the incident stayed in my head, and I made use of it in less innocent ways in my long narrative poem, *View from Mount Diablo*, where the hero's nurse, squint-eyed Nellie, who later becomes a ruthless political enforcer, is rather more definitely abusive:

> her black fingers roamed his private parts
> exciting them with predatory glee
> into a generous lather of carbolic soap.

In retrospect, it is astonishing that up to my sixth year Mother was still insisting that babies were brought by a stork sent by God. I am sure Mother consulted Uncle Bishop about our early sex education, but he seemed to think that no guidance was necessary until the child's seventh birthday, the traditional Jesuit age of reason. I am not sure that the Catholic church has ever formulated a theology of sex, certainly not with the same clarity that the encyclical *Rerum Novarum* deals with social justice.

In discussing culpability for wrong actions, Thomas Aquinas posits three modifiers of the volitional, namely ignorance, fear and concupiscence, the theory being that a person can only be held responsible for a free choice. Many examples of the role of ignorance and fear in limiting freedom are given, but I know of no detailed analysis of concupiscence, the word itself being difficult to spell and to pronounce.

Audrey and I lived in a state of unwilling suspension of disbelief, mired in ignorance about all things sexual. In conspiracy with next door neighbours of about our age we tried to unravel some of its mysteries in a secret hiding place under the house which I had created, lit by a single electric bulb and furnished with old blankets and the sides of cardboard boxes. It was here that we played "Doctor" until one of the servants reported us to Mother.

She ordered me into her presence and intoned with a frightening frigidity, "How could you do such a disgusting thing? There will be no more of it. Do you understand?" She started to cry.

Already awash in guilt, I stammered, "Yes, Mother."

But perhaps ignorance and innocence are somehow related. I have happy memories of Camperdown where the East Indian gardener harvested "blackie" mangoes for us, which we devoured skin and all. He had high cheek bones and a pointed beard and seldom spoke to the other staff, yet was always willing to do their bidding. He was called Babu, which we thought was an honorific title. It was there after Mass on Sunday that the ice cream bucket was set up on the back step to be churned by Babu, the gardener. When the paddle was withdrawn *we* were allowed to lick it, but not the black children.

Camperdown boasted a grass tennis court on which of an afternoon Uncle Mike and Uncle Tony, both over six feet tall, would do combat while I fielded balls. Their tennis styles summed up their personalities: Michael a crafty server with lots of spin; Tony a baseline player, his muscles toned to perfection from his daily bicycle jaunts. He was usually the victor. In addition to numerous bedrooms, Camperdown boasted a library and a billiard room. The walls of the dining room were decorated with dead birds mounted behind glass in cameo-shaped cases. Shadows were everywhere, the brightest electric light bulb burning at 25 watts. Few visitors crossed the threshold except for Mr. Philip Stern, a noted barrister in his nineties who, after dinner, reclined in a chair with a dirty damp handkerchief draped across his eyes. The Camperdown atmosphere was decidedly gothic.

My most frightening memory of Camperdown was the night of the great flood in 1933 when I had just turned six. Everybody gathered in the living room as lightning slashed like a silver sword through the house, intent on cutting it to pieces. Thunder shook the building to its foundations and rain in great waves of solid water sluiced down from the heavens, rising inexorably inch by inch. Holy candles were lit and one rosary after another collectively recited until, in the early hours of the morning, the storm abated.

For most of my youth Uncle Mike lived as a bachelor with us at Camperdown and other houses that we subsequently rented. There was some discreet courting which never quite came to fruition until, after I left for university, he married Mary, an English lady who taught Latin at Wolmer's Girls' School. He quickly fathered three children, making up for lost time.

I suppose Uncle Mike was, in a limited way, a substitute father figure for me. He was tall and handsome with soulful brown eyes. Suave, some might say unctuous, he spoke well, almost pedantically, his conversation sprinkled with phrases like "Dear Boy", "Mark you," "I put it to you," and "Balderdash." He seldom if ever took upon himself to discipline Audrey or me. That was left to Mother who kept a leather strap beside the Seth Thomas clock atop the china cabinet behind her seat at the head of the dining table. Not that she ever had to use it. A ruffle of the fingers of her right hand on the top of the table was sufficient to bring us to book.

Uncle Seymour, my mother's younger brother, may have been marginally mentally challenged. He had no interest in academic subjects, but became a self-styled veterinarian, his degree obtained by a correspondence course. He saved my horse, Dickie, from colic by administering an enema with the garden hose and by keeping the animal on its feet for hours, walking in circles. Needless to say, he was a favourite uncle. He had been excommunicated from the family for getting one of the Cavalier maids pregnant but was allowed to visit monthly to have lunch and collect a brown envelope that contained his maintenance allowance. At a relatively young age he suffered a stroke which caused him to walk with a limp.

One day when I was on vacation from school, I saw him swaying up the driveway sweating in a heavy jacket, its pockets bulging with tins of Epsom salts. He headed straight for the bathroom where he got down on his knees beside the tub and, cupping his hands, splashed water convulsively over his face. He was served lunch by a barefoot servant, rice and stew, but she was obliged to take the first taste to make sure the food was not poisoned. He rubbed lumps of rice between thumb and forefinger to detect if broken glass had been sprinkled in the meal as another method of assassination. When it was time for his departure he gave me a florin, but not before testing it with his teeth to make sure it was not counterfeit. He died in exile and there was only a subdued family funeral, which Audrey and I were not allowed to attend.

Years later, I wrote a poem called "Uncle Seymour" in *Moving On*, where in addition to some of the details mentioned above, I also imagined the circumstances of the need for the brown envelope. It was not an uncommon story in those days. My fictive Uncle Seymour observes the undulating buttocks of the maid polishing the floor. The temptation and power of a privileged white son proves too much:

He lifted her skirt, flipping it up like a shawl
around her shoulders,

surprised she wore no undergarments.
He stood for a moment
inspecting the articulation of her hips,
the muscles rippling in the haunches...
When her belly was too big to hide,
he confessed paternity
and gracefully accepted his own banishment.
No one saw the child. After the birth
a messenger came to the back door once a month
to collect a five pound note
tucked in a small, brown envelope –
unadressed.

My mother's elder sister, Aunt Bella, was a tall, handsome woman with a prominent nose. When we children commented on this, Mother insisted that it was a "Royal Roman Nose", a typical finesse about any hint of our Jewish heritage. Aunt Bella was inflicted with a strange disease that caused her hands to shake and her fingers to flutter like birds unable to perch, a condition she passed on to me and which began to manifest itself when I was in my seventies. She became the beloved chatelaine of every house in which we lived, a huge bunch of keys to cabinets, closets and cupboards hanging from her waist. She never married.

One of the few investments Grandpa Ralph had the foresight to make before his untimely death was a waterfront property known as Wherry Wharf, located at the foot of Pechon Street. A "wherry" is an open boat, manned by one or two oarsmen, used to transport passengers across water from one location to another, runt cousin perhaps of the more commonly known ferry boat. In the 16th century, nobs and their ladies from central London would cross the Thames in a wherry to Southwark, there to attend a new play by Mr. William Shakespeare at the Globe theatre. I have seen an old map showing a corresponding Wherry wharf at Port Royal that linked that notorious pirate city to the backwater that Kingston then was. The Port Royal wherry station was, as with most of the city, destroyed by the great earthquake of 1692. Kingston became the capital of Jamaica in 1872 and the building of the Palisadoes road around the lip of Kingston harbour to what remained of Port Royal put paid to the viability of a wherry service.

The wharf itself, which was meant to add some degree of value to Grandfather's investment in waterfront real estate, consisted of a jetty one hundred and fifty feet long, so pile rotted and shaky no ship larger than a canoe could safely dock alongside. On land, there were two rows of warehouses, painted black, on either side of a narrow driveway down which customers could approach the office to transact business. They came at desultory intervals, by foot, bicycle and even by motor car if the driver was prepared to reverse down the gauntlet of warehouses to the exit gate. The office, a two storey wooden building was on the water's edge. Uncle Mike was titular manager of the family partnership and he and Mother sat side by side at twin tables.

Uncle Tony, humorous eyes behind wire spectacles, was stationed on the opposite side of the room, but more often than not was in the yard receiving and delivering customer's goods into and from the warehouses. This afforded him also the opportunity to sip a tipple of rum from a flask carried in his back pocket. He was never drunk but developed a bleeding ulcer. One day he collapsed at his desk and was rushed by taxi to St. Joseph's hospital. There he was lovingly restored to health by a young nurse from Ballards Valley, a village settled in 1834 by German immigrants whose descendants looked like Europeans, which is to say white, but whose speech was the broadest of Jamaican patois. Back on his feet, Uncle Tony married his nurse, a union that produced four sons and a daughter, Barbara, who became a nun and the redoubtable principal of Alpha Academy high school. In his early eighties, Uncle Tony predeceased his younger wife. He had spent two years in a nursing home bravely fighting the ravages of cancer. One of his sons, a lecturer at Reading University in England, in a tribute at his funeral remarked: "Our father not only taught us how to live. He taught us how to die."

During his life, Uncle Tony established a reputation in Kingston as an eccentric. Except for a black tie, he dressed exclusively in white – white shoes, white socks, white shirt, white trousers and a white pith helmet. His only mode of transportation was a white bicycle with white sidewall tyres. On weekends he could be seen pedalling through some of the poorest areas of the city, collecting rents from a handful of slum tenements purchased over time from his meagre savings.

Dilapidated Wherry Wharf was incapable of providing an income as a functioning wharf, so the family was obliged to invent enterprises, other than storage fees, that could support its members. They displayed considerable ingenuity in this regard, and when I was allowed, during school holidays, to visit Mother at work, the scope of the business had already been expanded. Wherry Wharf was by then the exclusive manufacturer of canvas awnings in the island. The department was on the second floor, above the office, the clatter of three heavy-duty Singer sewing machines erupting at regular intervals. Aston was the artisan genius who ran the show. He had been born profoundly deaf but had taught himself to read lips. He was able to utter a few words, intelligible only to those who had to deal with him on a regular basis. Whenever my mother caught him in some minor mistake or, more often, when he proved to be right on some technical matter, he would take one of her hands in both of his, lean his head to one side and lift the clasped hand to his cheek. I often saw my mother, who loved him dearly, reciprocate the gesture by clasping one of his hands and lifting it to her breast.

It took me until late in my writing life to explore the nuances and complexities of race expressed in the closeness of human relationships. In my long poem, "The Colour of Conscience" I tried to deal with the kind of relationship that existed between Aston and my mother as it shaped my own perceptions. There could be no ducking my mother's unreflective racial attitudes, the scorn we were taught for "the barefoot, uneducated masses", the forbidden black friends, the glass reserved for black lips, but in the poem I write of witnessing Aston's and my mother's embrace:

> his cheek nestled against her breast, her fingers
> caressing his Brillo hair – a minute of grace
> that flickered only for a moment but still lingers.
> Why slow applause from me? Such special care
> deserved a special poem but I lacked the art
> to craft it then. I attempt it here.
> Mother, on this white page I cleanse my heart.

In addition to making awnings, Wherry Wharf rented out tarpaulins sewn up from flax material imported from Scotland. The tarps were used to cover open trucks carrying the treasures of Kingston – cement, lumber, flour and corn meal – to towns in the interior of the island. They were also in demand for St. Andrew cocktail parties, spread out on lawns to prevent ladies' high heels from sinking into the damp ground. Noel Coward often visited the wharf and referred to it as Jamaica's "old curiosity shop".

Beggars who came to the Wharf asking for water were never turned away, but they were served in a special mug reserved for black lips. Uncle Mike never hesitated to embellish on the phrase "filthy lucre", pointing out that black hands, previous handlers of notes or coins, might be infected with VD, TB, yaws or even leprosy. Audrey and I were scared rigid of contamination, for there was in fact a leprosarium in Jamaica and no cure had yet been found for Hansen's disease, the technical name of the affliction. Any transactions involving cash at Wherry wharf saw Mother or Uncle Mike dashing to the bathroom to wash their hands – the prototype of modern money laundering.

After Camperdown I vaguely remember a bungalow in Springfield near the residence of Mr. "Crab" Nethersole, founder of Jamaica's Central Bank. The steps and narrow verandah were concrete shined red with Rexo polish. The walls were concrete nog, standard building technique for residential houses before the advent of concrete blocks. The floors were all-heart pitch pine, polished once weekly with half a dried and waxed coconut used as a brush by a maid down on her knees, her behind swaying to the thumping rhythm of the brush. Near to Springfield was the Bournemouth bathing complex to which Audrey and I were able to walk and where we learned to swim.

At this Springfield location Audrey and I grew older but no wiser. In addition to sex, other topics that remained verboten included racial prejudice, our Jewish origins, the status of our father and family illnesses like Aunt Bella's trembling and especially Grandma Fielding's dementia, which was equated with madness.

One hot day, so hot the road asphalt was melting, Audrey and I reached home from swimming to hear the sound of conversation and laughter. We halted immediately, for this was a strange phenomenon. Avoiding the front door, we sneaked around the back of the house and peeked in. There we could see a balding gentleman in military uniform, a glass of rum in his hand, engaged in animated conversation with Mother.

"Who is it?" Audrey whispered.

"I don't know but Mummy is laughing. That's strange."

At this point Mother spied us and called out, "Ralph, Audrey. Come and say hello to your father."

Such a banal introduction for such a momentous occasion! I took Audrey's hand and we advanced into the living room.

He picked Audrey up and lifted her above his head, asking, "How are you, darling?" Then he kissed her on the forehead, put her down and turned to me.

"And how are you, big man?" he asked, sticking out his hand for a shake. Then he pulled me to his chest in a firm hug.

This was the man who in Poughkeepsie, during the early days of his marriage to mother, had cuddled and kissed us, his reward a happy gurgle and a smile. This was the ghost about whom nothing much was ever said, but whose absence haunted our young lives. But nothing of the honey of generation sweetened my Jamaican encounter with paternity. In truth, Audrey and I were more interested in the presents he had brought for us than in getting to know the kindly, balding man who had offered them. He smelled of cigarettes, smiled easily under a greying moustache. After the years of separation, Mother seemed at ease with him.

Like my uncle Vincent, my father had served in World War I, a member of the 11ᵗʰ Engineers, the first American regiment to see action in France. At one stage he had been gassed by the Germans and this, combined with heavy cigarette smoking, visited upon him a chronic cough. Now he was serving in another World War and had come on a brief furlough from his unit at Camp Lejeune in North Carolina.

During the two days of his visit, Aunt Bella surrendered her room to him. The conversation was generally polite, but whenever I could excuse myself to go outside and play I did so. On the third day he left for Vernam Field, the US air base in Jamaica, where he was able to "hitch" a ride back to his unit on a military aircraft. I was mightily impressed that he commanded such authority. In saying goodbye, he held out hope that one day we would be reunited – when I came to college in America and Audrey completed her secondary education at the Mt. Saint Vincent Academy.

Some months after Dad's departure, one morning I heard a woman screaming, the sound coming from Uncle Mike's bedroom. I rushed to see what was happening and there was Uncle Mike, one hand around my mother's throat, the other flaying her with the belt he had drawn from his trousers. Mother's knees had collapsed and she was begging for mercy. "Stop it! Stop it!" I screamed and rushed into the fray only to be tossed aside by a slap from my enraged uncle. Down on the floor behind him, I was able to take a large bite out of one of his calves. He bellowed in pain and kicked loose from me. In the encounter, Mother and I fled to her room and locked ourselves in.

I was too young then to appreciate the power of a bishop in the hierarchy of the Catholic Church. A bishop is a prince and like all princes enjoyed wide autonomy and wielded immense influence. It took only one telephone call from Mother to Uncle Bishop for Uncle Mike to be on a plane the next day to New York where he would live in a Retreat House until his nervous breakdown was cured. The treatment took over a year and during that time his name was seldom mentioned. Mother never explained what triggered his attack on her and life continued in its usual conspiratorial way. Some eighteen months after his mysterious departure, Uncle Mike surfaced again. He arrived on a Sunday in a taxi, carried his own bags into the house and retook possession of his bedroom. The next morning he started out for work at Wherry Wharf with Mother, as if his sabbatical had been a figment of our imagination.

Grandma Hannah was the legal owner of Camperdown and when Uncle Tony started his family, she decreed that he should have the right to occupy that house while the rest of us moved into rented quarters. After a brief spell at the Springfield house we moved to a larger rented residence on Upper South Camp Road, a house which is now the location of the Gun Court and prison. It was owned by a tough Syrian businessman who charged rent of $40 per month. When he was owed rent he dictated dunning letters to his secretary, brief and to the point. "Either you pay the money you owe me, or I sue your crotch." But, intimidated by the Isaacs' *hauteur*, he always came to the servant's entrance to collect the rent.

The house on South Camp Road fronted on the main line tramcar tracks from downtown to Cross Roads, separated from the street by a row of eight foot high cactus plants bristling with vicious, blue-tipped thorns commonly known as a dildo fence. There were four bedrooms in the house, but only one bathroom. Before school each morning I showered outside under a standpipe, which jutted like a gibbet from the kitchen wall. There was always a traffic jam for the toilet and to alleviate this the bedrooms were furnished with chamber pots, emptied daily by the servants. I was embarrassed by this ritual and the red ring around my ass when I stood up took on the status of an unwelcome stigmata.

With the advent of World War II in 1939, Kingston, once a bustling capital city, was reduced to a rural village, cut off from supplies of fuel requisitioned for the war effort. Jamaica, as the geographic "cross roads" of the Caribbean, was a special target for German submarines, which circled the island like sharks, forcing the Jamaican people to be as self-sufficient as ingenuity allowed. Lawns and backyards were converted to "Victory Gardens" where foodstuffs were planted, especially corn, which as cornmeal porridge was served for breakfast, and as cornmeal pudding was served for dessert after dinner at night. Motor cars were turned into buggies and the working-class population travelled on tram cars and rode bicycles.

As the war progressed, we acquired a menagerie of animals, the stallion "Dickie" saved by Uncle Seymour, a donkey named "Wally", three goats, one of which I had to milk each morning, ducks, guinea pigs and a chicken-run of white leghorns and Rhode Island reds. And of course there were dogs, Rufus the prince of the mongrels. Coal black and with a big head, he had a habit of looking at you through his large sad eyes begging permission to lick the back of your hands. If you so much as blinked or nodded he jumped forward to perform the anointment. When at rest, his belly on the cool tiles, he always crossed his front legs as if posing for a photograph.

During the war, the Isaacs family was especially fortunate that Grandpa Ralph, in the glory days, had imported from England a pony cart for the enjoyment of his young children. Shaped like a Roman chariot with large wheels on either side, entrance to its "well" through a small rear door, it was powered by Dickie whose feisty temperament matched that of Mother. Only five feet two inches tall and weighing a mere 85 pounds, she sat sideways on one of the benches, the reins looped over the backboard into one of her leather gloved hands as she trotted off to work.

Audrey and I, given the isolation of our domestic environment, paid scant attention to the war raging throughout the globe. It hardly affected our practice of playing "make up" games to escape boredom, games in which I extemporized the plots and Audrey, almost by magic, with no instructions from me, intuited the next chapter. There was a shortwave radio in the living room, art deco in shape, before which Grandma, dressed in black bombazine for the afternoon, would take tea sweating profusely under her heavy make-up. When she relinquished ownership of the radio, we rushed to listen to "The Green Hornet" and "Mr. Keen, tracer of lost persons".

Antoinette, lovingly referred to as Aunt Nettie, was the youngest of the Isaacs daughters. She had married Hans Schnoor, a young German commission agent who had settled in Jamaica in the interregnum between World War I and World War II. His agencies included kitchen cutlery, Bavarian crystal and German beer, the sales of which provided a comfortable living. They had two sons, Desmond and Raymond. Shortly after the outbreak of World War II, Uncle Hans was arrested by the colonial authorities and, together with other German citizens living in Jamaica, was imprisoned in a compound for enemy aliens established at Up Park Camp, the army base for a series of British regiments stationed there to protect the island from invasion. The Schnoor internment caused a rift in the family, for while Aunt Nettie, understandably, was desperately trying to get her husband released, my mother, while acknowledging that he probably was not a spy, nevertheless considered his internment by the authorities to be justified in the circumstances. There were other internees and she did not think it fair

that an exception should be made in the case of her brother-in-law.
Justice was for her more important than compassion. Uncle Hans,
fictionalised as "Uncle Johann" features in *The View From Mount Diablo*,
where I imagine the circumstances of his arrest:

> The regimental major who served the detention order
> addressed Johann in stilted, high school German,
> allowed him an hour to pack and say good-bye,
> saluted his wife and waited for him in the garden.

While war was being fought in Europe, another war of sorts was being
fought in Jamaica on the labour front. Alexander Bustamante, a fiery
labour leader, organized waterfront workers to go on strike for higher
wages, closing down the port of Kingston, including Wherry Wharf.
Mother would have none of this. On the morning of the general strike,
she trotted to work as usual in her bright yellow pony cart. A line of
pickets, mostly her own workers, blocked the open Wherry Wharf gate
and refused to let her in. She wielded her chariot up Pechon Street and,
standing in the "well" of the cart, whipped Dickie into a gallop, charging
the gate. At the last moment the line parted and she triumphantly
opened the office where she sat in solitary splendour for the rest of the
day. At closing time she trotted back home.

Because of the political unrest, schools were closed and by 10 a.m. I
was travelling home by tram. On either side of the tracks, and at
important intersections, English soldiers from Up Park Camp, shirtless
to the waist, were laying sand bags. I had never before seen white men
performing manual labour and the sight of these sunburned soldiers,
dripping sweat, increased my apprehension about what was going on.

The English Governor of the island considered the labour unrest
fermented by Bustamante to be subversive in time of war and he ordered
the labour leader's arrest. Bustamante was thrown into the same canton-
ment at Up Park Camp where Aunt Nettie's husband was interned.
They became good friends. Busta did the cooking for his barracks and
my German uncle-in-law washed the dishes. Most of the coloured
intelligentsia, some whites and nearly all blacks sympathized with
Busta's fight for the Jamaican working class and considered the Governor to be a colonial tyrant. Not so my mother. She thought it was
disgraceful of Bustamante, at a time when England's back was against
the wall, to be agitating for better conditions for workers.

Uncle Hans was eventually released from camp a year before the war
ended, presumably because it was known by then that the Allies would
be victorious. Our proximity to Up Park Camp provided Audrey and

myself a quixotic opportunity to get back at the Governor for interning Aunt Netty's husband. The British soldiers had adopted my sister and me as unofficial mascots and we often rode our donkey "Wally", me in front, Audrey behind, through restricted areas of the camp, one or two soldiers waving a greeting. To mark Empire Day or some such important occasion, a military march-past had been arranged, the Governor to take the salute. Temporary bleachers were erected for the comfort of invited guests, the elite of Kingston and St. Andrew. Black Mr. Byrd, who considered himself a socialite, but who had failed to get an invitation, attempted to breach the main gate on the day of the parade. When stopped by a Cockney corporal, he proclaimed in a loud voice, "I am Byrd. Byrd, do you hear," to which the corporal replied in an intense whisper, "You could be a fucking hawk. No one gets in without an invitation."

Riding Wally, Audrey and I strategically positioned ourselves on a side street watching the regiment muster for the grand occasion. Boots and rifles slapped the pavement as orders were barked in hoarse screams. In front, a gaunt drum-major flung his silver baton in the air, catching it behind his back. Then came the side drums and the bugles. In the rear, a sergeant beat the great bass drum draped in a tiger skin.

On the platform, the Governor sat in the front row in a cockaded hat, his aide-de-camp jingling with medals. As the troops came into sight, Audrey and I slipped from ambush into the lead, the donkey trotting briskly, three mincing steps to each beat of the drum. We could hear the voice of Empire hissing behind us, "Get out of it. Get out of it!" but we rode on, the battalion stretched out behind. "You little shits," the drum-major hissed again but we were now directly in front of the reviewing stand. There was a titter of laughter, followed by the thunder of applause as the Governor flashed us his salute and all the guests rose to their feet as one.

Concomitant with life at South Camp Road there was life at Shadowbrook, the Isaacs' country house at Green Hills, a rain forest in the valley a mile beyond Hardwar Gap, elevation 3,800 feet. Mountain retreats to escape the heat of Kingston were popular with the Jamaican upper-class, a colonial hangover from the days of the Raj in India. The wealthy were not interested in beach resorts. If you were passing for "white", who would wish to jeopardize this status with a tan?

The Shadowbrook cabin huddled half way up a steep mountain, hugging itself from the cold. If arrival was by motorcar it had to be parked in the garage at road level, passengers obliged to climb a series of steps terraced into the side of the hill, pushing through vines, bracken, bush and tree ferns whose tendrils curled into themselves like treble clefs in musical notation. The house was flanked on one side by hydrangeas massed like pale blue brains over an acre of garden lovingly tended by Uncle Mike. Mist from the rain-drizzled valley regularly drifted like a miasma over everything and the sun, only occasionally able to break through, lost its battle with mildew that seeped into clothes and books. There was no electricity at the cabin, meals cooked on a black cast-iron Dover stove that crouched like a bull frog in one corner of the kitchen, devouring cords of wood Malcolm, the caretaker, cut from the forest and stored under the house. Malcolm I remembered in my poem, "Carpenters" from *The Denting of a Wave* as "incalculably old/ and purple black", written in celebration of a boy's first awareness of the beauty of craft in the building of a house for Malcolm, "respectable/ enough in which to die" by the excellent Mr. Coombs,

> pegging out the new domain with such casual
> grace and squint-eyed wisdom as Penn & Venables
> would have envied, albeit this forest colony
> was twelve by sixteen feet of mildewed mulch.

How and when our new location was selected as a permanent residence owned in fee simple, as distinct from rented premises in Kingston, I never found out. Mother had to be carried up the steps by Malcolm on his back, and the perpetual damp that permeated the house could hardly have been the ideal environment for an asthmatic. Life at Shadowbrook was even more isolated and lonely than life at South Camp Road. But for an introspective like me, the imagination took a perverse pleasure in exploring all the damp and dark hiding places of the house, the mysteries of the surrounding forest, dense with underbrush and sinister sisal vines, fallen tree trunks covered with moss.

There was also the height of the place that came to inhabit my imagination. Perhaps it was to Shadowbrook I returned in a poem called "He Knows What Height Is", written about the special perceptions of the mountain dweller seeing himself in the flight of a bird. The last stanza went:

> The bird floats down the mountains, wings at rest,
> riding high currents over the ridges, swinging
> him between the peaks, feet dangling
> above the abyss filling up with shadows,
> elbows screaming at his sides,
> fingers frozen on the fog frayed vines.
> As it was in the beginning so, after all

these years, the sign and wonder – between his legs
the anus closing, the shrinking of the balls.

At Shadowbrook, Aunt Bella also made her contribution to my initiation
into the world of the strange and suspenseful by taking me on early
morning walks along the main road, mist clutching at the lapels of our
sweaters. We would stop at each milepost and she would read a passage
from Stevenson's *Treasure Island*, Poe's *The Gold Bug* or Jane Porter's *The
Scottish Chiefs*. This kindness in reading to me turned out to be counterproductive because I was content just to listen and not read for myself.
But when it became apparent that I was a slow reader, considerably
below the norm for my age, Aunt Bella came up with an effective
strategy by reading a story to the point of maximum suspense and then
refusing to read any further. I was handed the book and had to decipher
the *dénouement* for myself. In a very short time my disability was cured.

There were good times at Shadowbrook, too. Mother was especially
happy when Uncle Bishop spent a weekend. He cooked Irish stew for
lunch on the Dover stove and after dinner, kerosene lamps lit and
emitting a golden glow, we gathered in the living room, Uncle Bishop
in a large leather chair smoking a cigar, Mother on the floor beside him
buffing his nails. Uncle Mike would wind up the gramophone that
featured a "His Master's Voice" trumpet, the recordings released by
bamboo needles. We listened to scratchy opera arias sung by Enrico
Caruso and Amelita Galli-Curci.

Uncle Bishop was "lace curtain" Irish from Boston. His vocation
blazed early and never faltered. An arch conservative, he ran the Catholic
church in Jamaica with great administrative skill, relying to some extent
on Mother for her commercial know-how. Their relationship was
intimate but Platonic. On weekends at Shadowbrook, in addition to
Mother and Uncle Bishop, there were Uncle Mike, Aunt Bella, Audrey
and me. Uncle Mike employed a carpenter to make a portable altar,
which was set up in the living room for daily mass. I was the altar server,
Aunt Bella coaching me in some of the Latin responses.

Malcolm told my mother about a lad in his village, Nathaniel, who
was being bullied by a gang of older boys. He was a few years older than
me, was intelligent and anxious to escape the constant harassment.
Mother agreed to take him on as gardener and general factotum at the
South Camp Road house and at Shadowbrook when we were in
residence. He flashed an engaging smile, called me "Mr Son" and
became my close friend, sharing in my achievements and my failures.
We often spoke about religion and in due course he converted to

Catholicism. In time, Mother came to give him her complete trust, allowing us to go on camping expeditions overnight. He never betrayed my confidence or mother's total acceptance. What was extraordinary also was how much he loved Audrey and how much she loved him.

But friendships like mine with Nathaniel were condemned by our relative social positions and the passage of time. I was always destined to move away through education to a different world. I perhaps explored my own feelings about Nathaniel in *View from Mount Diablo*, where the picture of the friendship between the fictional characters, Nathan, the black groom and gardener and the white boy, Adam Cole, draws from the past I have described above, where the "boy/ and groom soon bonded like brothers, dauphin prince/ and companion of honour." In a wholly imagined later life, Nathan has become a cocaine baron who visits his old friend Adam, now a crusading journalist, to order him to leave Jamaica to save his life. Old love and bitter resentment fight in Nathan's mind, and he tells Adam:

> "When you leave for Oxford,
> it mash me up bad, leave me low. I feel
>
> you desert me, man."

One morning at Shadowbrook I found myself in the middle of a crisis. Running out to play, I jumped sideways off the front steps and sliced my shin open, down to the bone on the mud scraper. Mother tried to remain calm but we had no phone, no transportation except for a bicycle; the nearest doctor was at the Newcastle military camp three miles away. Nathaniel, who was helping Uncle Mike in the garden, offered to push me on the bike to Newcastle. I sat on the seat, feet up on the handlebar while Nathaniel walked beside the bike, steering it around corners and over the camber of the road. It took us an hour to get to the camp by which time the temporary bandage applied to the wound by Mother was soaked with blood. A British army sergeant who recognized me from Kingston appraised the situation and went to fetch the doctor, a major, who was just finishing lunch.

I was lifted up the encampment to the clinic where Major Twigger wafted me with breath that smelled like the dispensary, harrumphed his assurance that I would be a brave soldier, wouldn't I, and presented in a Petri dish an array of needles, one of which seemed longer than the sabre Governor Richards wore at the march-past. Then he squirted iodine directly into the wound, the pain of which served as a kind of anaesthetic for the actual stitching. The doctor selected a relatively small needle, thank God, and tried to thread it with cat gut, holding the eye up to the light as I had seen Aunt Bella do when attempting to sew a button on one of my shirts. He administered four stitches, the while continuing to harrumph about my being a brave lad.

Throughout the entire ordeal I managed not to shed a tear and reported this proudly to Mother when I got back home. But when she learned that I had not been given a local anaesthetic, she flew into a rage.

"As soon as we get back to Kingston I am going to write to that doctor's superior… How dare he treat my son like that. It shows disrespect for Jamaicans."

"Please Mother, don't do that," I implored, and it was only then that I broke down and wept inconsolably. I had been proud of the fact that there was no anaesthetic, that I had proven to myself that I could be brave. How could Mother take away my badge of courage? I began to regain my composure only when, after a week, she had not carried out her threat.

★   ★   ★

Romping in the garden of our South Camp Road, Kingston home, Audrey and I would play "make-up games". Our plots would unfold as if we were one imagination, one body almost, acting out the adventures with no need for coordination or instruction.

"Shhh," mother would call from her bedroom. "Be quiet. Help your grandmother to her room."

Grandma would balance by holding onto our shoulders, one of us on each side, but she would suddenly balk at a stream of water she thought she saw running down the middle of the living room. She was senile and I would humour her. "Just step over it, Grandma." She would smile and obey. We would deposit her in her bedroom and rush back to our game. Grandma was a continuing nuisance in our young lives, a daily penance to be endured. We were secretly delighted when, health failing, Uncle Tony agreed to take her in at Camperdown where his wife, the nurse from Ballard's Valley, could minister to her.

Grandma had been at Camperdown about a year when one night the phone rang. It was Uncle Tony. Grandma was dying. We had no transportation except my bicycle, so I was allowed to tow Audrey to Camperdown where I would drop her off and return for Mother. There was no traffic on the road; the finger of light from my bicycle's generator swung from side to side as we raced down Deanery Road, Audrey on the handle bars, head down into the wind.

Audrey later told me she was met by Uncle Tony's wife who, in a state of panic, locked her in the room where Grandma's body was stretched out on the bed, eyes still open. Because Audrey disliked Grandma, she was convinced that she was the cause of her death and would be punished for killing her. She escaped through a window onto the roof and thence back into the main house. By then Mother had arrived by taxi, but my sister, traumatized, neglected in the ensuing bustle, was condemned to spend the rest of her life trying to find a key to unlock her guilt.

At this stage of our elementary education, Audrey and I were both students at Alpha Academy, only a short tramcar journey from our South Camp Road house. Alpha was a girl's school but an exception was made for me and about four or five other boys waiting to enter St George's College, at the age of eleven or twelve, to complete our secondary education. Among them were Robert Patterson, a senior reporter for *The Gleaner*, who later became a priest, and Carol Thorbourn, founder of the Touche Ross auditing firm.

Puberty occurs early in the tropics, bestowing on a girl a certain secret maturity not available to boys of the same age, and I noticed that Audrey and I were starting to drift apart. We no longer played made-up games and she developed an inner assurance that I envied – now a beautiful girl, of above average height for her age, her head perfectly complemented by her tall frame. She had an infectious giggle that usually climaxed into a raucous laugh, sign of a wry sense of humour that endeared her to a wide range of friends at Alpha. After High School in Jamaica, she attended Mount St Vincent's academy, a prestigious Catholic secondary school in Tuxedo Park, New York.

It was at Alpha that I entered and won my first elocution contest with a selection from Tennyson's *Morte d'Arthur*. While I was there, Sister Legurie, a Cockney English nun, taught me fretwork and French polishing, hobbies that added significance to my lonely home environment.

When I was growing up, the state of race relations in Jamaica was puzzling to me. Prejudice was rampant, partly to do with colour and partly with class. In the Isaacs family, this was even more confusing. My black school friends were not allowed to enter the house, but Dr. Ludlow Moody, a decidedly black gentleman, was welcomed like a head of state when he visited to attend to Mother. For hours before his arrival the house had to be cleaned, especially the bathroom, in case he had a call of nature. I found it difficult to accept that what was good enough for us might not be up to his standards, but I was sensitive enough not to raise the issue with Mother who, after all, relied on Dr. Moody for her survival. Dr. Moody makes an appearance in my "The Colour of Conscience", again as one of the anomalous experiences of race in my boyhood. I wrote of how:

> He enters like an African prince
> come to bless a country cousin. She bares
> her breasts for the kisses of the stethoscope, a wince
> when his fingers massage her spine, hears
> his consoling voice as he prepares the morphine
> shot. When the heaving stops he stands
> aside, slowly turns towards the pristine
> bathroom to wipe her whiteness from his hands.

Like the odour of Mother's Kellogg asthma remedy, illness permeated the house, keeping its inhabitants on edge for an inevitable catastrophe: mother always on the verge of an asthma attack; Aunt Bella unable to find rest for her shaking hands; Uncle Seymour a candidate for a second stroke; Uncle Bishop diagnosed with dangerously high blood pressure. But even in this gloomy atmosphere I spent little time thinking of death. This was to change one afternoon when a car racing down South Camp Road hit and killed Rufus, our cherished dog, as he was crossing the street. The agony of his dying yelps, high pitched at first, then fading to a terrible silence brought Audrey and me to choking, uncontrollable tears. Mother was understanding and agreed that Nathaniel could dig a grave in the backyard for suitable burial. In a few days others in the family were recovering from grief, but for me not even the grave could provide closure. I became convinced that the only way I could assuage my grief was to fill the void of Rufus' death with words. So I wrote a poem.

Jamaica's first broadcasting station, call letters ZQI, was launched shortly before Rufus's death and I recalled Dennis Gick (1904-1962), the General Manager, requesting submissions of short stories and poems to fill air time. I printed out my poem on a lined sheet of paper and posted it to the station. Although it was perhaps what one might call doggerel, not a word of which I now remember, its acceptance came as no surprise to me, so strong was my sense of vocation.

I presented myself at ZQI at the appointed date and time and was met at the door by Archie Lindo, a well-known journalist, who introduced me to Gick. I was ushered into the studio; this consisted of one medium sized room, a heavy carpet on the floor, thick drapes on the walls to improve the acoustics. Seated at a small desk with a microphone in front of me, I waited for Gick's index finger to point at me to start reading my poem. I had taken the bus to the radio station, but I verily believe that I floated on air back home. From then on poetry became another tension in the working out of my destiny.

The Young Poet

CHAPTER TWO

ST. GEORGE'S COLLEGE

In January of 1939 I was enrolled at St George's College, founded by the Jesuits in 1850. Grandma Hannah's brother, Clem Fielding, had built the college's modern building. It was also he who had erected the Half-Way Tree clock tower and most of the important Catholic buildings in the Corporate area. He had ample talent but too many children, so long before it became fashionable to do so the Fielding tribe migrated to Canada where they prospered, one son ending his career as a high-ranking officer in the Canadian Air Force.

All but one of the teachers at St George's College was a Jesuit, so that students there, most of them black and underprivileged, received the benefit of a four-hundred-year Jesuit tradition on how best to educate young minds. The one non-Jesuit member of faculty was Adrian Chaplin, affectionately known as "Mr. Chaps", who taught mathematics. Even after the college, for financial reasons, was obliged to accept grant aid from the government and follow a syllabus geared to passing the Senior Cambridge Entrance Exam, it nevertheless tried to remain faithful to the idea of a liberal arts education.

Mother carefully monitored my overall progress at St George's, but was too busy and sick to help with homework problems. Uncle Mike had no interest in doing so. In this regard I was somewhat at a disadvantage to the four or five other white boys in my class whose parents could take a closer look at their sons' progress. I was academically and socially insecure during my first two years. Success at Latin, Chemistry and Algebra did not come as easily as home praise or the solace of "make-up games" in which I was always the hero. I did not hit my stride until third form, under the compassionate guidance of Fr. Welsh.

Outside the main gate of the College on North Street there was a gloomy Chinese shop where a "bulla" could be bought for a farthing. From a highly decorated handcart one could purchase for a penny shaved ice smothered in rich, red syrup. It was outside this gate that students were banished when "sent to Coventry" for relatively minor breaches of discipline. To be "sent to Coventry" meant that you were not allowed on the school compound before the beginning of classes or during breaks. Your fellow students were supposed to ostracise you, but often there were so many boys in Coventry at any one time that they formed an outlaw band with its own rules of camaraderie. I was successful in avoiding Coventry, fearful that I might be subjected to bullying there by some of the more aggressive boys.

By far the most beloved and interesting priest at St. George's College during my time was Fr. William Hannas, affectionately known as "Wild Bill". He taught Latin and would not hesitate to shy the blackboard eraser at the head of any boy talking in his class. A short, florid American of German extraction, he was genuinely devoted to the boys in his care, a love and respect which they reciprocated. A "man's man" who smoked cigars, he declined to wear his religious vocation on his sleeve and gave the impression of being a man of the world, reconciled to the reality of its imperfections. I think he considered me a bit of a sissy and tried to toughen me up by including me in his boxing class.

At the end of training, in my competition bout, although I was a good counter puncher, I was hit down twice. After what seemed like an eternity the fiasco mercifully ended and I was declared the undisputed loser. Hannas called me into his office, put his arm around my shoulders and congratulated me on a game defence.

I was not a particularly good student at St. George's College, doing well only in those subjects that appealed to me and failing those like Chemistry that I found boring. In fifth form, Fr. Ballou taught me English, my favourite subject. He awarded me an "A" for an essay on *Hamlet*, but expressed amazement that I managed to spell "Shakespeare" four different ways in the space of three pages.

I was never allowed to entertain black schoolmates inside our house. My best friend then was Chicki Ross, half Jamaican, half Cuban. He ardently wanted to become a writer and was editor of the school literary magazine. He was permitted to visit with me in the garden two or three afternoons a week, provided I had finished my homework assignments. Chicki and I would arrange two chairs behind the garage so we could sneak a smoke. He was able to produce a copy of Joyce's *Ulysses* at a time when it was banned in America for being pornographic. We spent hours ferreting out the juicy parts.

In my final year at St. George's College I managed to pass Senior Cambridge with one distinction in art. I became interested in painting one pre-Christmas weekend at Shadowbrook spent with two other boys – white – approved by my mother. There was an old Windsor and Newton set of watercolour paints and we decided to make our own Christmas cards. I found drawing poinsettia blossoms and holly leaves to be quite easy, but it was the interplay of colours that intrigued me – rich reds and cool greens interacting with each other in scintillating complementaries when the proportions of each were right. I graduated to oils and spent hours making copies of portraits of the famous wartime personalities who appeared on the covers of magazines like *Time* and *Saturday Evening Post*.

I was taught by John Wood (c. 1900-1970), an expatriate English artist, who came to Jamaica with his wife to escape the war in Europe. They lived in a small cottage on the way to Gordon Town in close proximity to what was then Mount Mansfield Hotel, known to the cognoscenti as a "short time house" – a place where gentlemen from Kingston took their inamorata for three hour trysts. Mount Mansfield Hotel and the Wood's residence were secluded locations in those days of no motorcars or public transport. John Wood supplemented his income as an artist by teaching painting to Jamaican students on weekends. To get to his studio I had to saddle up a horse, strap an easel on my back and clop up the hill from South Camp Road. The group painted on Saturday afternoons and Sunday mornings, the students sharing a dormitory room overnight and the Spartan meals Mrs. Wood managed to prepare.

Wood had started his career in Yorkshire as a landscape gardener. He had a fine sense of composition but his drawing was somewhat weak and Edna Manley often criticized his overuse of alizarin crimson in trying to capture the transparency of shadows in the tropics. But I learned much from him and am mentioned in *Jamaica Palette*, a book he published in 1955 on his return to England after the war.

The only short wave radio in the vicinity was in the open-air bar at Mount Mansfield, and it was part of our ritual to accompany John Wood to the hotel to listen to the war news from the BBC in London. Then came the long ride home. After the war, Mount Mansfield hotel was gloriously upgraded to Blue Mountain Inn, the most sophisticated restaurant in Jamaica at the time, and a watering hole with an international reputation. Princess Margaret once dined there.

Elocution contests were an important feature of the secondary education system when I was a schoolboy. They were conducted in age cohorts and, having won in all the early categories, my teachers at St. George's College proposed that I skip the penultimate group and enter the adult competition in which there was no age limit. Uncle Bishop was my secret weapon. He not only tutored me in voice and gesture, but was especially ingenious in choosing the selection I would deliver. While other competitors stuck to old chestnuts like "Invictus" and "The Charge of the Light Brigade", Uncle Bishop selected new material that surprised the judges. For the adult contest he assigned me a scene from Shakespeare's *King John* in which Arthur, the jailer of the little Prince, informs the boy that he has been ordered to put out his eyes with a hot poker – melodramatic stuff in which I pulled off a coup by taking both parts, Arthur and the Prince, changing my voice and turning my face from one side to another to signal the change. Uncle Bishop's strategy won the day and I was awarded first prize.

When I was in fourth form, my dad sent an American bicycle to Jamaica for me. Most of the George's boys rode bicycles to school, slim, sleek Rudges, Hercules, or Raleigh, all sold by Mr. Brandon whose showroom was at the foot of East Street. But my bike was different; rather than black, it was red with big balloon tyres, the valves for which, unlike English ones, were compatible with valves used in motor car tyres. This meant that instead of needing a special pump I could pull into a service station and fill up with "free air". There was no hand brake; this function was accomplished by pressing back on the pedals. I loved that bike. What a joy on school mornings to speed down South Camp Road on it, hands off the handle bars, mere wish sufficient to change direction. I remembered this joy in a poem I wrote many years later, "Cycling", from *The Denting of a Wave*:

> Then the glide –
> down South Camp Road
> spokes spinning in refracted light,
> such trust between the rider and the ridden
> no hands were needed...

I seemed to take naturally to acting and my reputation as an elocutionist led to a number of roles in local theatrical productions. I had a small part in *The Barretts of Wimpole Street*, staged at the Ward Theatre, but my starring role was as Puck in *A Midsummer Night's Dream*, produced and directed by Noel Vaz in an open-air production at the Holy Childhood Convent where, some years before, I had slept with the Mother Superior. A 100-foot stage was erected around three magnificent guango and mahogany trees. From a branch of one, an invisible harness was attached to my back that allowed me literally to fly off the stage, to "put a girdle round the world in thirty seconds".

But my role as a flying Puck nearly came to a tragic end. Riding my bike for a night rehearsal I pulled into a gas station to pump up my tyres. One sleepy attendant dozed in the office, the only light a 25 watt bulb. As I was riding in the dark towards the exit, I plunged into a deep hole, an unlit excavation for a new underground fuel tank. The attendant pulled me out but it was not until I saw the bone above my wrist sticking out from the flesh that I nearly fainted, overcome by shock. Sufficiently recovered, I phoned Mother and she came for me in a taxi. We rushed to St Joseph's hospital where we were met by Dr. Moody. In tears I explained that the opening night of *A Midsummer Night's Dream* was in two weeks and the play could not go on without me, for there was no understudy for Puck. Doctor Moody's solution was to form the cast in two halves, held together by tape, but which could be opened to allow a masseuse to massage the arm to prevent muscle atrophy. The play opened on time to a sold out audience.

Girls from the Hazel Johnston ballet school performed in the production as fairies and I was stricken with one particular beauty, whom I would chase around the curtilage of the stage during rehearsals. Mr. Finzi, maverick member of the rum company of the same name, had devised a unique lighting system for the production. Electric wires were connected to three iron ingots suspended over three huge rum casks filled with water. There was a wooden handle that Finzi used to lower the ingots into the water, which absorbed the electrical current, thus dimming the stage lights and creating "black outs" when necessary. One night on my chase after the ballet dancer, I bumped into one of the casks while taking a corner at excessive speed. Finzi draped me up with the warning: "Boy, mind pussy end your life before your time. If your hand touch a drop of this water, you stone dead. Electrocuted."

On Saturday mornings, Audrey and I were allowed to ride a tram car to Cross Roads to see a film at "The Movies" Theatre. Before the feature started Dudley McMillan entertained the audience with chalk drawings. The movie was a serial named *The Shadow*, the hero played by an out-of-work Shakespearian actor. Each reel started with his *basso profundo* laugh, which terminated in the terrifying certainty that "The Shadow Knows". I had mastered the timing of this dramatic introduction and, on returning home, wanted to share it with Mother. She was hunched over the dining room table working on the Wherry Wharf accounts and shooed me off. Still at her work two hours later, she explained that the books were "out" by a sixpence.

"That's not much money, Mummy. Go to bed," I urged.

"If the books don't balance," she explained, "the accounts may be out six pounds rather than six pence. Always remember that in life."

In retrospect I came to realize that, for Mother, love meant the sacrifices she gladly made to bring up her children, the desire for education she inspired in us, the search for perfection which, if I found it, was accorded her highest praise. There was little or no room in her emotional vocabulary for hugs and kisses, the sharing of childhood pleasures like parlour games or going to the movies. When I discussed this with Audrey, she concluded that Mother had done the best with what she had and I was able to take adult comfort in this.

After The "Movies" Theatre, The Carib theatre came into existence – a monumental white presence where Morris Cargill, the then manager of the theatre, dressed in a tuxedo, welcomed the patrons swirling through the lobby. This was the occasion for the Calypso jingle:

> Mongoose run in a Carib theatre,
> Swear to God him is de new operator,
> Morris Cargill say come back later,
> Slide mongoose.

The Carib was the first public building in Jamaica to be air-conditioned; I was astonished at the cool comfort it provided, but many men refused to remove their hats for fear that they would catch a cold in their "mole". When the show was about to begin, voluptuous curtains opened automatically to the strains of the Carib waltz, a melody lifted from a commercial for Carrier air-conditioning.

By the time I graduated from St George's College at the age of seventeen, the war in Europe was drawing to an end and the Jamaican economy starting to revive. After years of struggle, Wherry Wharf appeared to be making enough money to support the Isaacs family at a comfortable level. Mother still held the purse strings close to her chest and financial matters were never discussed with Audrey and me, but I could detect a slight weather change. A new family car was purchased, a Ford sedan that cost £700 – and my pocket money was increased to one pound per week.

In my final year at St George's College, I fell in lust and in love with Pam, an English girl whose father was stationed in Jamaica as the representative of a large international conglomerate. Pam and I met

Audrey, my mother Stephanie and me

through our mutual interest in horse riding. Audrey and I had taken lessons at Miss Steadman's riding academy, opposite the Constant Spring hotel, later to become Immaculate Conception High School. We were both good riders, but I was not in Pam's class. Tall and stately, with long blond hair, she often rode her chestnut stallion at the polo field at Up Park Camp where I encountered her from time to time and managed to initiate some stilted conversation. I could not contain my joy when one afternoon she phoned to invite me to a Saturday night party at her house. These Saturday night parties, held at different homes each weekend, were a feature of social life for middle-class youngsters in their last year of high school, or recently graduated.

Dancing was to gramophone records that featured the big band sounds of Tommy Dorsey and Artie Shaw, rumbas by Xavier Cugat and waltzes by Lester Lanin. These last afforded an opportunity for cheek-to-cheek dancing which, for some boys, carried with it the embarrassment of not being able to control an erection. The classic remedy for this was the wearing of a jockstrap that could be purchased openly, but purportedly for some athletic activity at school. No hard liquor was allowed, but the open smoking of cigarettes, sometimes dispensed from a silver case, was considered the height of sophistication. The parties ended at about 10:30 pm and young gentlemen often gave girls a lift home on their bicycles, the reward for which might be a good night kiss.

In retrospect, my infatuation with Pam was not only sexual but an important social triumph that allowed me to break out of the isolation and loneliness of life at South Camp Road. She performed for me the role of Robert Graves' "White Goddess", not just because she *was* white but because she was a symbol of the freedom and status I craved. Audrey and I had been brought up to believe that we were poor but aristocratic intellectuals, but I had begun to see through this charade. Mother never read a serious book and Uncle Mike, who had won every academic prize at Fordham, was more interested in gardening than in literature or philosophy. Dinner conversations could be stimulating but were often more argumentative than enlightening. Pam and her circle had no intellectual pretensions but seemed to epitomize the easy social graces that I associated with the truly aristocratic, persons to the manor and the manner born who knew the rules but were not hidebound by them. Pam was someone I could vaunt.

We eventually became formally engaged and the two families were obliged to meet. Protocol, thank God, dictated that this should take place at the residence of Pam's parents. I would have been mortally embarrassed had it been held at our South Camp Road ramshackle house with its one bathroom. But there was the problem of Aunt Bella and her shaking hands. There was talk of leaving her at home, but Mother, loyal to a fault, would have none of it. Aunt Bella, shakes and all, would attend the get-together, but with strict instructions to ask for a soft drink instead of tea, so as to avoid the clatter of cup and saucer. She followed instructions and when Pam's father went to the bar to fetch a ginger ale, I accompanied him. To my surprise, he took Aunt Bella's shaking hands in stride and suggested, with a wink, that a little vodka in the ginger ale might help. And it did. With each sip Aunt Bella's hands became steadier so that when it was time to say goodbye her handshake was as strong as a politician pressing flesh for votes. Mother voted the meeting of the two families a gratifying success.

What remained a deep mystery, however, and still is, was Mother's reaction to the courtship. In retrospect it is astonishing that the love affair was encouraged, despite the fact that Pam and I were both still only teenagers. Why was Mother so accommodating? There was no discussion about Pam's religion, if any, or how I would be able to support her. Could Mother's unquestioned acceptance have been triggered because Pam was white and her family socially prominent?

On the other hand, the reasons for my obsession were clear. I was not an attractive young gentleman. Now six foot tall, I weighed only 110 pounds, and was referred to by my few friends as "Bones" or "Pipe Cleaner". Behind glasses with tortoise-shell rims, the colour of my eyes in a certain light dimmed to a pale gray. My upper teeth, like Mother's, were slightly bucked and the bottom teeth were randomly tilted. I could hide my ugly lower teeth under the top ones, but the price for this compensation was having to keep my mouth shut, not an exercise that came easily to me. In these circumstances the fact that Pam seemed genuinely to find me attractive outweighed all other considerations. The truth is that our love was hardly more profound than heavy necking, as it was called in those days, and sharing the social trivialities which marked much of life in middle-class Jamaica.

Perhaps I laid too heavy a symbolic burden on my White Goddess, expecting more than was possible from the relationship. Pam's family was, it turned out, no more aristocratic than mine and she, like me, had her demons to deal with. We drifted apart while I was at university until, finally, the engagement was formally called off by mutual consent and the ring returned.

As ever, I created a poem out of the experience, not necessarily all factually true, but true at least to the "hot as first love" emotions of the young suitor I once was. In a stanza from "Straight from the Horse's Mouth", I pictured the couple:

> She wore jodhpurs and a silk blouse,
> the top two buttons open, a proper forward seat,
> pelvic bone braced to pommel, her body
> an exclamation mark. He was
> more a question mark, slumped
> on the cantle of the saddle,
> khaki pants tucked into riding boots,
> trying to woo her with mordant wit.

CHAPTER THREE

FORDHAM UNIVERSITY

Thanks to the Jesuits, I was awarded a scholarship to Fordham University in New York, not based on any scholastic merit, but because three of my uncles had been undergraduates there. I found the prospect less than exciting. I was nervous about leaving my little island for the first time and uncertain about what I wanted to do with the rest of my life. For most boys in Jamaica at this time, graduating from secondary school was the end of the education line. There was no local university and only the rich could afford to send their sons abroad to study. Amongst the minority of boys who attended secondary school, boys who "graduated" at 17 or 18 considered themselves to be "big men", ready to enter the work force, mostly the civil service. If successful, they looked forward to getting married and starting a family.

Mother finally persuaded me to accept the scholarship and it was arranged that I would fly to Miami, where I would be met by my dad. Having to cope with getting to know a strange father and an alien country simultaneously took its emotional toll, and my memories of the transition have almost completely faded. However, compared with the dinge of Nelson's Drugstore at Cross Roads, how brilliantly lit and extravagant was the Walgreens pharmacy where Dad took me shopping! We travelled by train to New York and at one stop I saw a rest room sign that read "Colored". I thought this was a spelling mistake, missing a "u" the way it would be spelled in Jamaica and I was astonished when Dad explained to me the dynamics of race relations in America.

In the hot July of 1945, a New York taxi deposited me in front of the entrance to Fordham University, marked by two imposing pillars. Cut into the stone over the one on the right was the name ISAACS. I was proud but intimidated by my uncle Vincent hanging over my head in more ways than one. I dragged my suitcase through the hallowed portal in a high state of nervousness, totally unprepared for the transition from a cocooned colonial life in Jamaica to the daunting intricacies of an alien American culture.

The Rose Hill campus of Fordham University, founded in 1843, was an oasis of calm and tranquility in the New York borough of the Bronx, inhabited largely by working-class families, many of them black. There were wide expanses of lawn trimmed by Brother Mark, riding a self-propelled lawn mower, the first of its kind I had ever seen. Squirrels – also the first I had seen – romped up elm trees that lined shady walks and paths. Dotted around the campus were imposing buildings, some approaching Gothic elegance, others that later, in my sophomoric arrogance, I came to denigrate as "Italian Wedding Cake" architecture.

My transition from country bumpkin to city slicker was cushioned somewhat by the fact that the Jesuits who ran the University did not consider the student body sufficiently adult to be afforded much freedom. No girls were allowed in the halls of residence and there was a Dean of Discipline, thin as an exclamation mark, who prowled the corridors at night in sneakers to guard against any hanky-panky. We were not allowed to leave the campus on weekends without the written permission of parents or guardians, and Mass on week days, as well as Sundays, was compulsory for Catholics. Checked off at the front door of the chapel like prisoners, the penalty for failure to attend was the issuance of demerits, an accumulation of which could result in the culprit being "campused" indefinitely. On theological grounds this galled me. Since I had been taught that missing Mass on Sunday was a mortal sin, the penalty for which was eternal damnation, I thought the punishment of demerits to be presumptuous and redundant. As a gesture of defiance, I sometimes purposely incurred demerits by missing Mass on campus, but going to the neighbouring parish church instead.

Eschewing the influence on American education of Dewey and other so called pragmatists, the Jesuits, for over 400 years, had adhered to their own vision of a liberal education based on Aristotelian logic and the magnum opus of St. Thomas Aquinas, which integrated every known branch of philosophy into one seamless, non-contradictory whole, capable, by dint of reason unaided by divine revelation, of being reconciled with Catholic doctrine. Scholasticism, sometimes referred to in derogatory terms, mostly by those who have never studied it, comprised apologetics, formal logic, epistemology, ontology, psychology, cosmology and ethics. Philosophy was compulsory for all Fordham students regardless of their so-called "major". In effect, everybody majored in philosophy and all other subjects were secondary, including English, my major.

At the time of my attendance at Fordham, the scope of a liberal arts education at a Jesuit university was somewhat curtailed by the demands of World War II, then drawing to an end. The usual four years of college in America were truncated to three, semesters converted to trimesters in order to cope with the normal four-year syllabus. Many young Jesuits were serving as chaplains in the armed services, so old stalwarts of an earlier generation had to be brought out of retirement to supplement the few young priests who had been denied military membership for reasons of physical disability.

My professors were a motley crew. The ancient priest who taught religion was nearly blind and could only read the attendance register by holding it two inches in front of his thick spectacles. Many students, after responding to their names, immediately escaped through the open windows that lined one exterior wall, leaving the priest to lecture to a nearly empty room. One of my philosophy professors, an alcoholic, rather than correct papers, rolled dice with his students for their year-end marks.

Overall, the academic standard at Fordham at this time left much to be desired, and I was not an outstanding student except in the philosophy subjects. Ironically, it was the philosophic emphasis of the Jesuits that nearly cost me my Catholic faith. The logic of Thomistic Scholasticism left no room for doubt. The concatenation of means to ends was made to seem utterly inevitable. If you wished to get to Chicago, you took the train. If you wished to experience the beatific vision, you kept the commandments. It was as simple as that. What happened, of course, is that when temptation trumped the means, I began to doubt the end. The inevitable linkage between the two became counterproductive, the one working against the other, negating itself.

What was missing in this teleological approach was acceptance of mystery as an essential ingredient of any religious experience. Religion, as taught at Fordham, was given only token attention, relegated to old, nearly blind teachers. Little recognition was afforded original sin or God's mercy. We were taught to think in syllogisms and in syllogisms there is no room for the sanctification of grace. This is not to detract from the vast wisdom of Scholasticism. What was lacking was balance, some awe of the numinous unknown as a counterweight to the intellectual muscle of philosophy.

My best friend at Fordham was Jack de Lisser, of that well known de Lisser clan, another youngster from Jamaica. I had not known him previous to our bumping into each other outside the letterboxes in Dealy Hall. Unlike me, Jack knew what he wanted to do in life, and after graduation from Fordham, he went on to study medicine in Dublin, eventually returning to Jamaica with an elegant Irish wife. The biggest decision facing Jack and I at the time of our Fordham enrolment was which one of only two available elective courses we should sign up for – physical training or ROTC. For years afterwards I dined out on the fib that I thought ROTC stood for Renaissance Overview Trimester Course and therefore signed up for it, whereas in fact I knew that it was an acronym for Reserve Officers Training Corps. The true significance of this I was only to discover at a later date.

Both Jack and I, having signed up for ROTC, were issued military uniforms, which we were obliged to wear to ROTC lectures. There were advantages. The war in Japan ended on September 2nd 1945 and a multitude converged in Times Square to celebrate victory. Decked out in our ROTC uniforms, Jack and I mingled with the crowd and soon found ourselves being soulfully kissed by strange young ladies who breathlessly exclaimed, "Thank you for saving America." Any further gestures of gratitude were foreclosed by our having to be back on campus before midnight.

All during our undergraduate days the lack of money was a problem. Exchange control regulations were still in force in Jamaica, prohibiting the export of US currency. Wherry Wharf sometimes earned dollars from its ship chandelling operation, and Mother would wrap a twenty dollar bill in carbon paper and slip it in a letter to me. Some got through the censors and others didn't. To bridge the gap, Jack and I worked at a number of part-time jobs – he setting up trays at Fordham hospital and me as a clerk in the campus bookstore. On weekends we both worked as ushers at the Grand Concourse Paradise theatre, decked out in Gilbert and Sullivan uniforms replete with white gloves, gold epaulettes and braided caps. We were paid the minimum wage which at that time was 50 cents per hour.

Given the demands of work and the protective policy of the university, our social lives were virtually monastic. In my second year, my roommate was an earnest Italian American who looked up to me as an exemplar of English manners and decorum. He was anxious to learn the correct knife and fork to use at formal dinners and I had rather to fudge my instructions. In my final year, seniors were assigned private rooms, each with a bathroom and a window overlooking the quad, guarded by a statue of the Virgin Mary.

My life at Fordham was a far cry from the "Joe College" fraternity frenzy experiences of an American university today. For one thing the shadow of war still lingered in the halls of academia and across the American landscape. Returning veterans were in deadly earnest about completing their education. For a callow youth from Jamaica like me, college was a combination of dread, curiosity and continued sexual frustration. During the brief term-time holidays there was no family to provide escape from the Rose Hill campus, and summer vacations were ungenerous, about three weeks, the first of which was disturbed by my break-up with Pam. The second summer I managed to save enough money to ride the Havana Special train to Miami, two days and a night sitting up in couch, thence by Pan American Clipper to Kingston via Camaguey. But even back home in Jamaica I was restless and found myself impatient to return to Fordham.

Jack de Lisser and I pooled our extracurricular earnings and bought an ancient Buick. On some Sundays we would drive to Tuxedo Park to see my sister Audrey, who was finishing her secondary education at Mt. St. Vincent Academy, which by this time had been relocated to a mansion in a wooded estate in Tuxedo Park, New York. It had been bequeathed to the Sisters by the family who owned the Piper Heidsieck champagne empire in France. Fifty-two students were in the charge of twelve nuns who lived in the servants' quarters.

After graduation, Audrey returned to Jamaica and lived there for a number of years, working at Wherry Wharf. She subsequently returned to America and went on to earn her B.Sc degree from Hunter College and her Master's degree from the Fordham School of Social Studies, becoming a dedicated professional psychiatric social worker. These were no mean accomplishments, achieved on her own with little or no help from home. Her speciality was troubled children and this vocation so absorbed her energies and so overwhelmed her generous heart that she, like Aunt Bella, never married.

My relationship with my sister was often rocky. I felt intimidated by the intensity of her feelings. Audrey's reaction to injustice, even in the abstract, was like the turning on of a light so blindingly powerful one was obliged to close one's eyes and to take a step back. Our arguments about Capitalism versus Socialism would come to a point like Lenin's beard, with me shouting and Audrey breaking into tears.

By the time of my senior year at Fordham I considered myself a hardened New Yorker. There was hardly any crime in New York in those days, and on weekends a group of us would take the subway to the

Village to listen to jazz at a variety of clubs. During term I managed to see a few Broadway shows, cheaper tickets for standing room only. I tried to capitalize on my acting skills by attending auditions of the Fordham Drama Club, but my sing-song Jamaican accent was incompatible with the rhythm of American speech and I was assigned only walk-on parts, such as the "Pen" in a production of Ibsen's *Peer Gynt*.

In my final year, I joined the fencing team and won my varsity letter in this esoteric sport; this was not much consolation when in a contest at West Point the Fordham team was routed by the army cadets.

In that year too an intriguing notice appeared on the bulletin board. It advised that a "Coming Out Ball" would be held at the Sherry Netherland hotel in Manhattan for a collection of debutantes sponsored by the American Polish Society. Fordham seniors, approved by the Dean of Discipline, could apply to be escorts if they possessed or could rent formal wear i.e. a tuxedo and were over 5 ft. 10 in. tall. They had also to be competent dancers, although how the Dean would ascertain that fact was a mystery.

Jack de Lisser and I applied and were accepted. We rented our tuxedos from Harry Harris who charged two different rates, $5 for tuxedos with previous stains, $7 for tuxedos if dry-cleaned after the last rental. We opted for the latter.

My assigned date at the Ball was one of the Zaplisky twins; Jack de Lisser was assigned to the other. They were both stunningly attractive, my twin a little plump, her magnificent breasts heaving out of the cylix of her green strapless evening gown. I attribute my success that night to being able to hold my liquor and being a good dancer. While the American escorts were stamp-footing on the dance floor, stuck in one spot, Jack and I and our partners were gliding around the ballroom like resurrected Fred Astaires and Ginger Rogers. We were applauded when we returned our ladies to their respective tables. When I asked Mrs. Zaplisky to dance she practically begged me to marry her daughter.

"Don't you just love his English accent," she exclaimed. Her husband agreed and ordered more champagne, which the twins downed with reckless speed. The Zaplisky parents had reserved two suites at the hotel, one for the twins and one for themselves. After more dances and more drinks and after consultation with her sister, my twin dangled the key to the girl's suite before my eyes, took my hand and led me to the elevators.

As was the case with Pam, this assignation was pre-pill agony and I was too unsophisticated and ridden with Catholic guilt to produce a condom. She attended a Catholic college in New Jersey and although equally inflamed we both knew the limits of the game. My tuxedo would be returned to Harry Harris the next day, ready for another rental with stains.

Whilst I was at Fordham, I made it a point of duty to visit my father on a regular basis. He, after being honourably discharged from the military, had returned to his civilian job as a conductor on the New York Central railway. As a senior conductor he was a member of one of the most powerful labour unions in the United States – the Brotherhood of Railway Engineers and Conductors. His was a position of considerable responsibility, especially on crack trains like the 20th Century Chief that ran between New York and Chicago. His union membership provided an important economic cushion during the great depression of the Thirties and may have influenced my mother's decision to marry him. He had never remarried after their separation and by the time I came to know him he lived in one room at the Elks Club in Poughkeepsie, New York, able to bid for the easier runs because of his seniority.

I had experienced the anomie of loneliness, and now I was at university I did not wish him to feel that he was being ostracized for his social status. We shared a double bed at the Elks club and in the morning, when the alarm went off at 5 a.m, I could hear him grumbling his way to the bathroom down the corridor. Through half opened eyes I peeked at him putting on his black serge uniform, shiny in patches from too many pressings. In winter, while I curled up in the bed and went back to sleep, he had to tramp through snow to the railway station over which a cold wind blew from the Hudson river. But all his sufferings were forgotten in the evenings when he escorted me into the bar of the club where his cronies were gathered. He proudly proclaimed, "This is my son who is studying at Fordham. Drinks for everybody on me."

I managed to maintain an overall B average during my studies at Fordham, getting all As in the philosophy courses and a scattering of Cs in subjects like German and Physics. From each graduating cohort, the University awarded six teaching fellowships, considered to be the pinnacle of academic achievement. The pay was $3000 per year. Philosophy professors, all priests, lectured in amphitheatre classrooms to about 150 students and the teaching fellows were obliged each morning to tutor groups of about 20 for two-hour sessions. They also assisted with grading end of term exam "blue books", which could run to as many as three per student. There were no "true or false" questions in those days. The answer to every question was an essay.

More as a lark than anything else, I applied for one of the teaching

Ralph's father, Lawrence Thompson

fellowships. It took some time for the decision to be announced and in the interim I was obliged, as an ROTC student, to attend a three-week final military exercise at Stewart Air Force base adjacent to the West Point Academy. The world was at peace and the authorities tried to flunk out as many candidates for a commission as conscience would allow. By some miracle I managed to get through and, by order of President Harry S. Truman, was commissioned a second lieutenant in the United States Air Force Reserves for a period of five years commencing July 1948.

After this, the formal graduation ceremony at Fordham was somewhat of an anticlimax. It was held in the gymnasium with Mother, Dad and Audrey in attendance. The invited commencement speaker turned out to be none other than Uncle Bishop. I never discovered what machinations behind the scenes had engineered such a conclave. I wore my academic gown over my Air Force uniform. The military uniform stirred patriotic pride in my father's breast and the academic gown was for my mother the fulfilment of all her dreams and aspirations for her son. Audrey's conviction that I was the most favoured child of the family never limited her magnanimous joy at my achievements.

In *Moving On*, I tried to sum up what Fordham had meant for me in a long poem, "Goodbye Aristotle, So Long America". The poem ended like this:

> Goodbye Aristotle
> So long America. Time to move on.
> The train is panting south, in my valise
> Newman once more wrapped in dirty linen
> to be washed in private. I slide
> the coach door open, stand straddling two cars,
> the couplings battling for direction.
> I sway to the message of the wheels,
> a splurge of hope riding the steel conviction of the rails.

CHAPTER FOUR

HOLLYWOOD

By way of a graduation gift to me, and to celebrate Mother's temporary release from the worst of her asthma attacks, Dad arranged free railway passes for Mother, Audrey and me to visit the Breen family in Hollywood. The original contact had been through Uncle Bishop's family, the Emmets, who shared an Irish Catholic bond with the Breens. The Breens had visited Jamaica on a number of occasions and Mother had extended to them the most lavish hospitality that she and Uncle Mike could offer. They naturally insisted on reciprocating as and when the Thompsons could visit California.

Mr. Breen was the head of an organisation set up by the American film industry to self-regulate acceptable conduct and moral values in the making of movies. It was known as the Breen office, later the Johnson office, and wielded enormous veto power. Without a Breen *imprimatur* no movie theatre would show the film and it would be doomed. This was considered preferable to regulation by the Federal government, which was poised to take action if the industry did not clean up its act. Breen censorship was based on strict conservative Catholic ethics that not only succeeded in cleansing sex from the cinema but neutering plot and motivation as well. Breen, czar of the nation's morals, was also a millionaire and lived in a Malibu mansion.

Mother was enthusiastic about the trip. However, we discovered that, for reasons of economy, the trains we had to take ran on coal. The locomotives belched black smoke from their funnels which, in the absence of air-conditioning, drifted in through the open windows covering us with a fine coat of soot. We sat on slatted wooden benches, like tramcar seats in Jamaica, and when the necessity arose stumbled through two cars to find a communal toilet. In parts of the country I noticed a surprising number of Native Americans on the trains; the many mothers with babes at their breasts reminded me of home. At this time I was not aware of the great injustices visited on Native Americans during the emergence of the United States as a sovereign nation.

One highlight of the journey lives in my memory. I had scoffed at the arrangements to visit the Grand Canyon, but when we came upon it I was astonished and mesmerized by its beauty and inconceivable size. A mile deep and ten miles across, it seemed like an inverted Mount Everest, descending in a series of golden layers and viridian ridges to a bottom shrouded in pink mist. This was pure space that welled up from the deep centre of the earth into a huge laugh, confident that anyone who came to behold would leave enthralled. We stood on the brink in awe.

The Breens met us at the railway station and drove us to their home. Mrs. Breen was a blonde Californian whose bouffant hairdo looked as if it had just been sprayed. Mr. Breen was given to wearing fawn-coloured sport jackets. I was asked to share a room with their son, Tommy, not to be confused with Bobby Breen, a Jewish child actor who had been given permission to use the stage name of Breen. I remembered him playing Little Lord Fauntleroy in the movie of that name.

The real Tommy Breen had been a member of the famous Merrill's Raiders during the recently concluded war, part of a landing party on a Pacific atoll defended by defiant Japanese soldiers. American troops scrambled off landing crafts, trying to establish a beachhead. Casualties were high. A sniper shot Tommy in the left leg, bringing him down. The first waves of American troops were repelled and Tommy had waited all night on the beach to be rescued. Every time he moved his injured leg, the sniper saw the movement and was able to blast another bullet into it. Japanese mortar rounds fell on either side of him. American soldiers were trained to change the mortar pattern every hour to hit the inter-stices of the previous rounds and Tommy expected this to happen at any moment, but the pattern never changed.

At first dawn, the second wave of landing crafts roared up the beach, disgorging personnel carriers and tanks, one of which ran over Tommy's injured leg. He regained consciousness in a ship's hospital, his left leg amputated just below the knee. The amputation had saved his life and when I met him he was nearly completely mobile, fitted with a prosthesis designed to look like a real leg.

Mrs. Breen took Mother and Audrey on sightseeing jaunts and Tommy included me in his social rounds, moving from one location to another in his specially fitted Cadillac convertible. We had coffee with Andre Previn, the jazz and classical pianist, went on a fishing expedition with a gaggle of actors including Brian Donlevy and Cesar Romero, and made the rounds of several famous nightclubs.

One night after a quiet dinner at home, Tommy was visited by his current girlfriend, introduced to us as Liz Taylor. She insisted on washing the dishes and I insisted on drying them. An astonishing young beauty with lavender eyes, she was dressed in a pair of shorts so scantily engineered around her bottom that had she appeared in a film so dressed, Mr. Breen would have vetoed it. She expressed a desire to visit Jamaica and I offered to be her escort if she did. We sat around chatting and Miss Taylor displayed moments of wit and wisdom beyond her age. The evening ended when Tommy suggested that it was time to drive her home.

We left for the return trip to New York shortly after this memorable evening. The two enduring images of the visit that later lingered in my mind were Elizabeth Taylor and the Grand Canyon but not necessarily in that order. Tommy and I exchanged a few letters before drifting apart. He starred in one movie, *The River*, directed by Jean Renoir, son of Auguste Renoir, the famous painter. It was a cult success. Thereafter Tommy deserted Hollywood to become a housing developer in Arizona.

With the passing years, Liz Taylor, my dish-washing companion, became a famous and genuinely talented actress. But as she grew older, wedded to and divorced from a number of Hollywood personalities, she suffered a series of serious illnesses. For these she was usually treated at the Harkness Pavilion of New York's Presbyterian Medical Centre where, years later, I was to have a hiatus hernia repaired. During my convalescence, strolling the corridors dragging my drip lines behind me, I often fantasised about bumping into Liz Taylor and reminding her of the night we did the dishes at the Breens. I like to think she would have remembered. Her death ended my fantasy.

CHAPTER FIVE

LAW SCHOOL

After the California adventure I returned to the Fordham campus, still undecided about what I wanted to do with my life. I was on the verge of returning to Jamaica when I read on the bulletin board that I had been awarded one of the teaching fellowships, my area of specialization to be Ethics, a subject taught to senior year students at Fordham. This was a considerable achievement, an opportunity that I did not want to miss. A condition of the fellowships was that the successful candidates must pursue a graduate degree at the doctoral level, either a Ph.D. or its equivalent in law, the Juris Doctor. I opted for the latter and was duly enrolled in the Fordham Law School, located in an ancient, ramshackle building at the opposite end of Manhattan from the Rose Hill campus where I would be teaching in the mornings. Mother was overjoyed that I was on my way to becoming a lawyer, unaware that the American qualification would not be accepted in Jamaica, which still had a Bar split between barristers and solicitors. Uncle Mike, himself a frustrated lawyer, sent me a long letter of congratulations and dear Audrey phoned to say how proud she was of big brother.

To position myself conveniently for my early morning teaching assignment I rented a small room on Park Avenue, an address with considerable *cachet* where it luxuriated in midtown Manhattan, but deteriorated notably as it travelled north to the Bronx, until on reaching my abode it became a virtual slum. My room was on the second floor, with one window, the bathroom down the hall. There were no facilities for eating or space for a refrigerator.

The textbook for the Ethics course I would be teaching at Fordham was brilliantly entitled *Liberty – its Use and Abuse*. Fr. Edward McNally, co-author of the textbook, was the assigned professor for the course. He had graduated from Fordham Law School before deciding to become a priest. As a personality he was not greatly gregarious, but we got on well enough.

The other five teaching fellows had all opted, like me, to study law, but their motives for doing so were quite different from mine. They intended to make a living from it, but in my case, the jurisdictional and geographical limitations of an American law degree were major obstacles. In truth, my embrace of the law had a touch of the dilettante about it, and my attention to its disciplines was further diluted when Fr. McNally became terminally ill in midterm and I was asked to conduct the main lectures.

My teaching fellowship carried with it the privilege of the Faculty Lounge and I enjoyed this academic oasis, a decided contrast to the cheap diner on Fordham Road where the instructors grabbed a bite to eat before taking the subway from the Grand Concourse station to the Law School on 14th Street in Lower Manhattan. Law lectures commenced at 2 pm and ended at about 5:30 pm. There was only one woman and one black student in my class. By a strange coincidence, the first case I was called upon to recite in my contracts class was *Harvey vs. Facey*, the venue of which was Jamaica. It remains a classic in contract law on offers and acceptances.

By the time I took over the main Ethics lectures, the class consisted mostly of returning veterans and I was conscious of how young and inexperienced I must seem to them. To look older I tried to grow a moustache, but the hairs sprouted sparsely. Relying on a trick from my days in theatre, I removed a cork from a bay rum bottle and held one end of it over the flame of my Zippo cigarette lighter. I then applied the charred end of the cork each morning to the hairs on my upper lip, darkening them.

My first year at Law school was stimulating but lonely. When I learned that to take the New York bar exam it was necessary for all candidates to establish formal residency in New York for a minimum of two years, I joined forces with two other law school students and we rented an apartment in Maspeth, Long Island, living together for the required period.

It was during this Maspeth period of communal living that I learned how enjoyable and stimulating male camaraderie can be, an experience denied me in the early years of my life. To handle transportation to the Rose Hill campus I bought a 1936 Plymouth motorcar for $100. It had an inordinately long bonnet, a bubble of a cabin that seated two persons and, in the back, an uncovered rumble seat. The few dates that I was able to garner loved riding in the rumble seat, even in winter, but its architecture did little for advancing my sex life.

While I was celebrating the Maspeth escape from anomie, Jamaica was slowly recovering from the deprivations of the war years. Mother's first priority was the purchase of a new car to replace the Ford sedan of our youth. The United Kingdom motor industry was slowly making the adjustment from tanks to motor cars and to earn foreign exchange the British government ordained that the first deliveries should go to Americans who could pay for the vehicle in advance in US dollars. The only proof of citizenship required for this special treatment was a photocopy of the purchaser's passport.

Mother had accumulated dollars during the war years from Wherry Wharf's ship chandelling business, and rightly concluded that since I possessed an American passport I would be the ideal candidate for purchasing a car. Exchange control was now relaxed so Mother was able to send dollars to me in New York. I concluded the purchase in my name and it was agreed that during the summer vacation of 1950 I would proceed to England by boat to collect the vehicle and see to its shipment to Jamaica.

I was delighted to learn that Mother and Audrey planned to travel by ship to France, there to meet for the first time the lady who had fallen deeply in love with Uncle Vincent while he was in Paris on leave from his regiment in World War I, and who had religiously placed a rose on his grave every year since his death. The plan was that I would rendez-vous with Mother and Audrey in Paris, able to report that we were now the proud owners of a new Vauxhall six cylinder sedan, safely garaged in London.

Uncle Vincent's faithful lover turned out to be a lady of considerable spirit but less than comely countenance. She had little English and we had no French, so the meeting was somewhat strained. We invited her to visit us in Jamaica but she claimed she was too old to travel.

Back in England, I escorted Mother and Audrey to their ship for the return voyage to America. I spent two weeks in London seeing the sights, sharing a flat with Normadelle, Jack De Lisser's sister and Tessa Prendergast, Jack's cousin. Elaine Dundy, the successful author of a novel entitled *The Dud Avocado*, was also a flatmate. They were all models and a man with a motorcar in postwar Britain was a welcome guest. They pranced about the flat in all stages of undress, unembarrassed by my presence.

It was in London that I received the results of my first year law exams. I had been awarded an A in Contracts, an A in Trusts and a B+ in Torts, three of the most important foundation subjects of the law school curriculum. I was ecstatic, finally convinced that I possessed a natural proclivity for the law.

The second year of law school was less stressful than the first and I welcomed the summer break of 1951 with a sense of accomplishment and excitement. I invited Lou DiDonna, one of my Maspeth flat mates, to come with me to Jamaica to meet the family. He eagerly accepted and was beginning to immerse himself in the local culture when the authorities unexpectedly announced that a hurricane named Charlie was headed directly for Jamaica. Lou was innocent of what damage a hurricane could cause. Mother made matters worse by suggesting that on the day before its expected arrival we go to confession at the Cathedral, rather than prepare our defences. The Governor, Sir Hugh Foot, was scheduled to address the nation at nine o'clock in the evening to entreat for calm. In the late afternoon I drove Lou to Cable Hut beach on the outskirts of Kingston to inspect the horizon. The air was still, the sunset a series of red streaks, like uncooked bacon.

Uncle Mike prepared for the hurricane by assembling a collection of tools, including hammer and nails, saw, axe and flashlights. Unfortunately, he neglected to batten the living room windows. In the middle of the Governor's radio address a giant fist of wind and rain smashed into the house from the north. The radio went silent, surrendering to the howling of the wind which was so strong it shifted the verandah roof off its columns.

One of the living room windows blew in. This called for emergency measures to save the main roof from sailing into Kingston harbour. Mother, Aunt Bella and Audrey were chanting the rosary. Uncle Mike used the axe to hack a wooden closet door from its hinges. He and I held it against the frame of the open window while Lou fastened it in place with four inch nails. Fear is a spur. Lou drove the nails home in four or five unerring strokes.

Except for the initial damage to the verandah, the house survived the hurricane. Others were not so lucky. When we were able to walk down South Camp Road, we could see into house after house, external walls blown away, in one a solitary toilet standing guard over the debris. Our landlord, Mr. Shoucair, repaired our verandah roof and increased the rent.

Lou and I returned to New York from our Jamaican adventure confronted by the reality of having to sit the New York Bar exam at year end. This exam, the most difficult in the nation, comprised one full day devoted to substantive law and one day devoted to adjective law, the quaint name assigned to procedural matters, with special emphasis on practice before the New York courts. Having been awarded a *Juris Doctor* degree by Fordham, I was in two minds whether to attempt the Bar exams at all, but at Mother's urging decided me to give it a try. But while my Maspeth flat mates were burning the midnight oil reviewing three years of study, I concentrated on substantive law, the meat of the Justice system, and neglected Adjective law as too parochial, relying more on memory than conceptualization, in short a drudge.

The results of the Bar exam are published in the *New York Times*, some two or three months after the exams. To pay the rent during this hiatus, I took a night job at the Brooklyn Navy Yard. My assigned section was no gleaming hermitage from whence sailors could transit ship to ship or ship to shore. It was an old basement area where I stood for eight hours a night manipulating the foot pedals and levers of a Hamilton pressing machine. Sailors would undress and stand in line in their skivvies while I tried to rehabilitate their uniforms. On the way home after my "graveyard" shift I would stop at a diner for an English muffin and a cup of coffee – all that I could afford. I had no friends, my only entertainment an occasional movie.

Then came the day when the Bar exam results were published in the *New York Times*. Because my name is toward the end of the alphabet, by the time my eyes rested there I had already seen that my fellow teaching associates had all passed the Bar. I had passed the Substantive part but failed the Adjective section.

I returned to Jamaica in disgrace. Mother's reaction was particularly vehement, not so much against me but against Lou who, she claimed, had distracted me from studying so that he would be acclaimed a better student. This was patently ridiculous, but there seemed always to be a fist in the Isaacs family preparing for defence or revenge. Still undecided what I wanted to do with my life and to assuage Mother's disappointment, I agreed to resit the Adjective section of the Bar exam. This meant returning to New York where I rented a basement room, in one corner of which stood the boiler that heated the house and which let out intermittent growls day and night. The basement was furnished with a small cot, a desk and a chair. I started a lonely but rigorous review of my Adjective law text books and class notes, resat the exam two months later and passed.

Shortly after graduation from law school, the Korean conflict erupted into a bloody war. In America the draft was reinstituted and just as I received news that I had passed the New York Bar, a letter from the United States Air Force arrived advising that my ROTC commission had been activated and ordering me to report in five days to an induction camp in New Jersey.

My first reaction to the summons was resentment at the awesome power of a nation that, with one short, unapologetic letter, could disrupt the lives of citizens and foreigners alike. To hell with it, I thought. I will return to my safe home in Jamaica. But my legal training informed me that as a citizen of the United States any such move would brand me as a military deserter and fugitive, the consequences of which I did not wish to contemplate. I had already concluded that America's intervention in Korea was justified and necessary to halt the spread of Communism in Asia. As a lawyer I was unlikely to see active frontline duty. Released now from the claustrophobia of my Jamaica life, the prospect of a global adventure was irresistible. Passing the Bar exams not only satisfied mother's ambitions for me, it very likely saved me from active combat duty in Korea.

CHAPTER SIX

LAW AND THE JAPANESE ADVENTURE

I had not yet been sworn in as a member of the Bar and some instinct warned me that this would be important. I put my case by telephone to the powers that be and it was arranged that Judge Nolan of the Second Judicial district would privately administer the oath of office in his chambers on the morning of 28 February 1952, the day I had to leave for my first military assignment at an early warning fighter interception squadron in Niagara Falls, New York. Judge Nolan was gowned in black and stood before a large American flag that flanked his desk. He reminded me that I would henceforth be an officer of the court and proceeded to administer the oath. Dad was the only witness to the anticlimax of a ceremony that lasted five minutes. He proudly saw me off at Grand Central station for the train journey north. When I looked back he was standing at attention on the platform, saluting my departure.

It was a cold February afternoon when I reported for duty at the fighter interception squadron on the Canadian border, three feet of snow on the ground. Four jet fighters were parked on the apron of the runway, their pilots in the "ready room", fully dressed for combat, drinking coffee, ready to scramble if the red light flashed and the alarm began to howl.

I was assigned to the Base Legal Affairs unit, headed by Captain Robert Feltner, a Harvard graduate whose speciality was marine law. He was punctilious but friendly, a good person to initiate me into the complexities of military justice. He explained that although I had been assigned to his small team, I could not function officially as a member of the Judge Advocate Generals department because I was still only a second lieutenant. He promised to put in train the paperwork necessary to correct this anomaly, which would require a promotion to first lieutenant, but warned that it would be a slow bureaucratic process. In the meantime I would be expected to perform general duties as an air force officer, including my turn as "Officer of the Day".

This duty should more properly be described as "Officer of the Night", because the designated officer had full responsibility for the night-time functions of the base, except for major emergencies, in which case the commandant was to be awakened, not something a junior officer would lightly do. The accoutrements of office were a band with the initials O.D. worn around the left arm and a .45 revolver strapped on the right hip. At four hour intervals the Officer of the Day was obliged to inspect the airmen guarding the jets and, as part of this exercise, to memorize a password. I pulled Officer of the Day three times while at the Niagara Falls base, and on each occasion it was snowing and bitterly cold. I drove a jeep along the perimeter of the base listening for the shouted challenge, "Who goes there?"

I shouted the password.

"Advance and be recognised!"

The guard pointed his rifle at my head.

Having disembarked the jeep, I stood freezing in front of its head-lights. On the one hand I was terrified that I would forget the password, in which case I might be shot dead, and on the other I found it difficult to take seriously the comedic rigmarole involved.

Each officer was assigned a private room in the Bachelors Officers Quarters, the BOQ, equipped with a refrigerator. Down the hall from me was Major Wilson, a crack pilot from World War II who had been recalled for duty during the Korean conflict despite his advancing years. More dangerous than age, however, was his drinking. His fridge was stacked with beer, which he kept downing, one after another, even when on scramble duty. He obviously had a death wish, because he would boast to me that on take-off, rather than lift the nose of the jet, he would retract the wheels instead, flying down the runway about two feet parallel to the ground. We became good friends and one night, in the intimacy of a dozen beers, he confided his story to me. He had become accustomed to the privileges and recognition that military service as an officer in World War II afforded him.

"Thompson," he asked, "do you know what I did in civilian life before the Air Force recalled me? I was a goddam taxi driver in Boston. The only thing I know how to do real well is fly a goddam jet. I ain't looking forward to going back to a cab, I can tell you." About a month later, he crashed into some high tension wires on take-off, failing to gain the altitude necessary to clear the obvious hurdle. He was killed instantly.

I spent about five months under the tutelage of Captain Feltner, but

Lieutenant Ralph Thompson in the US Airforce

before the paperwork for my possible promotion could be completed, overseas orders for a number of new officers, including me, came down from headquarters. Some of my friends were assigned to Europe, but I was not so fortunate. My destination, after two weeks' special leave, was to be Haneda Air Force Base in Tokyo, Japan, a major military Air Transport Command that flew long distance missions across the Far East. My mother was devastated by the news. Neither of us had any clear geographical idea of the difference between Japan and Korea, or what my duties might be in either.

She was convinced that I would be killed in combat on foreign soil like her brother, Vincent. In vain I pointed out that I was a lawyer, thanks to her urging, and would be "flying a desk". She insisted on coming to New York to spend part of my leave there with me. When she kissed me goodbye, choking back tears, I heard the words that would haunt me thenceforth.

"I know I will never see you again," she cried. "Wars always take the brightest ones."

Dad was cheerful and helpful, already calculating what medals I would be entitled to wear when my tour of duty was over.

The flight from San Francisco to Japan on a converted B-52 aircraft was exhausting and it took me a few days to settle in. Haneda Air Force base was a massive military complex on the edge of Tokyo Bay, bordered by the Tokyo river. From the BOQ where I was billeted I could see lone Japanese fishermen making for the open sea in their high-prowed boats, propelling the vessel with one long oar from a small platform in the stern. The JAG's (Judge Advocate Generals) office was on the second floor of a huge aircraft hangar that swayed whenever there was an earth tremor, an almost daily occurrence. We kept regular office hours from 8 am to 5 pm. The social centre of the base for commissioned personnel was the officer's club, equipped with a long bar, banks of "one armed bandits", slot machines and an upscale restaurant.

The Haneda JAG department was manned to cope with its general court martial jurisdiction, prepared to deal with crimes of the most heinous nature like treason and murder, as well as serious cases of fraud and negligence. The judge, the prosecutor and defence attorneys had to be qualified lawyers in civilian life. The findings and sentences of all cases were automatically reviewed by a prestigious civilian board in Washington that carefully inspected for proper procedure and adherence to the rules of evidence. Justice Felix Frankfurter of the US Supreme court was reported to have said that two years as a JAG officer at general court martial level was the best possible training for a civilian career in criminal law.

The Haneda JAG department, under the command of Captain Trabb, was overworked and undermanned. Immediately on reporting for duty I was thrown into the deepest end of the legal pool and expected to swim with officers who were experienced captains and majors. I managed to keep my head above water, but my rank as a lowly second lieutenant was a continuing embarrassment. Captain Trabb made it a high priority to accelerate the paper work started at Niagara Falls by Captain Feltner to bring about my formal appointment as a JAG officer. He wrote an enthusiastic letter of recommendation to higher command and this got results. My promotion to 1st. Lieutenant and my appointment as a JAG officer was approved in May 1953.

One Sunday, as I was taking a stroll around the base, musing on how a poor Jamaican boy from South Camp Road came to find himself in such strange circumstances and so far from home, a blue Chevrolet staff car speeded by, then braked to a stop. A bemedalled officer of high rank jumped out and approached me. I knew enough to snap to attention and salute, but he demanded to know why I had not saluted his car.

"I didn't know that I should salute a car," I replied with slight emphasis on the word car.

He flushed red in the face. "I am the Commanding General of this base. When I am in my staff car, my standard is flown and when you see that, you are to salute me, not the damn car. What kind of a soldier are you anyway?"

"Not a very good soldier, sir, but I hope a better lawyer."

He took a step back and examined me carefully. "You a JAG officer?"

"Yes, sir."

"What state bar?"

"New York, sir."

He stuck out his hand, inviting me to shake it. "Report to my office at 09.00 hours tomorrow. I was married in New York and have been trying to divorce my goddam wife for the past five years, but every JAG officer in my command has been from some shit ass jurisdiction like North Carolina or Arkansas."

I discovered that in the military, both lawyers and doctors were privileged to lead relatively autonomous lives; higher ranking officers were afraid of legal entanglements or catching a dose of clap. The next day I was obliged to inform the General that in New York at the time, the only grounds for divorce was adultery. He was not downcast. "Looks like I will have to hire a private detective, eh? We'll keep in touch."

Captain Trabb was succeeded as head of the JAG department at Haneda by Major Ralph Adams, a career officer with five more years of service before early retirement. His deep Alabama drawl camouflaged an alert mind and a true judicial temperament that usually came to the correct conclusion without unnecessarily bogging down in legal minutiae. There was also a strong fundamentalist religious streak in him and although he occasionally visited some of the better Tokyo brothels, I saw him one night, after too many bourbons, begging Fr. Bell, the Catholic chaplain, for absolution and, with tears streaming down his cheeks, insisting on kissing the priest's feet.

Major Adams also had strong political associations in his home state. He often talked about his partner in an insurance company that sold coverage to agricultural workers who payed their premiums in small monthly instalments. This partner had aspirations for national political exposure and was not paying sufficient attention to the profit potential of the insurance firm. Adams' long range plan on retirement from the Air Force was to call upon his political connections to get himself appointed president of a small southern university where, freed of military emergencies and excitements, he would live out the rest of his life in peace and tranquillity. Since I knew hardly anything about American politics, none of this meant much to me at the time. Often during our stay in Tokyo, Adams would suggest that after my tour of duty I should take over the management of his insurance firm and actuate its full potential. The starting salary figure that he teased me with seemed impossibly generous.

Whenever I exchanged the orderly pace of life at Haneda Air Force base for the bustle and ramshackle of Tokyo, I was surprised at the extent of the damage American long-range bombers had inflicted on the city. There were still piles of rubble at various intersections, reminders that a formal peace treaty with Japan had not yet been signed. It was still occupied territory and I, far from the comforts of Jamaica, was a uniformed representative of the conquering nation.

Except for the Ginza, nearly all the side streets were in a state of disrepair, lined with dingy wooden buildings that housed, cheek by jowl, restaurants, bars, groceries, pawn shops, hardware stores and a miscellany of small factories each lit by one desultory light bulb hanging from a rafter. The streets were jammed with bicycles and a scattering of vintage prewar taxis, so small that a Westerner could hardly fit in the back seat. We thought that the brand name "Toyota" was Japanese for toy. The din of an over-populated city was deafening – car horns demanding passage, bicycle bells warning pedestrians and the mournful cry of noodle vendors.

But Tokyo came to life at night, trying to compensate for its drab daytime existence. Written Japanese uses Chinese characters as its alphabet, each letter a tiny work of art in itself. With their curlicues and arabesques, Chinese characters are an ideal medium for neon signs and at night Tokyo became a blaze of flashing, blinking, flowing lights in a myriad of colours. No part of Tokyo was off limits to American servicemen, although some districts were visited at one's own risk. The one exception to freedom of movement was the Imperial Palace, a huge oasis of tranquillity in the middle of Tokyo surrounded by a water moat over which small bridges humped their backs like stretching cats. General MacArthur had wisely decided not to desecrate the image of the Emperor as a symbol of Japanese pride, custodian of its ancient culture and traditions. I was determined to find some way of getting into those off-limits Palace grounds.

The Imperial Riding Academy of Japan was located in the grounds of the Imperial Palace, under the watchful eye of Colonel Kido who had represented Japan in dressage at the 1936 Olympics. If I could qualify for membership in the Academy, this would be one way of crossing the magical moat into Shangri-La. Remembering my multitude of mounts in Jamaica on various donkeys and horses, not to mention Miss Steadman's tutelage in horsemanship, I was confident that I would qualify and, truth to tell, Colonel Kido was avid to receive the one hundred US dollar membership fee. The only condition was that I must be properly attired, including a custom-crafted pair of black riding boots.

I was issued with a pass to enter the Palace grounds, but the jeep driver had to let me off at one of the bridges, from whence I proceeded alone to the huge oblong pavilion where the *haute école* training took place. I was assigned a handsome mount, an Anglo Arab, and Colonel Kido called out his instructions from the stands over a public address system. There were tall mirrors flanking the walls of the arena so that riders could check their posture and for the rest of my life I will hear Colonel Kido's invocation, "Lieutenant Thompson, left shoulder down." During some sessions I rode with the Denka, the Crown Prince, who subsequently succeeded his father as Emperor. Exalted company for a boy from South Camp Road!

In my spare time, which was more bountiful than when I was teaching or studying law, I wanted to learn traditional Japanese calligraphy, but the only convenient Master, a Sensei, was a painter named Nakama who, before the war, had studied in Paris. His wife was also a painter and their studio in Hamada Yama was a half-hours' jeep drive from the base. I spent Sundays painting at the studio and another pupil, a girl named Yasuko, reasonably fluent in English, agreed to be my translator. She took a bus to Hamada Yama, but when the painting session was over I gave her a lift in the jeep back to her house.

She was an unusual Japanese woman, *sui generis* to the traditional female in that culture. Before the war her father had graduated from Columbia University in New York, converted to Christianity and returned to Japan to found a successful pharmaceutical company. Yasuko had been educated at a Protestant mission school and, after the war, accompanied her Father as his secretary on a trip to New York to renew old contacts there. On the sea voyage back to Japan he died suddenly of a heart attack.

Yasuko's hair was black, thick and shiny, her eyes heavy lidded but sparkling. When she laughed, which was often, she held her hand in front of her mouth. Exquisitely polite and demure, she was nevertheless forthright in expressing her opinions and over many painting sessions we became attracted to each other. The extraordinary characteristic of my relationship with Yasuko was that her determination not to surrender her virginity was as strong as mine to bed her. This resulted in a stalemate with interesting consequences. Over time we convinced ourselves that we were in love and should get married. How and when this could be accomplished remained vague. The *detente* I reached with Yasuko about the limits of our sex life bore some resemblance to my courtship with Pam. Before the advent of the pill, the fear of pregnancy was palpable. The mere thought that I might have to confess to my mother that I had fathered a child was enough to demolish the most potent erection. In those days the sexual geography was confined to what was euphemistically referred to as "necking" or "petting", a masochistic exercise. Yasuko was, within the prescribed bounds, an energetic lover, the sonata of our lovemaking orchestrated for finger and tongue.

To celebrate my twenty-fourth birthday, I invited Yasuko to the Haneda Officers club which, for the pleasure of dining and dancing, rivalled any American country club. A Japanese band played music from the current US Hit Parade and the menu featured meats and fish exquisitely prepared by a squad of Japanese chefs. There was a scattering of married officers dancing with their wives, but when Yasuko and I ventured onto the dance floor they all returned to their tables and subsequently took their leave of the club. As far as I knew there was no official policy against fraternizing with the enemy, but I am sure that the American wives regarded all Japanese companions as prostitutes. They undoubtedly felt that I had dishonoured the officers club by inviting Yasuko to enter its sanitized precincts.

But Yasuko was a graceful dancer and we were quite happy to perform solo, much to the delight of the Japanese musicians who, in our honour, played a few calypsos. After a delicious meal we departed, and perhaps because I was a legal officer there were no official complaints.

Mother wrote a special letter to acknowledge my birthday that ended:

"I cannot believe I have been spared to see my son live to the age of 24. Well, I thank God first for that but then doubly so because that son has so far never let me down. It's a grand thing, baby boy, to know Mother feels that way about you. Mother thanks God sincerely for her kids. May he keep you always as kind and as devoted to yours at home."

I replied telling her how sumptuous the dinner at the club had been but I neglected to mention Yasuko. In retrospect I think it would need a psychiatrist to interpret Mother's third person speech and the full impact of "baby boy" taking consolation from how his mother felt about him.

In other letters at about this time Mother began enthusing about a new house the family had purchased uptown in the Liguanea area. She was working so hard to restore and redecorate it that Audrey wrote to say she was fearful for her health, the asthma attacks increasing at an alarming rate.

CHAPTER SEVEN

THE PILOCARPINE CASE

The use of heroin by US military personnel was becoming a "sixth column", promoted and supplied by Red China, a staunch ally of the North Koreans in the bloody conflict which, isolated in Tokyo, I had almost put out of my mind. The higher echelons of the military were demanding more court martial convictions to discourage the use of drugs. Under normal circumstances this would involve taking as evidence a urine sample from the suspect. These samples could only be admitted in evidence, however, if the chain of their possession could be proved to be unbroken from the moment the military police took the sample for analysis at the central Tokyo CID laboratory, to its production in the courtroom at the trial. If it was possible for defence counsel to cast reasonable doubt on the chain of possession, an acquittal was almost inevitable.

In due course I was appointed defence council in the case of Adrian Greene, an airman accused of using heroin. By this time I was a seasoned JAG officer, having been involved in either prosecuting or defending some twenty cases, ranging from grand larceny to rape. In the case of Adrian Greene it became clear that the prosecution intended to rely on a shortcut to establish guilt. The military police had caught Greene in the women's latrine at midnight and as they approached he flushed something down the toilet. He was taken immediately to Captain Baker, the base medical officer, who examined him and found his eyes to be acutely myopic. It was the doctor's expert opinion that only the use of heroin could cause this condition. In a pre-trial meeting with the doctor I tried to shake his conviction in this regard, but he was adamant.

"Look here, barrister," he remonstrated, "maybe you don't know what myosis involves. The pupil of the eye is pinpointed. In fact when I gave Greene the standard accommodation test I couldn't find a pupil at all. You don't need any instruments to determine that. One quick look and you can tell."

"And on that basis and nothing more you would testify that the man was using narcotics?"

"Yes," he replied. "Frankly, I can't think of anything else besides a member of the opiate family that could cause such acute mycosis."

It all sounded too simplistic to me and smacked of pressure from the top echelons to get convictions in narcotics cases. Juries, and especially military juries, place great store on the testimony of an expert witness whose credentials the prosecution can establish. Captain Baker's professional background was impressive and the military code made no provision for the defence to hire a contending expert witness.

I paid a visit to Tokyo General Hospital, once run by Catholic nuns and now turned over to the military to handle the sick and wounded from Korea. I spent three hours studying a standard pharmacology text and making notes. Then I visited the eye specialist.

"What can you tell me about a drug called Pilocarpine?"

"Damn little," he shrugged. "It's rather rare. Sometimes used in the treatment of glaucoma."

"Would it cause acute myosis?"

"Possibly – if it didn't make you blind."

I asked if he could help me get a sample of the drug. "Not a chance, lieutenant. We might be able to source it, but you would need a prescription."

Back at the base I phoned Yasuko and asked for her help. Because of her father's pharmaceutical connections she tracked down a source, but wanted to know what solution I needed. I took a chance and requested 2%.

The case of "The United States versus Adrian Greene" began on a cold Tuesday. Greene was indicted under two specifications, the possession and the use of a habit-forming narcotic drug. The government's case was presented by Tom McCullan, a lawyer of equal rank to myself. Tom and I were friends, although there existed a natural rivalry between us. The jury consisted of eight military officers seated under a huge American flag attached to the wall. Major Hostettler, from another base, served as the Law Officer, the equivalent of the judge in a civilian case.

Adrian Greene pleaded not guilty to all charges and the trial got underway. Tom started by trying to introduce into evidence the results of the urine sample taken from Greene and sent to the lab for testing. As anticipated I had no difficulty in breaking the chain of possession and Hostettler refused to allow the test results into evidence. Tom was not discomforted by this because it was clear that the prosecution's case would rely on the doctor's testimony as an expert witness.

Captain Baker was called to the stand. His medical qualifications were established. Tom was very careful in his examination and when he was finished there could be no doubt in the minds of the jury that in the doctor's opinion only the use of a narcotic could cause pin-pointed pupils. Now I had to try to discredit the doctor's testimony.

"Doctor Baker, you must excuse my ignorance if I seem to ask some very obvious questions." He nodded.

"What is heroin derived from, doctor?"

"It is an opiate. A member of the opium family."

"What other narcotics are derived from opium?"

"Morphine. Perhaps codeine."

"Any others, doctor?"

"Not that I can remember."

'Have you heard of a text known as Williams Pharmacology?"

"I have."

"Do you recognize it to be an authority in the field with which we are dealing?"

"Yes."

"May I quote from page 236? The following nine narcotic drugs are opiate derivatives."

I read the list slowly. The court was listening but they were obviously not particularly impressed.

"Now doctor, would it be accurate to say that these derivatives of opium are known as alkaloids?"

"Yes, I believe they could be characterized as alkaloids."

"Would you tell the court, please, whether dycetlemorphine is a synthetic alkaloid of opium or a natural alkaloid."

The doctor twisted in the witness chair. "A natural alkaloid, I should think."

"May I quote from Williams pharmacology, page 237: 'Dycetlemorphine is a synthetic alkaloid of opium.' Do you disagree with that statement?"

"No. But this is medical school stuff. It's been a long time since I studied alkaloids."

"But you are testifying as an expert witness, Doctor."

"Yes, but I am not a pharmacologist."

The doctor was beginning to get testy. I could not blame him. No expert witness can cope with the minutiae of textbooks. But I continued to plague him and his answers became more and more hostile. At the same time the jury was becoming irritated with my nit-picking. I was losing them and the case. I asked for a five-minute recess, grabbed my briefcase and dashed for the men's room. I sat on the toilet seat and took out the little bottle of Pilocarpine Yasuko had found for me. My hands were shaking. I remembered vague warnings I had read that commercial Pilocarpine may not be sufficiently pure and should always be tested on rabbits before administering to the human eye. That was what I needed, to pull a rabbit out of a hat in the court-room. I leaned my head back and instilled a drop of Pilocarpine into each of my eyes.

It took about another ten minutes of contrived cross-examination of the doctor before the drug did its work. Suddenly I could see nothing. It was time for the denouement.

"Let me make sure I have your testimony right. You examined the accused on the night of October 15?"

"Yes." His voice boomed at me from the witness box.

"For five minutes?"

"Yes." I could hear the sneer in his inflection.

"Airman Greene's eyes were very pinpointed?"

"Hardly a pupil at all."

"And in your opinion only an opiate could cause such myosis?"

"Yes."

"So it is your professional opinion that the accused, Adrian Greene, had recently used heroin?"

"I have no doubt about it."

"Please stand up, Doctor."

There was silence and I could see nothing. I heard the scraping of his chair on the floor. I took a few steps forward in the general direction of the doctor, and then whipped off my glasses so that they clattered on the floor.

"Look at my eyes, Doctor. Look at them for as long as you examined Adrian Greene's eyes on October 15."

I could feel his breath on my face.

"Are they myopic, Doctor?"

"Yes." His voice was low, almost a whisper.

"Just as pinpointed as the defendant's eyes?"

"Yes."

"And would you have the temerity to suggest to this court that I have been using narcotics? Do you really believe that I am an addict?"

"No, Lieutenant. I don't."

"Thank you, Doctor. No further questions."

And that, of course, gained Adrian Greene his acquittal. A court martial is full of anticlimaxes and this one was no exception. I didn't faint. There was no applause. At the end of the trial my sight was beginning to return but I had a shattering headache and a touch of nausea. The military court martial review process is slow and it was not until I had been honourably discharged from the United States Air Force that I received a letter addressed to me at Wherry Wharf. It was an official letter of commendation that read:

> Your personal effort in the case of airman Adrian Greene which materially contributed to effect an outstanding job reflects favourably upon yourself and the United States Air Force. This case was particularly well handled and I am marking it for transmission to the Judge Advocate's school at the Air University for classes there.

It was signed by Albert Kokfeld, Brigadier General, USAF. The awkward prose not withstanding, I was grateful for the sentiments expressed and delighted that my efforts had been officially recognized.

CHAPTER EIGHT

FLIGHT TO ARABIA

The climate in Tokyo is similar to that in New York and by October 1952 it had turned cold at Haneda. I was obliged to swap chinos for the blue Air Force winter uniform and a few days later found on my desk 25 copies of Special Order #236 which read:

> Lt. Ralph Thompson AO 1849639, Headquarters 1503 Air Transport Wing, will depart on or about 9 October 1952 from his station as additional crew member on Embassy flight to Dhahran, Saudi Arabia and on return trip will depart aircraft at Manila and proceed by next available aircraft to Guam, Iwo Jima and thence to Haneda, for the purpose of investigating claims at Bangkok and Calcutta and coordinating legal assistance matters at Manila, Guam and Iwo Jima.

On its face, Special Order #236 was an amazing document, likely to throw a young lieutenant from Jamaica into shock. Even in the military, the life of a legal officer is generally routine and sedentary. The extent of his travel is from quarters to office, from office to court room (directly across the hall) and once a month to the base finance office to collect his pay. It was unusual, therefore, to be ordered half-way round the globe for no apparent good reason. When I reported to the commanding general for briefing it was evident that he was uneasy. He invited me to sit.

"You have been selected for the mission as much for the diplomacy that I hope you possess as for the military legal knowledge which I know you have mastered." It was a difficult sentence and I thought he got it out rather nicely.

"It's damned ridiculous of course," he continued, "but a corporal stationed at our base in Dhahran, Saudi Arabia, has been accused of larceny by an Arab merchant, and the damn-fool government, Saudi Arabian, not ours, has determined that the appropriate punishment is to cut off the airman's right hand. Even if he is guilty, such drastic recrimination is inconceivable. The American consul in Dhahran has expressed some concern in the matter and, besides, the corporal has made a request in writing to be represented by a qualified attorney."

Before I was dismissed, there was one more unfortunate task the General had to perform. Recent international developments involving Saudi Arabia and Israel had made the Arabs rather sensitive to the presence of Jews in their countries. In fact there was an unequivocal ban on Jewish members of an aircraft crew seeking permission to enter Saudi Arabian air space. The restriction applied also to anyone with red hair, why I never discovered. The General could see that the colour of my hair would not disqualify me but he had to make sure about the other condition. He blurted out, "What is your religion, Thompson, Protestant or Catholic?"

When I told him that I was a Roman Catholic his relief was visible. His last words were rich with unconscious irony: "Remember this calls for diplomacy. If they cut off the boy's hand he'll be sure to write to his Congressman about it." I left his presence worried that my mother's maiden name "Isaacs" might appear in my passport.

My journey covered twenty thousand miles through seven countries and three continents. In retrospect I marvel at how much the geopolitical face of that part of the world has changed since my sojourn there. Some countries have been re-baptized with new names – French Indo-China now Viet Nam, Siam now Thailand. But the Saudi Arabian empire was stable and the treaty arrangement by which the USA was allowed to maintain an air force base in that country was a model of elegance. The instant the wheels of a US aircraft touched down on the runway in Dhahran, title to the plane passed to the King. At the instant of take-off, title reverted to America. No unnecessary paperwork, easy to understand, easy to enforce. We travelled in a C-54 aircraft and except for the *dénouement*, my memory of the trip is a mélange of sights and impressions in no particular order of magnitude.

The first stop was Manila and I suppose it was no surprise that Clark Air Force Base made me nostalgic for Jamaica. The walk I took from the officer's quarters to the terminal induced a deep longing for home. It was early in the morning and shadows were just beginning to tremble into light as the sun climbed the side of the mountains that stood guard over the city. The air was warm, clear and sweet as only a tropical morning can be. The night dew was heavy on the grass and tall shade trees formed a lush canopy over my head. I passed tropical houses with generous verandahs, one-storey bungalows standing high off the ground to guard against termites.

Some foreign locations gush an atmosphere that speaks to you, force themselves upon you by persuasion. Most countries captivate by their physical arguments, through the sermons of great cathedrals, the cold dissonance of skyscrapers, the melody of strange dress. The tropics have a different approach. They never speak or persuade. The tropics are always listening. If you would know them, you must listen too – for the rest of your life.

On the second day of the flight we landed at Saigon, French Indo-China. The airport looked deserted and sinister, the French tricolour flapping exhaustedly in the humid breeze.

From Saigon we flew to Bangkok. On final approach we lost an engine and another was coughing consumptively. Pilots of a C-54 cannot see the plane's engines from the cockpit. To make an inspection they have to enter the main cabin. I was in a bulkhead seat and the captain knelt down on one knee beside me. I thought he was going to enjoin me to prayer, but instead he threw a fist at the choking engine and exclaimed, "Give out if you dare, you son of a bitch! Please God, don't let it give out." His prayer was answered, we landed safely and, because the engines had to be repaired, we were granted a three-day stay in Bangkok, considered by those who knew to be the closest place to heaven on earth.

We were told that Turkey and Siam were the only two countries in the world whose governments permitted legalized opium houses. There was time to visit one such den situated on a dark corner of a district where the smell of garbage in the streets mingled with the odour of contamination and disease. The house was an unpainted, three-storey structure, each floor divided into cells exactly like the inside of a jail. The interior walls were mesh wire and in each cell there was a raised wooden platform on which the customers, attended by young boys or old women, reclined, the left leg arched at the knee and the head resting on a wooden block. This was the traditional Buddhist position of contemplation. Nearly naked, except for a loincloth, the addicts progressed from the ground floor, reserved for the young, to the third floor where the permanent residents lived until they passed from temporary to permanent beatitude. The silence was overpowering and there was no objection to our voyeuristic presence.

Our next stopover was Calcutta. The pilot and co-pilot had both drunk too much cheap Scotch and could hardly climb into the cockpit for the early morning departure. They clamped oxygen masks over their faces which helped to sober them up sufficiently for take-off. As soon as we reached cruising altitude, the co-pilot collapsed into the hammock which, on military aircraft, hangs behind the flight deck. An hour later the pilot summoned me forward and ordered me to take the left seat while he too caught up on some sleep. The plane was on automatic pilot, flying over the great Ganges river, heading for New Delhi. When I was seated at the controls the pilot handed me an HB pencil and pointed to a small aperture on the instrument panel. "Follow the river, Thompson. If the plane starts to drift off course you can make a small trim tab adjustment with that pencil. Just stick it in that hole and turn right or left to make the correction." Shortly after I could hear him snoring in the other hammock and I knew I was on my own. At times it seemed as if the C-54 was flying sideways but it generally followed the river and I had only to make a few adjustments with the pencil. After about an hour the co-pilot returned to the cockpit and I was relieved from my assignment.

In New Delhi we were billeted at the Maiden Hotel, a central location in the city. I watched tall women in silken saris carrying water jugs on their heads. There were sacred cows roaming the streets, ox carts and camels. I walked down avenues with English names and passed shops with the pathetic legend: "By Appointment to His Majesty the King" still painted over the door.

From India the flight continued to Saudi Arabia, with a brief stop in Karachi. The U.S. base at Dhahran is built on desert sand, as I had imagined it to be. I went immediately into the air-conditioned operations building to confer with the Colonel about my client.

The Colonel informed me that the accused corporal had suddenly and without explanation been returned to U.S. military control just prior to my arrival. He had previously been confined in a local dungeon. In my view this was a face-saving ploy on the part of the Saudi authorities. I recommended that the young airman should be accorded his right to consult with counsel in the C-54 and if, during this conference, the weather forecast was in any way unfavourable, the plane should immediately take off for the return trip to Japan. So said, so done! Once it was clear that the prisoner had been returned to Japan, the Saudi Arabian officials dropped the issue. In Tokyo the airman had already been arrested and booked for a summary court-martial hearing. He was reduced in rank to a private and fined a month's pay. This seemed an absurd anticlimax to my odyssey but an international incident had been avoided.

CHAPTER NINE

A CLOSE ESCAPE

A voice bellowed, "Telephone call for Lieutenant Thompson." In my skivvies I ran down the corridor to where the telephone receiver dangled on its cord. In those days overseas calls relied on radio transmissions and through the trans-Pacific static I could hear my friend in New York saying, "So sorry to learn… your mother's death…" The static got louder. "Are you saying my mother has died?" I screamed into the phone. "Jesus, I'm sorry. I thought you knew…" The phone went dead.

Audrey had indeed sent me a cable asking me to return to Jamaica as soon as possible, but it had disappeared into the military maw. Mother's prophesy that she would never see me again, uttered when I said goodbye to her in New York, had come true. But it was her death, not mine, that now froze our last New York meeting in my memory – the tears in her dark, sickness-circled eyes, the final clutch of her emaciated hands.

I was worried about my sister, Audrey, whom Mother, by many subtle investitures over the years, had entrusted to my care and protection. How would she manage the shock and confusion? What legal steps needed to be taken to probate Mother's will? I returned to my room and flung myself on the bed, sobbing. It was not her passing that wrenched my heart – given her chronic asthma, her death was always imminent. But I had hoped to be at her bedside when it happened. Japan now seemed so foreign and far away from Jamaica.

Thanks to the kind cooperation of Major Adams and the Commanding General, still tied to his New York wife, I was able to get myself temporally assigned to the JAG office at Hickham air base in Honolulu, considered to be a domestic posting. From there I was able to proceed on thirty days leave to Jamaica.

Just before my departure, Audrey's delayed letter advising me of Mother's death was delivered to me. It read:

I had become Mother's night nurse. I was in the bed next to her the
night she died. I awoke to the realization that she was gasping for breath,
was ice cold, the veins at her temples protruding and pulsating at a rapid
rate. I knew what to do. Telephone Dr. Moody and ask him to come
immediately. He arrived within thirty minutes, a suit jacket worn over
his pyjamas.

He injected mother with morphine – the usual procedure. Very soon
she was breathing normally. I hugged Dr. Moody and he left. I thought
the crisis was over. I had only to wait for the morphine to wear off.
Always when Mother would awake after a serious attack she would whisper,
"That was a bad one, wasn't it?"

I waited and waited for Mother to say those words but she never did.
I performed the mirror test and there was no fogging. Dr. Moody was
by then in the cane fields at Caymanas and could not be contacted. An
ambulance eventually arrived from the University hospital and the doctor
who came with it pronounced her dead as the result of heart failure.

I was in deep shock, unable to release the body to the undertaker.
The maid brought me a glass of iced tea and insisted that I go out on
the verandah to rest for awhile. Nathaniel tried to console me. He was
so devoted to Miss Steff. He reminded me he had been with the family
since he was about eleven years old. He always referred to himself as
Miss Steff's black son.

Mother was not conscious when she died, which was a great blessing.
Had she been conscious she would have fought death to the bitter end.
I don't have to tell you what a big time fighter she was. I am grateful
that after so much suffering her exit from this life was so peaceful.

By the time I arrived in Kingston Audrey had recovered from the first
shock of the death. My limited stay in Jamaica was taken up with
mundane tasks. I visited Mother's grave at Calvary cemetery and
attended a meeting with her lawyer about her will. Although she owned
a one-third interest in Wherry Wharf, Mother was afraid that a demand
for such a payout in cash by her children would be detrimental to Uncle
Mike carrying on the business. Her will specified that any monies to be
paid to her children would be entirely at the discretion of Uncle Mike,
the only remaining member of the original partnership.

This struck me as being legally suspect, and after my eventual return
to Jamaica I was able, on an originating summons, to get the Jamaican
court to order a distribution. The sums involved were relatively small,
but sufficient for Audrey to go to New York to further her education and
to start her career as a psychiatric social worker.

The return journey to Japan was interminably long, giving me time
to debate with myself about my relationship with my mother. My
respect for her was profound – the bravery with which she clung to life,
her acute Jewish sense of duty, her unquestioning loyalty to the doc-
trines of the Catholic church, the sacrifices she made for her children's

sake. But did I truly love her? There seemed to be a lack of warmth in our relationship and, mistakenly, I felt that I could only earn her love by seeking perfection for her approval. When I fell short of her expectations or my own I was riven with guilt.

But I soon readjusted to the routine of life at Haneda Air Force base. I prosecuted and defended a number of cases, winning some and losing others. But the end of my military service came more quickly than I expected. Five months after my return from Jamaica to Japan, the Base personnel officer telephoned me.

"Shit, Lieutenant, I have been checking your records and you become a civilian in two weeks. Please prepare to leave Haneda for the States at once, unless, of course, you want to sign up for another hitch."

I declined. My original ROTC commission had been for five years and its fifth anniversary was at hand. I was booked first class on a flight for Parks Air Force base in California where I would be processed, paid off and given an honourable discharge from the United States Air Force.

Yasuko was understandably upset when I told her of my imminent departure and reminded me of my commitment to sponsor her entry to the United States and thereafter to marry her. That said, she accepted the news with a degree of stoicism. I promised to get in touch with her as soon as I was settled.

I bid farewell to Major Adams who again urged me to accept employment with his insurance company in Alabama and insisted that I carry with me a letter of recommendation to his partner in Clayton.

I walked one last time to the edge of the base to watch a solitary boat cut from the river into the harbour, probably to reap seaweed rather than to catch fish. In Jamaica it would have been a cotton-tree canoe, rowed blindly backward. This squint-eyed craft looked where it was going, the blade of the oar unscrolling in Japanese a wake that I could not decipher.

The separation procedures at Parks Air Force Base took about two weeks, involving a full medical and information on veteran's benefits including what military decorations I was entitled to wear on formal occasions. I was now officially a United States veteran entitled to free schooling under the GI Bill, a house mortgage guaranteed to 95% by the government and free medical care for the rest of my life at a VA hospital. But I felt unable to accept such largesse. My military career had been a dream, an unreality that warranted no such rewards, a fantasy like the "make up" games my sister and I played in Jamaica. It was I who was indebted to the US Air Force for seasoning my immaturity and instilling in me a sense of discipline. My relationship with Yasuko had been another kind of dream from which I was only now awakening. With the passing of time since leaving Tokyo, I became more and more confused and less resolute about what to tell Yasuko, so I did nothing, immobilized between realism and guilt. Even now I cringe at the image of her greeting the postman every day, hoping to receive an envelope addressed to her in my lawyer's scrawl.

Years later, in my first collection of poetry, *The Denting of a Wave*, I wrote a poem called "The Other Island", which among other things memorialised how:

> Yasuko perfumed his exile
> bringing her consolations with tiny steps
> to his off-duty hours, alleging
> her love in English less tenuous
> than his limping Japanese.
> Their body language tested every
> consonant and vowel, slurring
> only when they talked of islands.

After my discharge in California I used some of my severance pay to buy a second-hand Chevrolet coupe in which I would travel to Clayton, Alabama to present Major Adams' letter of introduction to his business partner. I arrived on a hot August day at high noon, the Chevy coated in white dust. The town square was deserted except for an old man hunkered on the sidewalk, whittling on a piece of wood. I asked for directions and he pointed to the courthouse, a white wooden building with false Palladian facade. It, too, was deserted, except for a clerk behind the counter swatting flies. Major Adams' partner was on the second floor and greeted me affably. I presented my letter of introduction, and while he read it I examined the office.

On the wall there was a picture of a pretty woman, his wife I assumed, leaning back on a garden swing dressed in a crinoline skirt and bobby socks. Beside it was a boxing trophy in his name for the welterweight State championship. His hair, black and thick, was combed back without a part and made his head seem too big for his body. He had dark, deep-set eyes under bushy eyebrows and a dimple in his chin like a button.

"Well," he drawled in a high-pitched voice, "Adams sure thinks a lot of you, son. Ah congratulate you on a distinguished career to date and ah feel sure you will do just as good in the insurance bisness."

He proceeded to tell me about the operation, emphasizing how much commission I could earn if I concentrated on group agricultural policies. Even in dealing with such details he was passionate and persuasive, obviously a person of some intellect and considerable drive.

He wanted to know when I could start working and I explained that I would be returning to Jamaica for a visit, but would let him know as soon as I had settled my affairs there. He stood up.

"Ah think that's very reasonable, son. Look forward to hearin' from you."

We shook hands and I left.

Clayton was not what I had expected. Compared with Kingston it was a backwater town with a spooky feel about it. I had already rejected any idea of living and working there and had an almost biblical desire to shake off its dust as I crossed the city limits and headed for Miami. Little did I know how close I had come to being sucked in by a personality of cyclonic proportions, a category five hurricane that, shortly after our meeting, was to cut a swathe through America's political and social landscape.

Major Adams' partner was George Wallace, later four-times governor of Alabama, once described by Martin Luther King Jr. as "the most dangerous racist in America today." In 1958, beaten in his first bid for the governorship by a well-known segregationist, Wallace declared, "No other son-of-a-bitch will ever out-nigger me again."

Bitterly opposed to school integration, Wallace physically tried to block admission of two African-American students to the University of Alabama, forcing President Kennedy to "federalize" the Alabama National Guard, to give it the power to carry out the court order. Wallace appeared on television shouting "Segregation now! Segregation tomorrow! Segregation forever!" During the civil rights march from Selma to Montgomery, he ordered State troopers to use dogs, whips and tear gas to break up the demonstration. The resulting violence provided President Johnson with enough ammunition to get the landmark 1965 Voting Rights Act passed by Congress. But so fierce were Wallace's ambitions, he decided to run for the presidency. He made two surprisingly successful attempts. In 1972 he swept Florida in the primary and was campaigning in Maryland when he was crippled by an assassination attempt and spent the rest of his life in a wheelchair.

All of this came to light after my encounter in Clayton, but I could still hear the billiard balls clicking on the table as the cue stick of providence saved me from the acute embarrassment of being counted a member of the Wallace entourage.

Upon retiring from the Air Force, Major Adams was appointed President of Troy State University and I was able to contact him there. We never spoke about George Wallace's career but he did confirm that one of my paintings hung on the wall of his university office.

CHAPTER TEN

LOVE AND MARRIAGE

On my return to Jamaica from Japan in 1953, Jack de Lisser's sister introduced me to Doreen. I was entranced not only with her beauty and style but with her unusual background. Her father, Francis Emanuel Lyons, known to friends and colleagues as "Mr. Frankie", was a wealthy Jewish wharf owner and merchant who in his 46th year had the good sense and moral courage to marry Ermyn Ellis, his secretary whose antecedents remain a mystery to this day. Mr. Frankie proudly enthroned her as queen of "Mayfair", a gracious mansion on seven acres of land in St. Andrew, adjacent to King's House, the official residence of Jamaica's governors. So unshakable was the Lyons' social status, not only in Jewish circles but in the community at large, no one refused an invitation to dine and dance at the parties hosted by Mr. and Mrs. Lyons. From entire visiting cricket teams to leading Jamaican politicians and business tycoons, a large cross-section of the *haut monde* were the beneficiaries of the Lyons' hospitality. Mr. Frankie imported peacocks to grace the Mayfair lawns and, under the guidance of Millard Ziadie, one of Jamaica's leading horse trainers, established a racing stable on the back lands of the residence. The favourite horse to race at Knutsford Park in the Lyons colours was Sunnymorn, winner, on one occasion, of the coveted Governor's Cup.

Ermyn was a Catholic convent girl but, committed to the marriage and determined to make a better life for herself, agreed to bring up the children as Jews, knowing deep down that since she was not a Jew they could never in any rabbinical sense be truly Jews. In time they would choose whatever religion appealed to them. She insisted on going to Mass regularly and despite Mr. Frankie's rumblings, this set a subliminal example for her children.

Frankie and Ermyn had two offspring, David the first-born and Doreen two years later. Frankie doted on his son, found it difficult to refuse his extravagances and spoiled him. Ermyn showered special love and care on Doreen. The mother was determined that the social graces

Ermyn Lyons

Frank Lyons, son David and daughter Doreen, with champion horses

and good breeding that she had worked so tirelessly to acquire would come instinctively to her beautiful daughter. In due course David went off to Northeastern University in Massachusetts to study chemical engineering. Doreen, after graduating from Wolmer's, was enrolled at Mary Burnham, an elite American prep school. After two years there she was accepted at Wellesley College, an even more elite, all-girls college whose graduates read like a "who's who" of famous women. Doreen fitted in at Wellesley and majored in political science. She had returned to Jamaica only shortly before I met her.

My return to Jamaica convinced me that tropical islands exert an ineluctable attraction for those exposed for any length of time to their charms – so much beauty enshrined in such small spaces, a melodrama of white sand beaches, lush scenery, muscled mountain ranges and peaks, the highest of which in Jamaica soars to seven thousand feet. No poisonous snakes crawl in Jamaican forests, no lions roar or wolves howl, only the nightly chorus of barking dogs and, in the morning, the crowing of arrogant roosters welcoming another sun-splashed day.

Before the Black Power movement in America influenced Jamaica, racial tensions undoubtedly existed, but on the fringes of society. On gaining independence from Britain, Jamaica's official motto was "Out of many, one people" and Whites, Blacks, Browns, Chinese, East Indians, Jews and Syrians appeared to be living together in harmony. There were class barriers, to be sure, but these were becoming more permeable as education became more accessible to the population. Nevertheless, as I relate a few pages later, there were areas of Jamaican life where an informal colour bar persisted.

The existence in most Caribbean islands of a servant class is one of the most difficult and subtle relationships to define. The availability of inexpensive household help contributed significantly to the lifestyle of the middle class. Later, this was seen as a remnant evil of colonialism and Michael Manley, as prime minister, abolished the Master and Servant law. There were, no doubt, many abuses. Among the upper classes as well as among the emerging middle class there were some heads of households who exploited their servants, insisting on long working hours and paying substandard wages. This was not the case among our friends and certainly not in the Thompson or Lyons households. Esme Williams was a sainted cook, who incidentally loved cricket and knew more about it than I did. Lurline, our housekeeper, has been a part of our family for over fifty-five years. Edna was her counterpart in the Lyons household. They were servants in the Biblical sense of that status, constituent members of the family and as such entitled to special respect and support. Some would see this as paternalism, but for many of the working class who could not survive in the commercial jungle it provided a humanistic environment in which to earn a living. Such live-in servants had few personal expenses and over the years embraced the social skills and world views of their employers who inevitably became the godparents of the servants' offspring, children who grew up with and were often, though not always, treated in the same manner as blood children of the household.

Perhaps it took me a good while to think beyond the norms of my upbringing, but in my most recent collection of poetry, *Taking Words for a Walk*, published in 2012, there is a long poem, "The Colour of Conscience" that explores in a way that I found satisfying some of the complexities of class and colour in those intimate family relationships. Of the "fictional" housekeeper "Carmen" I wrote:

> But certain
> bondages refuse to slacken, no
> eating with us at table, her meals taken
> in the kitchen, callalloo and sweet potato
> dished from pot to mouth. Nor would she address us
> by first name. I was "Da" for "Dad"
> (invented by Eunice); my wife "Miss P" or "Missus";
> yet she hugged us and for the children a chiliad
> of kisses. After fifteen years Carmen accepts us
> as mere mortals, part of a vaster
> congregation of eccentrics. We had ordained
> her to the rank of sisterhood, encouraged
> to tweak the humdrum.

I knew with certainty that the quality of life in Jamaica, including the support of domestic help, would provide me the greatest opportunity of perfecting my potential as fully as possible. No great riches perhaps, but ample time and freedom to read, to reflect, to enjoy surpassing natural beauty and to lead an examined life. In honour, it also imposed on me an unconditional obligation to perform public service and to give back to the community. This had been a tradition in my family as far back as Grandpa Ralph and I was proud to be a part of it.

It was against this background that I fell deeply in love with Doreen and I was content, in the choices I made, to sacrifice a career in law – which in any case I could not practice in Jamaica without requalifying. During our early courtship, Doreen exclaimed one day, "Edna likes you, my darling! Edna likes you!" – an elated proclamation that, as far as her old nanny was concerned, I had passed the litmus test.

On my return to Jamaica I took up residence at the new house the Isaacs family had bought before Mother's death. It was from here that

I wooed Doreen. By the time of our courtship, Uncle Mike had married and set up his own dark nest on Hopefield Avenue. When Aunt Bella's health began to deteriorate she became a paying boarder with a cousin. So Audrey and I were the sole inhabitants of 133 Hope Road, hosts to an exciting coterie of young Jamaicans. It became a centre for high jinks.

When I asked Mr. Frankie for permission to marry his daughter he seemed quite pleased, but insisted that he would never enter a Catholic church. But at the church rehearsal, on being presented to Bishop McEleney, my future father-in-law bobbed a little curtsy, grabbed the Bishop's hand and kissed the Episcopal ring with such vigour I thought he might swallow it.

★   ★   ★

After a relatively short engagement, Doreen and I were married on June 26, 1954 at SS Peter and Paul Roman Catholic church at five o'clock in the afternoon. There were nineteen priests present at the altar, marking the special relationship that had existed for many years between the Jesuits and the Isaacs family. Bishop McEleney performed the ceremony.

The reception was a grand affair on the lawns at "Mayfair", the Lyons' residence, attended by some three hundred guests. Uncle Mike transported carloads of hydrangeas from Shadowbrook, which provided a dramatic backdrop for the head table. There were speeches aplenty as was the custom in those days. Abe Issa was Master of Ceremonies; Douglas Judah, a leading lawyer and legislator, proposed the toast to the Isaacs family; Arthur Myers, scion of the family that introduced Myers rum to the world, proposed the toast to the Lyons family; Jack de Lisser toasted the Thompson family and my father and Mr. Frankie made tidy speeches in reply.

Hans Schnoor, after release from detention during World War II, had established a successful mining operation in Brown's Town which supplied the white lime used to spray bananas and sugar cane as protection against insect infestation. After dinner and much champagne, he took me aside:

"Herr Thompson, a wager."

"What?"

"Ten pounds sterling you have a child within the next six months."

It is theologically wrong to bet on a certainty, but far from taking umbrage at the implication, I needed the money. I accepted the bet.

Stephanie was not born until October of the following year, delivered by Caesarean section.

Shortly after our marriage, as often happens, Doreen's brother, David, married Kay and they had two children. The marriage soon came under stress as the Lyons' fortune began to dissipate, despite David's best and sometimes misguided efforts. The Lyons' enterprise included ownership of a private wharf on the Kingston waterfront, but by the time of my marriage to Doreen this once grand merchant bastion of wealth was beginning to crumble. David had little business experience and his naturally adventurous and erratic nature led to a number of misadventures that took their toll.

Mr. Frankie was now too old to exercise control but, ever generous, he offered a lot of land each to David and me, valuable real estate that he would cut off from the large family spread in upper Saint Andrew. David accepted and built a splendid house on the parcel, which he designed himself. Anticipating problems and wishing to maintain my independence, I declined Mr. Frankie's offer and Doreen and I established ourselves in a small rented cottage on Oxford Road. The Lyons financial problems continued to worsen until Mr. Frankie was forced to sell the wharf. This was followed shortly after by the sale of "Mayfair", the family residence. Frankie and Ermyn relocated to a modest bungalow on Allerdyce Avenue.

All of this put a strain on David's marriage, which eventually ended in divorce. He migrated to Miami where he became a successful stockbroker and married Ann who was to become his devoted second wife and salvation. Tragically, Kay, his first wife, committed suicide some years later and in his middle eighties David, who had been a heavy smoker, succumbed to emphysema and died in 2013.

CHAPTER ELEVEN

ABE ISSA

In 1954 there were few companies in Jamaica that could offer me employment at a level commensurate with my qualifications. The Issa family owned one of the largest trading organizations and I was fortunate to be interviewed for a job by Abe Issa. Newly married, I resigned myself to having to start in the bottom ranks. Thus my business career began, not in accordance with any plan, but by the happenstance of what was available.

Short and with slightly bowed legs, Abe had the constitution of an ox and the social sensibility of a Jane Austen. He was urbane, witty and charming. His voice had a distinctive rasping quality and his speech reflected a slight American accent, acquired no doubt during his student years at Holy Cross College in Massachusetts where he was an outstanding scholar. At his graduation in 1926 he was class valedictorian and delivered his address in Latin. Among his notable skills was an incredible memory for names.

Abe Issa hired me as his executive assistant at a salary of ten pounds sterling per week. As a family business, the Issa organization lacked formal structure, a situation often exacerbated by policy differences between Abe and his younger brother, Joe. These differences often had to be arbitrated by their father, Elias, who had founded the empire. He lived in a modest bungalow on South Camp Road and came to rely on me for information, which I conveyed to him in a series of private meetings at his home. He was nearly blind and when accounting figures were involved I would set up a blackboard in his living room and print on it in chalk the key financial details he needed to make a decision.

In such a loose organization, I learned how things should be done and how things should not be done. Progress was by emergencies. If a crisis occurred when Abe was off the island and I dealt with it satisfactorily, that automatically became a part of my portfolio. Michael Manley, destined to become prime minister of Jamaica in the Seventies, was then a power in the trade union movement. He was targeting hotel workers in the emerging tourist industry and, in Abe's absence, tabled an outrageous wage claim on behalf of the workers at Tower Isle, the premier Issa hotel, now known as Couples. I knew the hotel was only marginally profitable at the time and although the principle of not disclosing audited accounts to a trade union was sacrosanct, I prepared graphs and pie-charts, all in terms of percentages, to demonstrate inability to pay. Hitherto such research and presentations were un-known. Negotiating sessions with a union were a series of informal and unprepared shouting matches on both sides to impress the worker delegates whose presence the union insisted upon. At one joint session with the Jamaica Tourist Association in Montego Bay that I attended on Abe's behalf, Michael Manley proposed maternity leave for female workers in the industry. Dick de Lisser, who owned several leading hotels in Montego Bay, declared, "I have no intention of subsidizing fucking" and stormed out of the room. I urged the meeting to give the Manley request careful thought and John Maxwell, a leftist journalist, in one of his subsequent columns in *Public Opinion*, hailed me as a capitalist liberal, which I took as a compliment.

Abe's adventures in tourism began with the purchase of Myrtle Bank Hotel for forty thousand pounds sterling, a price that barely covered the value of the silver, crockery and glassware that were part of the sale. In 1949, Abe built Tower Isle Hotel, now Couples, Jamaica's first modern resort in the sleepy village of Ocho Rios, midway between Kingston and Montego Bay. Jamaica had only one international airport then, and that was in Kingston. Abe thought that Tower Isle Hotel would attract guests who did not fancy the long drive from Kingston to Montego Bay. This gamble backfired when a second International Airport opened in Montego Bay. Many thought that Abe's investment in Tower Isle would be in jeopardy, but he single-handedly and with his own money visited scores of travel agencies in America, marketing Jamaica and its hotels as a premier tourist resort. He became a legendary figure in the industry known far and wide as "Mr. Jamaica".

The Myrtle Bank Hotel had been built by the United Fruit Company to accommodate tourists travelling on banana boats from Boston to Jamaica. Painted cream with green trim, Myrtle Bank featured a deep front verandah scrolled with arches that gave it a vaguely Spanish look. The lobby opened onto an esplanade lined with royal palms leading to a swimming pool on the edge of Kingston harbour, the Palisadoes airport in the distance. On one side of the hotel grounds there was a modern two storey annex, an in-bond tourist shop on the first floor, and two offices on the second floor, one for Abe and one for me. In addition, Abe had a bank of phones installed on a table under an umbrella at the pool side and, attired in his swimming trunks, often conducted business from this temporary headquarters, much to the amusement of tourists staying at the hotel.

The Myrtle Bank Hotel pool played an important role in the evolution of race relations in Jamaica. It was out of bounds to non-guests, a not so subtle strategy for preventing anyone who was obviously black from using it. Then one day Evon Blake, decidedly black, an ex-policeman and journalist-entrepreneur par excellence, managed to evade hotel security and plunged into the pool at lunchtime. The white tourists in the pool or on the deck paid no particular attention to him as he completed his laps. In fact, a few of them engaged him in conversation. The taboo had been broken and the Evon Blake splash created waves across the island. One by one, all hotels in Jamaica lifted their swimming bans and so history was made.

Between my eagerness to solve old problems and Abe's insatiable appetite for new adventures, my plate was soon fuller than I could rightly say grace over. From giggles to gravitas, I was involved in every aspect of Abe's life. I wrote letters to his children when they were away at school urging them to work hard and keep the faith. He appended the word "Dad", hardly glancing at what I had written. I wrote first drafts of his speeches, in his personal capacity, as Chairman of the Tourist Board and as a member of the Legislative Council. When he travelled abroad I packed his bags, which I handed over to him at the airport.

Cruise ships came regularly to Kingston and anchored in the harbour. Passengers were ferried to Myrtle Bank by tender and spent the day drinking rum punches and shopping in-bond. The liners did not sail until midnight and there was little to amuse the tourists after dinner. Abe requested, or I volunteered, that I would produce and MC floorshows in the Myrtle Bank gardens whenever a cruise ship was in port. I held auditions and among the performers whose careers I helped to launch was the late comedian, Charles Hyatt, who mimed a lady wiggling into her girdle and the late Reggie Carter who rendered a soulful version of "Ruby" on the harmonica. He subsequently became an advertising executive and a leading classical actor, a career cut short by his untimely death.

Whenever time permitted, Abe would pace the sidewalk outside the Issa retail department store on King Street, greeting customers, many of them by name. He kept an eye on the sales clerks to make sure they were courteous and efficient, but he also kept an eye on Nathan's, the adjacent department store, which he coveted. Nathan's and the Nathan family represented old money whereas the Issas, in the eyes of some Jamaicans, were *nouveau riche* Syrians. When it became known in commercial circles that Major Nathan wished to sell the store, Abe correctly calculated that, given the prevailing prejudice, it was unlikely that Nathan would welcome any offer put forward by him. He turned to his old friend John Pringle, a Montego Bay socialite, to front for him in negotiating a purchase – on the basis that Pringle would be given a 20% interest in the venture for his efforts if the sale was concluded.

Pringle was successful in getting from Nathan a verbal commitment to sell all of the shares in Nathan and Company Limited for sixty thousand pounds sterling. But when Nathan learned that Pringle was fronting for Abe he tried to renege on his agreement. I pointed out to Abe that although a contract involving real estate must be in writing, a verbal contract, although difficult to prove, could support a sale of shares. Pringle advised Nathan that if he did not honour his commitment to sell the shares he would be sued and the case taken to the Privy Council in England if necessary. This would tie up any possible sale for years.

Nathan eventually capitulated and Abe, Sir Neville Ashenheim, his lawyer, and I repaired to the Myrtle Bank bar to celebrate. At one time in his career and for many years Abe had been a prodigious drinker, although alcohol never seemed to affect his work. Then he suddenly gave up drink, as a promise to his dying mother, it was said. On this occasion champagne was ordered and I saw Abe take a tiny sip. The acquisition meant more to him than a commercial venture. It was also a metaphor for arrival and social acceptance.

By this time I had gained Abe's complete confidence and trust. We shared the bond of a Jesuit education and a commitment to inordinately long hours of work. Doreen and I were always invited to Abe's soirées and on one occasion, when he arranged a party for the cast of the James Bond film *Dr. No*, then being filmed in Jamaica, Doreen and Joan de Lisser found themselves sitting on either side of Sean Connery. Joan later reported that despite her best efforts to flirt with him he had "nothing good to say for himself". At this same party Ursula Andress asked me to teach her the ska, a dance recently invented in Jamaica. We were making good progress until she remarked, "Why we dance so far apart?", and pulled me to her ample bosom. At this crucial moment I developed a "stitch" and had to retire from the lists. I have never been able to live down this embarrassment.

When Bishop Fulton Sheen, the renowned and hypnotic Jesuit preacher visited Jamaica, Abe offered complimentary accommodation at the Myrtle Bank. I was there when they met in the lobby. They exchanged a few pleasantries about Holy Cross and then Sheen focused his penetrating stare on Abe and asked him when last he had been to confession. While Abe stumbled for an answer, Sheen took him by the hand and propelled him to his suite. When Abe returned to the office he was as white as a sheet and presumably as white as his absolved soul. He could hardly contain his joy.

My portfolio now included three hotels in Jamaica, two department stores, in-bond shops, real estate developments and shopping centres, as well as the scores of companies in which Abe had a financial interest. I was also involved with his chairmanship of the Jamaica Tourist Board and his role as a member of the Legislative Council. It was therefore a vicarious thrill for me when he was awarded the CBE by the Queen, although I suspect that he was disappointed at not having been recommended for a knighthood for almost single-handedly establishing Jamaica's modern tourist industry.

In the centre of what is now New Kingston, part of the Liguanea Club lands, there was a charming race track owned by Knutsford Park Limited, all the shares of which were held by Mr. Audley Morais. A grandstand with thin iron columns and balustrades of black wrought-iron was reserved for the elite. The track itself was circled by a wooden railing around which the groundlings gathered, interspersed with vendors hawking drinks and tricksters with wily accomplices gulling country bumpkins into betting on the three-card scam. There was one race day a week, on Saturdays, and four sweepstakes a year authorized by the Government, tickets for which were sold throughout the island, the proceeds allocated to the upkeep of the Kingston Public Hospital.

The Lyons' racing colours were white with a blue slash and it was at Knutsford Park that horses from the Lyons' stables often performed brilliantly, the victorious mounts led to the winner's circle by Doreen and her brother David. Uncle Seymour was the only member of the Isaacs family who frequented the track. On a few occasions his offer to take me with him was grudgingly accepted by Mother and we mingled with the *hoi polloi* in the shade of a lignum vitae tree that had managed to survive despite the countless initials carved into its bark.

Ladies in the stand wore elegant hats, some white gloves, and the men were suited and sported colourful ties. Abe Issa was attracted to the glamour of horse racing and counted among his acquaintances a number of international personalities connected with the sport. One in particular was a Canadian racing mogul. So when on a Monday morning early in 1958, Audley Morais visited Abe in his office at Myrtle Bank Hotel and asked him to sell Knutsford Park on his behalf, the logic of the request was taken for granted. The matter of what commission Abe would be paid for his efforts was another matter and I was a witness to the haggling, Jew versus Arab. I helped to end the stalemate by suggesting that Abe be granted a thirty-day option to buy the shares in Knutsford Park Limited for the price Morais had nominated, any amount in excess of this to be Abe's profit on the deal. Morais agreed and I was asked to draw up the option immediately. I crafted a ten line agreement that Abe and Morais signed. Auditors for Knutsford Park were Carman and Bruce, later to become Price Waterhouse. Morais authorized Caswell Harry, the account manager, to turn over to me the last three years' audited accounts of the company.

I would be Abe's ambassador in negotiating a possible sale of the track to a Canadian mogul and accordingly booked a flight to Toronto on Friday. My task before departure was to try to make adjustments to the audited accounts, which would appear to be reasonably achievable, and so justify Morais' asking price. I doubled the number of race days, increased the price of sweepstake tickets from five shillings to ten shillings and reduced expenses by fifteen per cent. None of this was good enough. But on the Thursday night before my scheduled departure the next day, balance sheets spread out on the dining table, it suddenly came to me with growing excitement that the value of the land and buildings were shown as assets at cost. What if Knutsford Park was more valuable as a real estate development than as a racing operation? I needed Abe's confirmation of how much he thought land in this area would fetch. If my guess of about twenty pounds sterling per square foot was correct, the development, including two hotel sites, might provide a gross income as high as thirty million pounds sterling.

I phoned Abe immediately. He was already in bed but agreed to see me. He sat in pajamas, a cup of black coffee before him and listened to my calculations. It took no more than half an hour for him to decide to exercise the option to buy Knutsford Park. Neither of us slept much for the remainder of that night. When on the Friday morning Morais was summoned to Abe's office and informed that Abe intended to exercise the option, Morais was furious and stormed out of the meeting, threatening to sue. Abe and I rushed to the law offices of Judah and Randall on Duke Street. Judah studied the option I had crafted for an agonizing fifteen minutes, pronounced it enforceable and asked Abe if he would consider letting his firm purchase 25% of the venture. Judah's partner, Harry Randall, was a leading conveyancing lawyer and real estate speculator so his advice would be a decided advantage. Abe readily agreed. Randall arranged for a land surveyor, a Mr. Jobson, to design the subdivision, which turned out to be an unimaginative mosaic of domino-shaped lots arranged side by side and back to back.

While the partners revelled in the coup they had pulled off, I was awarded the privilege of naming the new location. I baptized it New Kingston and, at a press conference held at the Myrtle Bank Hotel on October 27th 1958, Abe distributed a press release I had drafted that formed the basis of *The Gleaner*'s front-page story the following day. It captured the vision in these terms:

> A modern "city within a city" complete with two hotels, multi-storied office buildings and apartment houses, 18 parking areas, 300 commercial sites, modern street lighting which will make New Kingston a city of lights. The planned development will be at Knutsford Park which has been Jamaica's premier racetrack for nearly 60 years. New Kingston will be the first scientifically planned expansion of metropolitan Kingston. Lots are priced at £20 to £30 per square foot. New Kingston will be of equal importance to downtown Kingston where the lack of adequate parking space has become an insurmountable problem.

But that was not the end of the New Kingston saga. Its subdivision, like all subdivisions, required the approval of three Government agencies. Shortly after submission of the plans, Norman Manley, then Chief Minister of Jamaica, telephoned Abe to advise that he was not prepared to deprive the citizens of Kingston of a race track. There would be no subdivision approval forthcoming until the Knutsford investors built an alternative facility. The Chief Minister understood that Mr. Alex Hamilton was prepared to sell land at Caymanas for a reasonable price. Abe should get on his horse and contact him.

Surrendering gracefully to this blackmail, the Knutsford Park consortium purchased the Caymanas land and, to ensure that the new track would be up to world-class standards, consulted with Sir Neville Ashenheim and his son Richard, a renowned sports statistician. The Ashenheims, after studying the figures, asked if Abe would consent to their participation for 25% of the project. He once again agreed and the Caymanas track, with its dramatic cantilevered stand, opened a year later.

Shortly after the birth of Larry, our son, it was time for me to claim entitlement to long leave. When I told Abe that we planned to tour

Europe he arranged for complimentary hotel accommodation in all the cities we were to visit and generously instructed the Issa Confirming House in London to provide me with five hundred pounds in cash on arrival.

The trip was a spectacular success. One of the highlights was Hamburg. We stayed at the Vier Jahreszeiten hotel, our room overlooking the Alster river. This was where Hans Schnoor, Aunt Nettie's husband, had lived before migrating to Jamaica. The hotel itself was one of the most luxurious in Europe, a favourite of Konrad Adenauer, the postwar Chancellor of West Germany until 1963. Upon checking in early on a Saturday afternoon we booked a car and chauffeur for a night club tour but made the innocent mistake of asking the times of masses on Sunday. With German attention to detail the receptionist passed on this information to our driver who came to the correct conclusion that we were Catholics. We had been looking forward to seeing the fleshpots of St Pauli and the Reeperbahn, naked girls wrestling in mud, but our driver, "Papa Fritz" as we named him, would have none of it. "No good for you," he kept insisting. "I take you to good German beer garden." And so he did, to an establishment where we sat at table with men dressed in lederhosen downing beer. One asked Doreen to dance a polka and Papa Fritz gave his permission. We returned to the hotel exhausted, but our innocence still intact.

For the return trip we booked first class passage on the *SS. Mauritania* from England to New York. We were a curiosity for not many couples as young as us could afford such a prestigious transatlantic voyage. We were seated at the table hosted by the ship's doctor and invited to a round of cocktail parties.

In more sober moments we missed our two children who had been left in the capable care of Grandma Ermyn. Larry was only a year old and we had some misgivings about deserting him at such an early age. We were able to make a ship-to-shore telephone connection with him in Jamaica and hearing his tiny voice on the other end of the line only increased our guilt. Having burned our candles and our bridges at both ends, we returned exhausted to Jamaica and the demands of my career as Abe Issa's Executive Assistant.

CHAPTER TWELVE

INVESTMENT CONSORTIUM

It was now apparent to me that the estrangement between Abe and his brother was growing systemic, exacerbated by a severe cash shortage that confronted the Issa enterprises, because too much money was tied up in obsolescent inventories at the department stores. The Bank of Nova Scotia demanded Abe's presence in Toronto and he asked me to accompany him. One of the bank's balance-sheet experts, a Mr. Kent, lectured Abe on the importance of fiscal discipline. Abe sat chewing his lower lip and when, after wiping his mouth, he returned his handkerchief to its accustomed home up one sleeve of his jacket, I noticed that it was discoloured with blood. The bank was going to put in place an unofficial receiver to take control of the core business, a serious blow to Abe's authority and pride.

Abe was still a man of substantial means and at Harry Randall's urging he joined an investment syndicate, owned 50% by himself and Harry and 50% by two Americans, Richard Cowell and Murray Koven. Cowell was an international water-ski champion and playboy, though constrained by Koven, his lawyer and investment advisor. Now, investment opportunities that would ordinarily have been channeled to the House of Issa were increasingly being taken up by the new syndicate under the name of West Indies and Caribbean Developments Limited, registered for tax purposes in Nassau. As the name implied, the investment thrust of WIC, as it became known, was to focus on the Eastern Caribbean, in addition to substantial hotel, shopping centre and hardware interests in Jamaica.

I now found myself trying to divide my loyalties between the core Issa enterprises and the new ventures controlled by WIC. Sometimes the lines of demarcation became blurred and often there were internal adjustments in the ownership of various projects. In the case of WIC, I also found myself trying to maintain a balance between the Jamaican and the American investors, who often espoused different business philosophies and ethical values.

WIC had already acquired some 305 acres of land in the Eastern Caribbean islands which, at the urging of the American partners, were slated to be sold in the United States as lots that could be paid for over time in monthly installments. Abe was of the view, and I agreed with him, that the development of the real estate would not succeed unless seeded by a hotel in each of the islands. Accordingly plans were drawn up for three hotels, an 80-room unit in Antigua that would occupy a prime section of land fronting on Jolly Beach; a 70-room unit in St. Lucia with frontage on Reduit beach and in Grenada, a 60-room unit fronting on Grand Anse beach. I estimated that it would cost just over one million pounds sterling to build the three hotels and it was thought that the Colonial Development Corporation in England might be prepared to put up the money.

Abe was distracted with other problems, and more as a lark than anything else agreed that I should go to London on my own to make the case. I stayed in a single room at a Mayfair hotel which had a basin in one corner but no bathroom. I found my way through Berkeley Square to Hill Street where CDC was headquartered, there to keep an appointment with a Mr. Minetzhagen whom I expected to be of German background. He turned out to be quintessentially English, about my age and we soon discovered a shared interest in the theatre. He recommended that while in London I should see a show called *Irma La Douce*. "I am sure you will love it," he assured me, "It's all about a prostitute." Then realizing that this had been a minor *faux pas*, he apologized and we both had a chuckle. He was later to be knighted and as Sir Minetzhagen became the head of CDC, whose initials had, by then, migrated from Colonial Development Corporation to the Commonwealth Development Corporation.

Minetzhagen helped me to refine my rather rough feasibility studies and this obliged me to work late at night in my hotel room, revising figures. I often pissed in the basin rather than stagger down the hall to the communal bathroom. Finally, I was assured that the application would go to the Finance Committee some time in the future. Bemused and exhausted, I returned to Jamaica. I do not know who was more surprised, Abe or me, when a letter arrived about a month later, advising that CDC had approved the loan.

This put the WIC strategy into a new perspective. Someone, on a full time basis, would have to negotiate with the various island governments

and supervise the construction and staffing of the hotels. Not without
further aggravation between Abe and Joe, it was agreed that I would
resign from the Issa organization and take up duties as Managing
Director of WIC, operating out of rented offices on Slipe Road. The
transition from executive assistant to line management was sudden and
traumatic.

Prior to my WIC appointment, a gentleman in a heavy serge suit,
florid of face and sweating profusely, presented himself at Abe's office
and introduced himself as the Managing Director of British Overseas
Stores, a London company. Part of its investment strategy had been to
purchase enterprises in ex-colonial territories and in Jamaica it had
acquired D. Henderson and Company, the island's largest hardware
store, and Leonard deCordova, a large, wholesale lumber operation,
located almost directly opposite Henderson in lower King Street. The
gentleman confessed that managing these enterprises from London was
becoming increasingly unprofitable. Theft was rampant and collecting
accounts receivable seemed an almost impossible task. Would Mr. Issa
please buy British Overseas Stores' investments in Jamaica? He could
name his own terms. A figure that corresponded to the amount of
receivables shown in the balance sheet was agreed. The Issas already
operated a hardware store, so to avoid a conflict of interest the new
acquisition became part of the WIC portfolio.

The day-to-day operations of Henderson and Leonard deCordova
settled down under my direct supervision and appeared to be on the
verge of profitability. Then came a telephone call at 3 a.m. that Henderson
was on fire. I rushed to the scene, but from the intensity of the inferno,
started in the paint shop, it was obvious nothing could be saved.
Henderson was insured, including a loss of profits policy. Since the
claim was going to be one of the largest in Jamaica's history, the insurers
appointed an internationally famous loss adjuster to minimize the
amount of the claim.

Along with Whiskey Gordon, of Myers, Fletcher and Gordon, I led
the negotiations and a figure was eventually agreed. It was decided not
to rebuild the Henderson building and the proceeds of the settlement
remained in the WIC coffers as working capital. This allowed me time
to concentrate on WIC's investments in the Eastern Caribbean.

In their initial negotiations with the various Eastern Caribbean
governments, Abe Issa and Harry Randall had been selling a vision of the
rewards to be gained from promoting tourism, citing the Jamaican
experience. This enthusiasm intoxicated the local politicians whose

agreements in principle to cooperate fully resulted in a series of very elastic and in some cases unrealistic undertakings. My job on the ground was to tie down the details. This involved the formation of local companies that would hold title to the hotels and through which their financing could flow. I choose the name Caribeach Hotels Limited, in which WIC held the majority shares. The final decision makers of the various governments were V.C. Bird, Chief Minister of Antigua; John Compton, Minister of Trade and Industry in St. Lucia and Herbert Blaise, Chief Minister of Grenada.

During construction of the three Caribeach hotels I was away from home three weeks out of every month; Doreen and my then three children became almost strangers. The hotels were opened on time, but other factors began immediately to impact on their viability. Strategically, not sufficient thought had been given to the lack of airlift in the various islands. Only Antigua had an international airport; the other islands were limited in the type of aircraft that could serve them. The remarkable DC 3 was still being flown by BWIA, but I was somewhat nervous about being a passenger on an aircraft older than I was.

The island governments had no funds for advertising and promoting themselves as tourist destinations, a burden that the hotels themselves tried valiantly to bear. This and low house counts put a strain on working capital, and CDC was becoming reluctant to put more money into the venture. I was summoned to London and given a nasty reception by Lord Rendell, who advised that CDC's hotel expert, a Mr. Hall, had been instructed to take the Caribeach hotels under his wing and, in about three months, would make a final report on what had gone wrong.

Mr. Hall, a man of Napoleonic stature and hubris, ran a number of successful hotels for CDC, in particular a highly profitable commercial property in Lagos, Nigeria. Unfortunately, he knew nothing about the resort trade in the Caribbean and the psychology of American tourists. He thought that what worked in Lagos would work in Antigua, St. Lucia and Grenada. He was ignorant of and astonished at so called wholesale tour operators who sold package tours to tourists for which they expected the hotels to pay a commission of 15%. He was convinced that I was getting a "kickback" from some of the tour operators and proceeded to cut them out of the reservation system.

I had no doubt that his report would recommend that CDC take over the hotels and place them under his administration. My pride apart, this actually suited the overall WIC game plan, which was to have hotels operational in each island, no matter who owned them, in order to seed the contemplated programme of land sales. Besides, my executive portfolio remained full to overflowing with other projects in Jamaica.

One of these was the acquisition of the Arawak Hotel in St. Ann's Bay, Jamaica's first five-storey structure, designed by Ted Lapidus, the flamboyant Miami architect. The entrepreneur behind the investment was a Mr. Ornstein from Toronto, who provided finance to the project secured by debentures issued to himself. Shortly after the hotel opened, the manager of the English construction company that had built it tried to collect a substantial amount of money still outstanding. Ornstein kept him waiting in the ante-room to his office for an hour. When he was finally ushered in, Ornstein asked him, "Have you ever been in the hotel business?", to which the manager replied in the negative. Ornstein stood up, shook his hand and exclaimed, "Well, congratulations. You are in the hotel business now."

The Arawak was placed in liquidation and a receiver appointed. A date at which it would be publicly auctioned was announced and needless to say Abe was salivating to get control of it. At a WIC strategic planning session it was decided to try to buy the debentures held by Ornstein for fifty cents in the dollar, which meant that a bidder at the auction would have to come up with cash for the total bid, whereas WIC would be bidding "paper" for at least half of its bid. Negotiations with Ornstein took place in Toronto, spearheaded by Murray Koven and me. Ornstein was represented by Deryck Stone, one of Jamaica's most brilliant legal minds, but someone emotionally feeble under stress. The all-night sessions wore him down. Eventually he broke down into tears and returned to Jamaica. I was near exhaustion myself but Koven remained remarkably fresh. Eventually a deal was struck, and at the auction title to the hotel passed to a WIC subsidiary and its supervision to me.

The only way a resort hotel can ensure 100% occupancy is to over-book by about 10%. This is usually a reasonable gamble, as there are inevitably cancellations and "no shows". Even if one or two rooms are short on a particular night, guests are usually prepared to accept alterna-tive accommodation at a comparable hotel. This was not to be on one occasion when a couple with confirmed and deposited reservations refused to transfer to another hotel. The architectural centrepiece of the hotel lobby was a huge chandelier under which two facing couches were arranged. The lady began unpacking her suitcases and, climbing on one of the couches, was able to hang her panties and bras on the chandelier. She then telephoned *The Gleaner* and suggested that if they wanted to photograph a nude lady in the Arawak lobby they should dispatch a photographer as soon as possible, for she intended to change into her pajamas in about an hour.

As this drama unfolded, other guests were gathering to watch the spectacle and in desperation the reservations manager summoned me. I tried to reason with the lady, but to no avail. I pointed out that what she intended to do was a criminal offence. If she wished to bring a civil suit against the hotel for breach of contract that was her privilege, but if she did not start behaving herself I would summon the police to remove her from the premises.

"I don't give a damn about your stupid island laws," she shouted at me. "I am from New York where the contract was made and I know my rights."

At this point I advised her that I was a member of the New York Bar so she had better heed my advice. She collapsed on the couch, a look of amazement on her face. Her long-suffering husband intervened at this stage. He helped her repack her underwear and I dispatched the couple to another hotel. The crisis was over.

As I had anticipated, "Napoleon" Hall recommended that CDC take over the Caribeach hotels under his administration. I was relieved of portfolio responsibility for them, which was fortuitous as WIC was seriously over-extended, outstripping its relatively small capital base. An injection of new equity capital was urgently needed and I was sent to England to explore with the London and Yorkshire Trust, an issuing House, how it might help us in this regard.

I presented my letter of introduction to Sir John Keeling, titular head of the Trust, and he turned me over to Ted Parsons, a hard-working technocrat with an accounting background. In the rigid class structure that then prevailed in Britain it was obvious to me that Parsons, though doing most of the work, was under-paid and not likely ever to head the organisation. But he was quite at ease with me and quick to grasp the investment opportunities that WIC might offer.

I had arrived at the London townhouse in which the Trust was located at 10 am and was shown into a drawing room heated by burning logs in a fireplace, above which was a gilded mirror. Parsons and I examined figures in a small conference room until 12:30, at which time he escorted me to his office. There was a bar set up on a side table and we had time for a whiskey before lunch, which was served in the dining room on the fourth floor. The dining table, gleaming with crystal and silverware, was set for about fifteen of the Trust's directors to whom I was introduced.

I was seated to the right of Sir John, and worried about being able to decipher the complexities of the feast. A butler in livery served white wine with the fish course and red wine with the meat. After dinner a bottle of port was passed around the table. I declined a cigar. Negotiations with Parsons resumed at 3:30 pm, by which time I was enveloped in an alcoholic fog, barely able to speak. Parsons confirmed that the type of lunch to which I had been invited was a daily affair during the working week, leaving me convinced that the ritual was a negotiating ploy to get the better of any bargain.

I survived the ordeal and was advised that, subject to another meeting, the Trust might be interested in taking a 10% equity stake in WIC and providing seven year loan funds by way of a debenture. So important was it to bring the negotiations to a successful conclusion that the full WIC team, headed by Abe, flew to London to reinforce the case.

Abe, who had not visited London for twenty years, was greeted by the majordomo of The Savoy hotel by name. The Savoy had no thirteenth floor, whether for reasons of superstition or because the hotel is built on two levels I don't know. Abe was assigned a suite on an upper floor and brought to the old hotel a surge of energy – early morning working breakfasts with his American and Jamaican colleagues, business appointments throughout the day, lunches with old friends he was able to contact, nightclub hopping until the wee hours of the morning. This pace was sustained for a week, and while Parsons, Koven and I hammered out the details of the proposed deal, Abe kept Sir John enthralled with stories about his adventures. Eventually a finance and promotion agreement was signed.

Two days before our planned departure for Jamaica I received a call from the hotel manager advising that Mr. Issa was not well; the house doctor had been summoned and would I go immediately to his suite. Abe lay on his bed with eyes closed, pallid and covered in cold sweat. The doctor drew me into the living room.

"I believe Mr. Issa may have had a mild heart attack," he advised me.

More tests would be needed to confirm this, which would mandate his staying in London for an extended period. Abe would have none of this and, under the circumstances, the doctor reluctantly agreed that it would be safe for me to accompany him back to Jamaica as soon as possible.

The reservations were changed accordingly and Abe and I sat in first class bulkhead seats on the BOAC flight. He hardly spoke and drifted off to sleep from time to time, leaving me to imagine a series of dreadful scenarios. Brown, the family chauffeur, was at the airport to meet him.

"Ralph, not a word of this to anyone," Abe ordered as he sank into the back seat of the Chrysler.

"Of course," I assured him, "I'll be in touch."

On the following Monday he swept into his Myrtle Bank office as if nothing had happened. He turned over his accumulated mail to me for reply and repaired to his swimming pool office. He would dip in the pool a few times but always with a lit cigarette between his fingers. "Helps me avoid the temptation of swimming," he once confided in me.

WIC's cash flow improved, but tension between the American and Jamaican partners did not. Abe as Chairman of the board of directors was not adroit at dealing with the various arguments that arose. Eventually, after some behind-the-scenes lobbying on my part, it was agreed that Parsons would take over as Chairman. Board meetings were held once a quarter in Jamaica.

My three year employment contract with WIC was due to expire in 1965 and I proposed a substantial salary increase as a term of renewal. The scope of my administrative responsibilities covered five hotels with a total capacity of 832 beds, including the Arawak hotel on the North coast and the Terra Nova hotel in Kingston. I was also responsible for Henderson, Leonard deCordova, Tropical Plaza and Liguanea Plaza shopping centres in Jamaica and the Hofus hardware company in Honduras. I was beginning to feel the weight and wear of such a large portfolio and thought that my remuneration should reflect both my endeavours and my considerable successes. The salary proposal was the last item on the agenda of a directors' meeting held at Terra Nova hotel. I was asked to leave the room and paced the lobby for about half an hour before being recalled. There was a strange silence when I entered the room. Without further ado Parsons said, "The Board finds it impossible to meet your demand for such a large salary increase and since you would hardly be comfortable carrying on without it, the Board has decided not to renew your contract and suggests that you resign. A formal letter will be sent to you expressing the gratitude of the directors for your years of service. The meeting is adjourned."

I stumbled from the room, shocked to the core. Abe refused to look me in the eye and hurried to his car. I was never able to get him to talk about the decision and I am not sure whether he supported me, but was outvoted. In retrospect, I should have realized that the Americans would feel that I sided too often with the Jamaicans and would be glad to see me go. It also turned out that I was already being paid almost twice as much as Parsons, which undoubtedly irritated him. After the tremendous time and effort I had invested in WIC, I felt sure that without me it would collapse. Of course it did no such thing. Doreen was traumatized by the news that I was suddenly unemployed. This was the first time that this had happened but, sadly, it was not to be the last.

Some years later Abe died of cancer after a long and brave battle. Doreen and I attended the funeral which, in accordance with his wishes, featured his favourite music, lighthearted songs like "The Object of my Affection". I wrote a remembrance for *The Gleaner* in which I pointed out that making money *per se* did not stimulate Abe. It was the game, the challenge of taking an idea and seeing it become reality that revivified his towering imagination and motivated his success in so many fields, all of which made an enormous contribution to the economic development of his beloved Jamaica.

CHAPTER THIRTEEN

WHERRY WHARF

The course of my life till this point seemed to be decided more by fate than by any intelligent planning on my part. But I now faced a serious crisis. I was suddenly unemployed and with no savings, currently running a modest overdraft. It was ironic that I, so scrupulous in protecting and enhancing the assets of those for whom I worked, was cavalier in how I handled my personal finances.

My mother had predicted that I would be a spendthrift, a prophesy I did not take seriously until, some years later, I noted that Dante had consigned spendthrifts to the Fourth Circle of Hell. But my extravagance was not in the acquisition of things – rather in satisfying my sybaritic propensities, flying first class, gourmet restaurants, fine wines and over- tipping, which was still an unexplained defect of my character.

Reasonably adept at playing whatever cards I was dealt, my departure from the ranks of professional management became the opportunity to go into business for myself. Out of what was sheer panic and desperation I found a way to buy Wherry Wharf, the old family business that had been such a significant part of Mother's life but which I never expected to be a part of mine.

This involved entrusting the purchase negotiations to someone with whom Uncle Mike would deal. To have approached him directly would have been fatal, for he seemed always to be threatened by me. In truth, I had no moral or legal claim to any interest in Wherry Wharf and even less capital with which to make a serious offer. Taking a leaf out of Abe's book for the purchase of Nathan's, I entrusted the negotiations to Maurice Facey, a friend and one of Jamaica's most creative entrepreneurs, who had the appropriate temperament and credentials to deal with Michael.

As it turned out the negotiations were frustratingly slow and always in danger of collapse. Whenever Maurice agreed a purchase price, Michael increased it. Eventually, however, he agreed to a figure of £100,000 sterling, and since Michael was willing to leave most of it on mortgage for seven years at 6% interest, I was able to subscribe for 70% of the equity with £10,000 borrowed from Doreen's father. Maurice received 20% of the company as promoter's fees for successfully concluding the purchase and Hans Schnoor, Aunt Nettie's husband, took up the remaining 10% interest. Without any formal arrangement, I accepted the moral obligation that a half of my investment in Wherry Wharf belonged to my sister, Audrey.

The task of building Wherry Wharf, the "old curiosity shop", into a viable modern business was a formidable one. Basically, success hinged on converting what I had purchased into what it was meant to be – an operational wharf. Although there was in existence a semi-decayed pier teetering tentatively over the sea, it was useless as a wharf because the maximum draft of water alongside was only eleven feet.

My business plan was to launch into the lumber trade, the dynamics of which I had learned when, as Managing Director of WIC, I was responsible for the activities of Leonard deCordova, one of its subsidiary companies. I recalled that the Georgia Pacific Corporation, one of the largest paper and lumber companies in America, had been interested in entering the Jamaican market, which at that time had a potential for about forty million board feet of construction pine per annum.

The time now seemed right to contact Howard Driver, GP's Export Manager. We arranged to meet in Miami at the then respectable Columbus hotel. It was only GP's determination to break into the Jamaican market that made a deal possible. GP agreed to extend me 180 days credit, interest free, which meant that if I could collect my receivables in 90 days the game could be played successfully – in theory anyway.

But how to rehabilitate the wharf?

Seprod Limited, an acronym for "Soap and Edible Products", was one of Jamaica's largest manufacturing companies, producing soaps, cooking oil, margarine and animal feeds for the local market. Bulk corn for the feed plant was discharged at one of the public wharves, sucked by a vacuvator out of the holds of the ship and blown into open dump trucks which transported the corn over a considerable distance to the feed plant. In the process a fine layer of dust blanketed everything in the area and this was a considerable nuisance to other users of the public wharves.

It so happened that the Seprod plant was geographically located only a few hundred yards away from and almost opposite the Wherry Wharf site. With more guts than grounds, I proposed to John Harrison, the General Manager of Seprod, that he should use my wharf to discharge his bulk corn. That the corn boats drew 18 feet of water whereas Wherry Wharf had only 11 feet of draft was no problem. I would have a channel dredged. That the wharf was so dilapidated it would collapse under the weight of a motorcar, much less a truck, was no problem either. The Seprod trucks could park at the foot of the wharf on *terra firma* and the corn could be blown into them through a lightweight plastic hose. That the wharf was not an approved sufferance wharf for the unloading of commercial cargoes was also no problem. I would get permission from Mr. Edward Seaga, the Minister of Welfare and Planning, whom I considered to be approachable. Finally, that I had no money to undertake the dredging was no problem. Seprod's only obligation would be to lend me the amount of money involved, in exchange for which I would enter into an agreement with it to land its corn at a 40% discount off the commercial wharfage rates it was now paying.

The fact that I would be using Seprod's money, earned from wharfage, to repay its loan and end up with a usable lumber wharf did not seem to discourage John Harrison, so powerful are the logistics of geography. Harrison persuaded the Seprod Board to approve the loan.

Each phase of the improbable plan presented difficulties. We started the Seprod arrangement using the eastern channel only. The first ship with corn, correctly attempting to approach at an angle, ran aground. It had to be refloated and berthed with the help of a tug. The voluble Spanish captain swore on his mother's grave that he would never return to Jamaica, much less to Wherry Wharf. But by some miracle we operated bi-monthly discharges at the old wharf for over a year.

Until this stage of my life I had always been subject to the jurisdiction of someone with the power of control – my mother, the US Air Force, Abe Issa, Ted Parsons of WIC. Now I was my own man for all intents and purposes. One spin-off of this was the freedom to speak my mind as I saw fit, without having to toe a corporate party line. Because I controlled my own working hours, I was also able to accept positions of public service to which I could devote the time they demanded.

Not long after purchasing Wherry Wharf, Edward Seaga asked me to take over the job of Chairman of the National Volunteers Organization. Under the umbrella of the NVO, island-wide programmes were to be established headed by local community leaders. Golden Age clubs would provide hot meals for the elderly delivered in Volkswagen vans, which I persuaded the Federal Republic of Germany to donate to the cause. The oldsters put on plays and quadrille dances which, as head of the organization, I felt obliged to attend. There were youth clubs that organized football and cricket competitions for which I begged equipment from large local corporations. There were outings in the country for inner city kids and a miscellany of cultural and educational activities, often organized on an *ad hoc* basis.

I catapulted myself into this new experience with enthusiasm and energy and in Kingston the programmes achieved a modicum of success. I soon learned that the venture had to overcome two main problems. Because of NVO's broad grassroots reach, the then People's National Party opposition was convinced that it was a cynical Seaga move to generate support for the JLP (Jamaica Labour Party). The media speculated that I would soon announce my candidacy for a seat in Parliament. Since I had no knowledge of or interest in Jamaican politics, I worked scrupulously to avoid any politicization of the NVO. Some years later at a dinner party at John Pringle's flat in London, Michael Manley confided to me that he had infiltrated the organisation and was pleased with reports of my neutrality. "Otherwise," he declared, "we would have mashed it up."

I ran NVO for some four years and, fortuitously, resigned a few months before the next General election at which the PNP was returned to power.

With profits earned from the Seprod contract I was ready to rehabilitate the wharf, subject to government approval. This approval seemed doubtful since there was now a plan that envisioned the reconstruction of the entire Kingston waterfront, and this would involve the government having to acquire the Wherry Wharf site by right of eminent domain. In my efforts to get permission for rehabilitating the wharf I kept bouncing from one government department to another, even as the bank kept eyeing the Wherry Wharf overdraft with increasing unease, and my friend Mr. Seaga became more and more unavailable.

I was told on a Friday that the Ministry of Communications and Works, whose portfolio included the passing of the actual construction plans, intended to reject my application on Monday. Once the rejection became a *fait accompli*, Mr. Seaga, as a matter of protocol, was hardly likely to reverse the decision. I tried desperately for an appointment on the Friday only to learn that he was in Parliament.

On Saturday, discouraged and dejected, my dream of landing lumber at my own private wharf about to be shattered, I decided to take Doreen to dinner. She suggested Blue Mountain Inn, but I insisted on a new restaurant just opened at Devon House. Devon House was deserted when we arrived. We sat at the bar and I was nervously playing with my

Scotch when Doreen nudged me with her knee. When I looked up there were Mr. and Mrs. Seaga walking in. They greeted us like lost relations from Lebanon and asked if they could join us. We had dinner together, and while Doreen skillfully engaged Mitsy in domestic conversation I was able to broach the subject of Wherry Wharf. He whipped out one of the IBM cards that he kept in a breast pocket and wrote himself an *aide memoire*. I was still trembling when we said our adieus and I drove home to Doreen's accusation that I was a warlock.

Under pressure from the indefatigable Mr. Seaga, the Kingston Waterfront Development proceeded much faster than anyone could have imagined. I was advised by Moses Matalon, Chairman of the Kingston Waterfront Redevelopment Company, that the government wished to "swap" the existing Wherry Wharf premises for a four acre site at Newport East. Newport East had been created by dredging the harbour and the proposed site would provide a new ships channel 250 feet wide and 30 feet deep. The prospect of such navigational generosity for my lumber ships was irresistible. The Newport East area was even closer to Seprod than the existing site and therefore the swap would not adversely affect the contract I had negotiated with John Harrison.

Since the government was only swapping land for land, albeit on a four to one ratio, my real problem was to find the finance to build an entire new operational centre at Newport East. The new wharf would be no problem. I had the Seprod loan for that. But I still needed lumber sheds, a factory and offices. I decided to gamble on being able to finance the move out of working capital which, in time, I could replace with a long term loan secured by a second mortgage on the new complex.

It took one year to complete the move to Newport East and there was a three year interval exactly between the first corn ship that parked alongside the old Wherry Wharf and the first lumber ship that docked at the new wharf. I had taken possession of the old Wherry Wharf from Uncle Mike on the very day that Elizabeth, our fourth and last child, was delivered by Caesarian section at St. Joseph's hospital. She was now three years old and I forty.

I had come to a milepost in my life in more ways than one. While engaged in the Wherry Wharf adventure I had not really been conscious of the passing years. But then neither had I counted the days during the WIC adventure, the Issa adventure, the Japanese adventure, the university and law school adventure or, most significantly, the "how to survive as a boy in the Isaacs family" adventure. In fact I had plunged from one episode to another in my life, passionately engaged in each with little overall perspective. Only now was it beginning to dawn on me how much I owed to others in this succession of excitements, especially the quiet loyalty and support of Doreen.

At 6 am Sunday, April 7 the bedside phone exploded. I grabbed it on the second ring. It was Doreen's mother, her words cold and controlled. "I can't seem to wake Frankie. Can you and Doreen come immediately?" We dashed out of the house in our pajamas. Mayfair had been sold and the Lyons residence was now on Allerdyce Drive. By the time we got there Dr. Wong had confirmed that Frankie's death was the result of a heart attack. David had arrived a few minutes before us and we all huddled at the foot of the bed. In life, Frankie's personality was so strong that one thought of him as a large presence; in death, the soul departed, the remaining clay seemed fragile and shrivelled in the bed, his mouth the empty entrance to a cave, his dentures snarling from the bedside table.

Frankie had a morbid fear of being buried alive and had extracted a promise from his son that he would slash his wrists to ensure that he was dead. While David was arguing about this with Dr. Wong I ushered Ermyn and Dody from the room. When I returned fifteen minutes later there were bandages around Frankie's wrists but I saw no signs of blood.

Two days after Frankie's death, the funeral procession left from the Sam Isaacs funeral parlour on Hanover Street – this Isaacs was perhaps an outside child of one of my Isaacs forbears. There were two police outriders as we drove up Duke Street and along North Street, past the old Lyons residences and thence to Kingston Cricket Club, of which Frankie had been President. The club members stood at attention as we passed on our way to the old Jewish cemetery donated to the community by Emmanuel Lyons, Frankie's grandfather. By coincidence, this was where my great grandfather, Henry Isaacs, is buried.

A huge crowd turned out to honour Doreen's father – of every colour and creed, two nuns and two monsignors. Our three eldest children were devastated, especially Deborah who was his favourite. He always referred to her as Debbie Lyons. Dody, David and I mourned the loss of Frankie and tried to console Ermyn. The realities of commercial life helped to distract me from grief.

★ ★ ★

Part of the development of the new Wherry Wharf complex was the installation of an Osmose pressure treatment plant to protect construction lumber from termites. François Petot, an Osmose vice-president, was sent to Jamaica to conclude the purchase contract and supervise the installation of the plant. Petot was short, egg-shaped and dapper. A transplanted Frenchman, he also spoke fluent Spanish. Although his educational background was somewhat vague, he was well travelled and a cultured gentleman, possessed of great Gallic charm. I was tendered a standard Osmose operating contract but insisted on certain changes to which Petot grandly agreed. After the signing, his boss in Buffalo telephoned to advise me that Petot had no authority to make any changes but, under the circumstances, he would reluctantly ratify them. This was a grave embarrassment to Petot. The Gallic shrug with which he reacted to it would have required a paragraph by Proust to describe, body language that signified both that the rebuke was not worth more than a shrug, and disdain for a stupid American superior. But I also suspected there had been an injury to his *amour propre*, because I knew that he was not all that he pretended to be. The shrug might also have been a warning that revenge is a meal best eaten cold.

CHAPTER FOURTEEN

SELLING WHERRY WHARF

Doreen and I planned a vacation in Mexico after the plant was success-fully installed and the new complex in full operation. Petot, who liked the grand gesture, offered to accompany us since he knew the territory intimately. He was able to secure an invitation from the daughter of a former wife or mistress of Diego Rivera to meet her mother, whom I knew was an iconic presence in so many paintings by the master. This woman had formed a construction company after Rivera's death and, now in her sixties, had become a multi-millionaire. Her *residencia* in Mexico City housed the largest private collection of Rivera paintings. We entered the grounds, driving through immaculate lawns on which peacocks strutted, fanning their tails. We passed a private bull ring built by the mother so that her current lover could practice one of his other special skills.

In the middle of the entrance hall there was a table on which a cast of the painter's right hand was displayed, the thumb obviously deformed. On another table was his death mask, like all death masks ghoulish and cold. But the walls were ablaze with Rivera paintings, more subtle and complicated than his public murals that bore the burden of revolution-ary social realism. After an hour of inspecting the paintings we were told that the lady of the house was sleeping late and would not be able to receive us. We were nevertheless grateful to Petot for arranging the visit.

On our return to Jamaica, my most pressing management priority was to ensure that I collected my accounts receivable to avoid running out of working capital. This entailed travelling one week every month into rural Jamaica to visit the retail outlets through which lumber was sold. I was driven in a new Morris Oxford by my salesman, Sarju, a dark East Indian with aquiline features and thick black hair pasted back with Brilliantine. He had a perfect set of white teeth, and when he splashed a smile it was difficult for customers not to reward him with an order.

He performed better as a salesman than as a debt collector, so it was necessary for me to take up the slack.

Sarju planned the route and we set out on a Monday morning, the weather and the landscape unfailingly beautiful. We stayed overnight in rural guesthouses patronized by other travelling salesmen. We would eat in cold supper shops, the tables covered with plastic tablecloths, cutlery wrapped in a paper napkin. Sarju was delighted when the tables were decorated with a bottle of hot pepper sauce. When we knew from experience that there would be no restaurants available at midday, we would buy a loaf of hard dough bread, a half-pound of butter, a tin of "bully" beef, a bottle of cream soda for Sarju and a Red Stripe beer for me. This meal we consumed in the shade of some magnificent mahogany or guango tree by the side of the road. With a gentle breeze flowing down the side of a mountain – which often was the case – Sarju and I would nap for half an hour, reclining in the front seats of the Oxford. A sweeter siesta it would be hard to imagine.

We had unexpected encounters and adventures aplenty. I recall one visit to Grange Hill, a village above Lucea, where a Chinese shopkeeper with the exotic name of Israel Williams served the community with grocery and hardware items as well as lumber. In typical fashion he would be dressed in shorts and clopped around behind the counter in open sandals. Like most Chinese shops of the time it was dimly lit and featured a cashier's cage protected with mesh wire. Inside the cage was a lady with long blonde hair and sparking blue eyes whom Israel had met and married when he was at school in Germany. Her accent was an interesting mix of German and patois. If one peered through the gloom, on a shelf above the cage you could see a display of silver cups and trophies, won by Nonsuch, Israel's famous, locally-bred race horse. One visit, he asked his wife to prepare a cheque for me, then wished us good-bye as he was off to Montego Bay to play in a polo tournament.

The first year of operation of Wherry Wharf at Newport East produced a profit after tax of £40,000. During the course of the year Maurice, Schnoor and I personally purchased two lumber ships, the *Dominion Trader* and the *Dominion Pine*. They had both been in the Scandinavian lumber trade and I was given the privilege of taking delivery of the *Dominion Trader* in New Orleans. After the formalities had been completed I was allowed to stand, holding the helm, as the ship made its way slowly up the Mississippi river, an imaginary voice from the bow calling out "Mark Twain, Mark Twain!"

In the late Sixties, under the prime ministership of Hugh Shearer, a rash of social tensions began to break out in Jamaica. There was admiration in radical quarters for the revolution in Cuba. Amongst students and sectors of the Black urban poor the ideology of Black Power, then sweeping through America, attracted adherents. Amongst the various sects of the fast-growing Rastafarian movements were some whose motivations were seen as seditious. There had been the Coral Gardens uprising in Montego Bay in 1963, during which eight persons were killed. This had unnerved the Government, and magazines and books deemed to be subversive were subject to censorship and confiscation.

Horace Levy, a young Catholic priest steeped in Liberation Theology and a student of the radical German philosopher, Herbert Marcuse, began publishing a revolutionary broadsheet called *Abeng*. He asked me to help defray some of the costs of printing and, seeing myself as an enlightened liberal, I was happy to do so. Horace and I shared a progressive religious perspective on Catholic doctrine. Often, when he came to dinner at the house he would hear my Confession and grant me absolution. Then one afternoon he arrived unannounced and explained that he would not place me in danger by visiting again. Shearer was about to ban *Abeng* and the Prime Minister's secret service men were monitoring his movements. There were, he said, two sets of cars parked as he spoke, one at the top and one at the bottom of the avenue where we lived. He bestowed his blessing and departed. This sounded like the script of a Grade B movie and I was sceptical. Doreen and I got in our car and drove up the avenue and there, sure enough, was a Ford Zephyr, with two men wearing dark glasses in the front seat. Horace subsequently left the priesthood and married. He is now a respected social worker.

Under Robert Lightbourne, as Minister of Trade and Industry, the Jamaica Labour Party had adopted a policy of import substitution. New local manufacturers – "screw-driver" industries in reality - were afforded heavy protection which resulted in factory inefficiency and pushed up the price of goods to consumers. Such protection did not apply to established industries such as the manufacture of awnings and tarpaulins by Wherry Wharf. When it was announced by the Trade Board that whilst there would be a tax placed on flax cloth used in the manufacture of tarpaulins, finished products imported from abroad would be duty free (to support the transportation sector), I went ballistic.

The JLP bureaucracy was becoming intolerable. The only way to sort out business problems was to line up outside Mr. Lightbourne's office at 6 am. He usually arrived at about 7 am, unfailingly polite, greeting everyone by first names. If you were not too far down the waiting line you were granted an audience and he usually dealt with the matter in a sensible way. But one was always subject to his mood and mercy, something that irritated me.

I refused to pay duty on the raw flax used in making tarpaulins, as required by the new law, and was advised by a bailiff employed by the Lightbourne ministry that he would be coming at 3 o'clock the following afternoon to place a levy on my office furniture and other equipment. I decided that I would strap myself to my desk and invited the television station to set up a camera in the office to film me being physically carted off to jail. The staff in the tarpaulin department fully supported my stand because their jobs were at stake. I arranged for them to parade in front of Wherry Wharf with signs that read, "Lightbourne unfair to Jamaican workers" and "Duty on raw material must go".

The bailiff arrived on time, astonished to see me trussed up at my desk, lashed down with awning cord, a TV camera rolling the while. He executed an about turn and departed. The event made the main news that night and Lightbourne was furious. He phoned me demanding an apology for the signs and placards. I insisted that I had nothing to do with them. The workers had taken action on their own. Disbelieve me as he might, there was nothing Lightbourne could legally do about my protest, and I heard nothing more about the incident or the tax claim.

About this time, Michael Manley was becoming a hero to the working classes and had persuaded the middle class that he was not a Communist. Handsome, charismatic, a master of political rhetoric, he appealed to the electorate as a welcome change from the growing arrogance of the JLP administration. In late 1968, Doreen and I hosted a dinner party for Manley at our home, attended by about sixteen persons. In those days his libation of choice was gin and tonic and after about three drinks, just when our guests were settling down to a lively political debate, there was a knock on the front door. It was one of Michael's political activists, come to tell him that a mob was burning down buildings in Kingston and had been confronted by the police at Torrington Bridge. The riot was led by students from the University of the West Indies at Mona to protest the government ban from Jamaica of Dr. Walter Rodney, a radical Guyanese who, the Shearer government believed, had been stirring up unrest throughout the island and the government, rightly or wrongly, had decided to move against him.

The rioters were hampering fire brigade personnel in their efforts to put out the fires, threatening to kill them. Manley made one or two telephone calls, issued instructions to the messenger and returned to the party as if nothing had happened. I could not decide whether this was dictated by prudence or whether it suited him politically to stay out of the mêlée. From our house we could now see flames from the burning buildings lighting up the night sky, a signal for our guests to say their good-byes. Michael was one of the last to leave.

My fear of Wherry Wharf falling into the category of an overtrader without a sufficient equity base seemed every day to become more of a reality as sales continued to show impressive growth. When the over-draft climbed to £80,000 sterling I began to give serious thought to selling some shares to raise additional capital. To this end I contacted my friends at the Commonwealth Development Finance Corporation, CDFC.

CDFC was a British development agency distinct from the Com-monwealth Development Corporation, CDC, which had financed the Caribeach hotels and with which I had parted company on less than friendly terms. CDFC operated on strictly commercial lines and was headed by Dennis Pearl, a dapper Englishman in his early sixties who was married to a new, young wife, but who still confessed to having a roving eye, from afar, for brown-skinned Jamaican beauties.

As part of my approach to CDFC I dispatched audited Wherry Wharf accounts to London and was surprised to receive a quick response, suggesting that, based on CDFC's analysis of the Jamaican stock market, they considered a PE ratio of 10 times after tax earnings would be an appropriate basis on which to make an investment. I considered this generous and would gladly have sold them 10% of Wherry Wharf on these terms, but they insisted on a minimum equity participation of 30%. This provoked the thought that rather than accept such a large dilution, why not sell the entire company? I thought Pan-Jam might be interested because, although the Trust was asset rich with land and office buildings, it was shy on cash. A combination of the two entities seemed a logical match that would enhance the value of Pan-Jam shares on the stock market.

I had already consulted Jim Lord of Price Waterhouse on the value of Wherry Wharf, suspecting, rightly, that he would pass on to Maurice Facey a recommendation to pursue the acquisition. If a sale was to take place there was no doubt in my mind that it would be to Pan-Jam, not only out of loyalty to Maurice for having helped me to buy Wherry

Wharf, but because, under his leadership, a culture was emerging at Pan-Jam that I found congenial and which was unique in Jamaica at the time. Unlike the introspective merchant mentality of even progressive family firms, Pan-Jam, from the beginning, welcomed professional management and was international in outlook. Maurice had an uncanny ability to spot talent and to surround himself with a highly qualified management team that was given extraordinary leeway in the scope of its responsibilities and authority. There was a lightness of touch, a grace and style, in the way Maurice exercised his authority as chairman of the board of directors. But I confess that I also knew that if Maurice felt Pan-Jam was the only potential purchaser of Wherry Wharf, he might not deal with the matter with any urgency and, when it came to price, I had to remind myself that I would be up against his astonishing negotiating skills.

In the event, I also consulted Darryl Ashenheim, who was a key advisor to the Matalon group, hoping that perhaps he would mention the opportunity to Mayer Matalon, the head of the clan. He did this and, without either party knowing, I held preliminary discussions with both. The figure on the table was £400,000 which, in the case of Pan-Jam, would be satisfied by about 25% in cash, the balance in Pan-Jam shares at par. I would be given a five-year management contract, the first year to be spent as a transitional period at Wherry Wharf, the remaining four as group managing director of Pan-Jam.

Matalon, made to feel he was the front-runner, set up an appointment to meet me at Wherry Wharf at 4 pm on a Tuesday. Facey and Charles Adams had promised, but failed, to get back to me the previous day with a final document. I phoned Maurice, told him that Matalon was coming to see me and that I had decided to conclude the purchase with him. Maurice begged me to give him an hour. He had, he said, called a directors' meeting to approve the terms of the sale. It was now underway and by the time I arrived the final document would be ready for signature. As I was driving out of Wherry Wharf to go to Pan-Jam I could see Mayer's long black Cadillac turning into the gate. At Pan-Jam the final document was agreed and initialled and the following day the news broke in the press. The television station, in announcing the purchase, emphasized that Pan-Jam had made a profit of £2,000 for the year 1968 compared with £50,000 for Wherry Wharf.

The relative speed and relief with which I sold Wherry Wharf confirmed once and for all that I was not at heart a true entrepreneur. My greatest corporate strength was as a "back room" tactician rather than as

Pan-Jamaican – Wherry Wharf Merger
BR, LR: Charles Adams (Pan-Jamaican Director), Hans Schnoor, Maurice
Facey, Ralph Thompson.
FR, LR: Audrey Thompson, Cecil B. Facey, Antoinette Schnoor, Doreen
Thompson.

a strategic visionary, and as such my most important contribution to corporate government seemed to be pulling chestnuts out of the fire and extinguishing the fire itself. Thanks to my Jesuit training, I was quick to see relationships that allowed me to walk into strange territory and take control of it. At the board level I was a passionate defender of whatever position I held. No "yes man" me. In corporate structure I was more at home as a managing director than as chairman of the board, a position admirably filled by Maurice Facey. Maurice was not stingy in setting salary scales for his senior executives and for the present life was good.

In 1967, Pan-Jam faced a severe cash flow problem, the solution for which was to go to the fledgling Jamaican capital market with a "rights" issue. While the underwriters and accountants shilly-shallied over technical matters, I bullied Maurice to take immediate action. The placement was a success, providing Pan-Jam with a cash injection of one million pounds sterling. Two weeks later the market collapsed; had there been any further delays, the ability to raise the needed capital would have been foreclosed. There is a difference between taking risk for gain and taking risk for survival. Maurice was a genius at the former, my strong suit the latter. At the Pan-Jam annual awards dinner that year I was named "employee of the year" and presented with a suitably inscribed plaque.

CHAPTER FIFTEEN

FAMILY

Our first child was due in October 1955 and Doreen was admitted to St. Joseph's Hospital into the tender care of the nuns and special skills of Dr. Ivan Parboosingh. He was head of Kingston's Jubilee Hospital, an institution so overcrowded with newborns they had to be wrapped in towels and lined up side by side, like sausages, on trolleys parked in the corridors. He was probably more expert at delivering babies under adverse circumstances than any obstetrician in America. Once he agreed to take on Doreen as a private patient I felt more comfortable. But she was two weeks overdue and one day I saw Nurse Hamilton pressing her ear to Doreen's bulging stomach. She detected some foetal distress and Dr. Ivan was advised immediately. He scheduled a Caesarian for that afternoon.

I was shattered, suddenly conjuring up a series of horrible possibilities. While the procedure was in progress, I knelt in the St. Joseph's chapel praying to God to save my wife and baby and trying to bribe Him with outlandish promises, few of which I have honoured. Thankfully, my prayers were answered. When I was allowed to see our daughter Stephanie, she looked at me through sad, brown eyes set in a perfectly round head, which is a characteristic of Caesar babies.

Seventeen months after Stephanie, our son, Larry, was born. No Caesarean was necessary this time. Doreen was joyfully awake as they wheeled her out of the delivery room. As I bent to kiss her, she whispered, "We have a son! A beautiful son."

There was a longer gap of three years between Larry and Deborah, our second daughter. Deborah's advent to the world was frighteningly dangerous. Hers was a breech birth and Dr. Ivan had to try to turn her during labour, a painful and delicate manipulation. When she was born the umbilical cord was wrapped around her neck, but by the grace of God and Dr. Ivan's skills the final outcome was successful.

Doreen's courage in labour became an emblem for me of all women who embrace motherhood. Her faith in the Lord and Dr. Ivan's skills were such that again, after a further gap of five years, we decided to try for one more child. Perhaps subconsciously, we wanted to have another boy, a brother for Larry. We understood the dangers and consulted Dr. Ivan. With Quaker calm he set out the pros and cons and in the end Doreen, in an act of faith, decided to invite another pregnancy. On the occasion of this birth it was Doreen's health that tested Dr. Ivan's skills. Her blood pressure was dangerously high and she had developed oedema. There was nothing for it but to perform another Caesarian, which was scheduled for March 31, 1965. Doreen, with sly humour, requested that the operation be postponed to April 1st – the month of my birth. Thus Liz became a Tom Fool's child whose birthday is never forgotten.

To help with the Thompson brood we recruited an eighteen year old nanny from the Crèche Training programme. Pearl was intensely black, with a bashful smile. She was immediately inducted as a member of the family and lived with us in the home we built on Dillsbury Avenue prior to Larry's birth. She was devoted to the children and made a signal contribution to their upbringing. When she was sure there would be no more offspring, Nanny Pearl announced that she was migrating to America. There was wailing and beseeching but we could not in good conscience dissuade Pearl from a move that would afford her more opportunities for advancement than would be available in Jamaica.

Even during the vicissitudes of childbearing, Doreen had channelled her unbounded energy into volunteer social work. She was a founding member of WEE CARE, a visiting service to provide nutrition for malnourished children at the University Hospital of the West Indies. Her interest in the welfare of children lead to her appointment by the Government as a member of the Adoption Board. For many years she distinguished herself as principal presenter on the radio programme, "Morning Magazine". Sometimes she could be heard on radio in the morning and I could be heard that same night on the public affairs programme, "The Verdict is Yours". This was a programme that started on radio and graduated to television. It dealt with topical subjects and the guest roster included, inter alia, Frank Barrow, Pat Mar Johnson, Viv Blake, David Coore, Ken Hill and Emil George.

Perhaps in gratitude that her four children came into the world sound in mind and limb, Doreen has always reserved a special place in her heart for the disabled. She serves on the Board of the Mona Rehabilitation Centre, originally established to care for polio victims, but now a centre for all orthopedic disabilities, many resulting from gunshot damage. For the past twenty years she has been Chairman of the Friends of the Centre, its principal channel for private fund-raising for the Foundation. She ritually claims that she hates begging for money, but does it surpassingly well.

Doreen shares with me an interest in the arts and the theatre in particular. Over the past twenty-five years, as a member of the Ward Theatre Foundation, she has struggled to save this treasure of a Victorian theatre from decay and government neglect. For four years she was Vice-Chairman of the Foundation's Executive Committee and has refused to desert the cause despite almost insurmountable odds.

Other Doreen interests have included the Jamaican Historical Society, for which she served as President from 1997 to 1999, the Jamaican Georgian Society, the Women's Club and the Royal Commonwealth Society. I estimate that she has given over fifty years of public service, working tirelessly behind the scenes, a key organizer and diligent worker for all the organisations with which she is connected.

On the Thompson domestic front, she is our Martha, always available to entertain visiting family, important dinner guests and any stray visitors I might invite for supper. The Lord gently chided the Biblical Martha for not being sufficiently introspective. Doreen claims there will be time aplenty for that in the future.

In 2008, long overdue and, in my view, in a rank lower than she deserved, Doreen received a phone call from the office that administers the awarding of Jamaican National Honours advising that she had been conferred with the Prime Minister's Badge of Honour. The official letter from the Prime Minister read:

> It gives me great pleasure to inform you that acting on my advice, His Excellency The Governor-General has awarded the Badge of Honour for Meritorious Service to you, for voluntary service to Jamaicans in the fields of Education, Child Care and Theatre Arts. The Ceremony for the presentation of the Badge of Honour will be held at King's House on Heroes Day, Monday 20th October 2008. Please accept my warm personal congratulations on your well-deserved award.
>   Yours sincerely
>   Bruce Golding
>   Prime Minister

★

After Mother's death and my return to Jamaica from Japan, it became obvious that my father was becoming more and more depressed. Retired, without any relatives or close friends, surrendering grudgingly to old age, he still lived in one room at the Poughkeepsie Elks Club. He received a generous pension from the railroad, but whenever I was able to visit him in New York on one of my business trips, I could tell that he was desperately lonely. He was also fiercely independent and brushed aside any suggestion that he move permanently to Jamaica. But time took its toll and I was able to convince him that a pension, payable in American dollars, would allow him to live comfortably in Jamaica without being a burden on anyone. He arrived in Jamaica, all his belongings in two suitcases. To preserve the façade of independence I arranged for him to live with Aunt Val, an Isaacs cousin, and to pay his own rent and upkeep.

However, with some prescience, I began to build a cottage a short distance from our main house on Dillsbury Avenue, separated from it by a swimming pool. Its design incorporated a comfortable bedroom and bathroom, divided by sliding doors from a large living area. I envisaged that my father would live comfortably in the cottage, and after his death it would serve as my studio.

Not long after settling in Jamaica, Dad developed Parkinson's disease and the cottage was waiting to receive him. He was still able to join the family for meals in the main house and to play happily with his grandchildren. In time the shaking and shuffling associated with Parkinson's disordered his mobility to such an extent that he was confined to the cottage under twenty-four-hour nursing care. Independent to the end, he decided one night to get out of bed without help, fell and broke his hip. Even with the best care at Medical Associates Hospital he developed pneumonia, fell into a coma and died. Consumed with guilt that I had not been a filial son, I wept on the drive home. He was so proudly American it was ironic to think of him buried in foreign soil. He was interred at Calvary Cemetery, not far from Mother's grave, his coffin draped in an American flag.

CHAPTER SIXTEEN

SAN SAN

In America, parents send their children to professionally run summer camps; in Jamaica wealthy middle-class families own or rent villas on the north coast of the island, often setting up residence there for the three months of summer, husbands commuting from work in Kingston at week-ends. We had been in the habit of renting a house in San San, an enclave favoured by the international jet set and a small group of senior Jamaican businessmen including Desmond Blades of Musson, Deryck Stone, one of Jamaica's leading lawyers, Oswald Dunn, another well-known lawyer, and the Faceys.

Our children learned to water-ski in the famous Blue Hole, sailed their Mirror dinghies in San San Bay, played Monopoly in the evenings and undoubtedly explored the relatively innocent outer territory of sex. Parental supervision was responsible but not unduly restrictive and, fortunately, there was never a problem with drugs. We rented a house owned by Denis Smith-Bingham, a mysterious Englishman rumoured to be in British Intelligence and a relative of the Queen. After living for many years in Jamaica, he had returned to England, entrusting the sale of "Gremlin Hill", his San San home, to Colonel Gayson, a real estate agent and ex-army officer who addressed all male acquaintances by their last names. When he turned the keys over to me at the beginning of the summer rental, he had intoned, "Smith-Bingham has decided to sell Gremlin Hill. I have some rich Texans flying to Jamaica in their private jet to inspect the property when your rental expires. I have to emphasize, Thompson, that you must be out of the house by 11 a.m on the last day of your stay."

The price being asked for Gremlin Hill seemed reasonable. Doreen and I conferred and decided to buy it because we had been seduced by its charms and because ownership would allow us to extend our present vacation by another month. This involved having to outflank Colonel Gayson and his Texas millionaires. I had to guess which law firm in

Kingston was the most likely to have been appointed solicitors for Smith-Bingham. Calling on my warlock gift, I picked Judah and Randall – which turned out to be correct. I phoned Douglas Judah to inform him that I accepted Smith-Bingham's asking price, wanted to continue in possession and would arrange for a cheque for the full purchase price to reach him that afternoon. Formal transfer of title could take place at his convenience. Judah phoned Smith-Bingham in London, who readily agreed to the deal. I was now the proud owner of Gremlin Hill, much to the delight of Doreen and the children.

On the final day of the rental, Colonel Gayson arrived in his Land Rover and was obviously upset to see me in a bathing suit lolling on the verandah. "Thompson," he barked, "I thought I made it clear that you had to be out of here by 11 am. I have someone who wants to buy the house."

"That's strange", I replied, "because I haven't decided to sell it." I advised him of what had transpired and suggested that he check with Douglas Judah.

"Well," he exclaimed, "you have certainly taken the wind out of my sails." He turned on his heels and departed.

These were heady days. The intellectual challenge of helping to guide the fortunes of Pan-Jam became a series of corporate adventures involving local and international negotiations at the highest level. I began reading books on management theory and finance and this, combined with my legal background, balanced Maurice's creative flights of imagination.

I also began to paint seriously on week-ends in the cottage occupied by my father before his death. Oil paint was my favourite medium, although over time I became competent with water colours. I set up still life studies in the studio and could became so involved in the work that when Doreen called me for lunch I refused to stop painting, settling for a chocolate bar to keep me going. Whenever I spent time at Gremlin Hill, our new home in San San, I would pack up my painting gear and venture forth for a day of *plein air* painting of the lush Port Antonio landscape. My painting, *Pavilion,* was accepted for one of the annual exhibitions mounted by the National Gallery and, after some years working on my art I was able to stage a "one man" exhibition of eighty paintings at a private gallery. I am now sorry that so many of them sold.

In truth, painting had taken the place of reading in relieving the high level of stress that was now a feature of my business life. Reading was too passive a pastime; a business problem was quite frequently able to interject itself into a chapter of a novel, no matter how exciting. Painting absorbed me completely and perhaps saved me from a heart attack.

Pavilion: San San

San San Beach

Lovers: oil and gesso on hardboard

Port Antonio

CHAPTER SEVENTEEN

JAMAICA'S FIRST CONTESTED TAKE-OVER

The dynamic of Pan-Jam's management style was best demonstrated in its contested take-over of Hardware and Lumber Limited. This made corporate history in 1969. One day at a directors' meeting, which included Charles Adams and Robert Lake, I presented a detailed plan for the take-over of H & L. I outlined enthusiastically the synergistic benefits that a management amalgamation of H&L and Wherry Wharf would provide, not the least of which would be the use of Wherry Wharf for unloading H & L's lumber cargoes. Maurice caught the take-over fever and the Pan-Jam board approved the attempt.

Hardware and Lumber Limited, founded in 1927, was the island's largest distributor of construction lumber and hardware items, selling at both the retail and wholesale levels. It occupied a commanding commercial presence on 18 acres of land at the junction of the Washington Boulevard and the Mandela highway. From this location its fleet of trucks traversed the island making deliveries to a network of village shops and general retail stores. For many years it had a monopoly on the supply of pitch pine lumber from Honduras, both rough and dressed, which had become the preferred type of wood used in the building industry. H & L's only drawback was that it did not own a private sufferance wharf and was obliged to discharge its lumber cargoes at the public wharves at commercial rates.

Shares in H & L were informally traded before the Jamaica Stock Exchange was formed. They were popular with a group of investors referred to as the "widows and orphans" – a safe haven for capital accumulated by well-off middle-class Jamaican families. Over the years H & L's shareholdings had become widely spread and when the Kingston Stock Exchange started trading in 1962, it was one of the first companies to be listed.

The board of directors of H & L comprised some of the leading business and professional personalities of the time. Mr. Fred Harris, an

Englishman who sat on the boards of some ten Jamaican companies, was chairman. Other directors included Lionel deCordova, Dossie Henriques and Leslie Ashenheim. In 1969 Harris was in his seventies and the character and direction of the H & L board was heavily under the influence of Ashenheim, an astute lawyer and a highly respected leader in the Jamaican Jewish community.

A combination of circumstances and coincidences contributed to the success of the H & L take-over. First National City Bank of New York (now renamed Citibank) had recently opened a branch in Jamaica and the current manager was William Rhodes, a rising star in the Citibank system. He took a shine to Maurice and me as the new breed of Jamaican entrepreneurs who would shake up the "commission" mentality of most trading houses in the island. Because of his junior status at the time, Rhodes was given limited local banking authority, but was an ardent advocate for Pan-Jam at Citibank headquarters in New York. After leaving Jamaica, Rhodes climbed rapidly up the Citibank corporate ladder and ended his distinguished career as its President.

Another fortuitous circumstance, which seemed trivial at the time, but turned out to be fortunate, was Ashenheim's absence from the island during the take-over manoeuvering. He appointed Deryck Stone to handle the legal ramifications of the take-over and to advise Harris, but there can be little doubt that Ashenheim's absence from the battlefield helped to ensure Pan-Jam's victory.

At a preliminary meeting with some of the directors of H & L, Maurice and I outlined the proposed bid. This comprised cash, Pan-Jam shares and unsecured convertible debentures. This worked out to 10/- per share for the H & L stock, a total purchase price for the company of £1,600,000 sterling – a sizeable sum in 1969. Deryck Stone announced that no offer from Pan-Jam would be considered unless the H & L shares were bought for cash. When we pointed out that this would not be possible, he closed his papers and the meeting ended. Pan-Jam was now confronted with the prospect of engaging in a hostile take-over battle, something that had never before occurred in Jamaica. The situation was further complicated because the Stock Exchange, still in its infancy, had not formulated any take-over rules, leaving the combatants to the bare-knuckled dynamics of the market and their own sense of ethical proprieties.

Pan-Jam's opening salvo was an advertisement in *The Gleaner* on July 8, 1969, setting out the terms of the offer made informally to the directors of H & L. In response, H & L published a series of advertise-ments advising shareholders not to accept the Pan-Jam offer. The business community in Kingston was agog as to what was going to happen.

In America there are companies that specialize, for a fee, in getting proxies from targeted shareholders in a take-over fight. No such companies existed in Jamaica, so Maurice and I and other Pan-Jam directors began the intriguing task of trying to contact H & L shareholders, mostly by phone, but often over lunch, to persuade them to accept our offer. One large shareholder, a Chinese gentleman, had left Jamaica and retired to his home province in China. Maurice eventually succeeded in getting a radio long distance phone call through to him and he agreed to sell his block.

Acceptances were coming in at a perilously slow rate, and based on the market's reaction to the initial offer it became clear that it would have to be improved if Pan-Jam was to win the contest. Conservative shareholders in H & L, many of them Jewish, relied on Ashenheim's advice not to sell and there was general uneasiness about having to accept shares in Pan-Jam as part of the purchase package. Founded in 1964, it was seen as a "Johnny-come-lately" company. Its published accounts for 1968, the year before the take-over attempt, showed audited profits of a mere £3,254! And who were these aggressive young men, Maurice Facey and Ralph Thompson, to whose management skills the destiny of the company would have to be entrusted?

A revised offer needed to increase Pan-Jam's cash payout, but this would need the approval of Citibank in New York. My assignment was to rush to New York to negotiate increased financing from the bank. Rhodes continued to support our attack, but the amount involved was now beyond his sphere of influence and, in any case, the figures of the proposed revised offer kept changing, because the value of the Pan-Jam and H & L shares on the stock market were both moving, sometimes up and sometimes down.

I stayed at the Waldorf Astoria Hotel on Park Avenue, a few blocks from Citibank's headquarters. The loan officer with whom I had to deal was a lady of gigantic proportions, attired in a long black dress. She looked as if she had just stepped out of a Wagner opera. It was a painful and slow exercise to explain to her the positive dynamic that would result from the merger. In those days, even companies quoted on the Stock Exchange, like H & L, were not required to disclose "turnover", a key figure used by banks in projecting bottom-line profits. I was obliged to demonstrate to the Valkyrie that because of my overall knowledge of the lumber trade, I could accurately estimate turnover from the accounts receivable figure shown in the balance sheet.

Facey could not authorize publication of the revised offer until I had obtained bank approval and the figures I was submitting to the loan officer kept changing with every passing day. Finally there appeared to be some acceptable alignment of the risk factors involved. Citibank approved the additional financing and Pan-Jam's revised offer was published in *The Gleaner* on August 11, 1969, the day I returned to Jamaica.

In reporting the terms of the revised offer in a news item on August 12th, *The Gleaner* abandoned its journalistic objectivity. The opening paragraph of the news item read: "In a fantastic bid to acquire the entire company of Hardware and Lumber Limited, Pan Jamaican Investment Trust has revised its offer made to H & L shareholders early last month." What made the revised package more palatable than the first was Maurice's inspired decision to arrange an underwriting that permitted any H & L shareholder to convert his Pan Jam-shares immediately for cash at 8/- per share.

With only a few days left before the expiration of the extended acceptance date, it was still uncertain whether Pan-Jam would get the amount of shares necessary to declare the offer unconditional. Was it possible that after all the hard work and ingenuity with which we had conducted the campaign, the take-over bid would fail at the last moment? I was distraught. Although the decision to do battle with H & L was a collegial one, it was I who had persuaded Maurice to enter the fight and I imposed on myself the moral responsibility for its success or failure.

Some tactic was needed to prod the holdout shareholders into action, to raise the spectre that if they did not accept the offer they would be locked in as minority shareholders in a subsidiary of Pan-Jam. In the event I crafted an advertisement which, although not untrue, gave the impression that the take-over bid had been successful. The advertisement read:

NOTICE TO STOCK HOLDERS OF H&L WHO HAVE NOT ALREADY ACCEPTED PAN JAM'S OFFER OF AUGUST 1969

The directors of Pan Jamaican Investment Trust Limited announce that the merger of Wherry Wharf Limited and Hardware and Lumber Limited will proceed on the basis of acceptance by 51% of the H & L shareholders. However the offer has been extended to Friday 22nd August 1969 because Pan Jamaican Investment Trust wishes to secure as large a percentage of the stock of Hardware and Lumber as possible.

The subtle threat of the language was not lost on the H & L shareholders and my ambiguous statement did the trick – but only just, for when the final deadline expired at 4 pm on August 24 1969, the count showed that 50.6% of the H & L shares had been tendered – technically a majority. We accordingly declared the offer unconditional and thereafter the flow of acceptances increased, so that by September Pan-Jam had acquired 58.4% of the H & L shares – a close but clear victory.

There was joyful celebration in the Pan-Jam camp. Valerie Facey graciously presented me with a document entitled "The Thompson Take-Over Kit", but the drama was far from over. A take-over bid concludes with the board of directors of the targeted company transferring the acquired shares into the name of the successful bidder. The old board is then supposed to resign, turning over the reins of management to the new directors. I made an appointment with Ashenheim to complete the formalities, but to my chagrin he declined to register the Pan-Jam shares on the basis that the Articles of Association of H & L provided that any transfer of shares needed the approval of the board of directors and the board of H & L was not prepared to grant such approval. I pointed out to him that such provisions in the Articles of Association were common and mere formalities in the circumstances. In my opinion he had no discretion in the matter. He replied, "You are right, Ralph, but I would prefer to be so instructed by a judge rather than you."

To avoid a long drawn out stalemate, Pan-Jam accepted Ashenheim's position in principle and it was agreed that although we would be allowed to take over majority control of the H & L board and management of the company, Ashenheim, deCordova and Henriques would remain on the board until an acceptable financing solution was worked out. This would involve some form of instrument to be issued by H & L to the minority shareholders that would provide them with protection, but which would not directly burden Pan-Jam with more debt.

Preference shares seemed to be the answer. The financing advantage of this kind of instrument was that banks would consider preference shares to be part of the equity of a company, thus improving its debt to equity ratio. Its disadvantage was that the coupon rate of the preference shares, unlike interest payable on a debenture, would not be deductible as an expense for the purpose of income tax.

I decided to approach Arthur Brown, my old neighbour on Dillsbury Avenue and now Governor of the Central Bank, to see if the coupon rate of preference shares might not be designated tax free and deductible as an expense. I waxed eloquent that in developing economies like Jamaica, preference shares were ideal instruments for raising capital. He agreed in principle and, perhaps chagrined that there had been no take-over rules on his watch, promised to get legislation through Parliament to facilitate the H & L situation.

We had given Ashenheim a date for issuing the preference shares and he was impatient. On the day Parliament was to deal with the new legislation I presented myself at Gordon House at lunch time to see Brown and seek reassurances that the bill would be passed. His office was in the back of the building and a sleepy policeman at the door made no attempt to halt my entrance. I found myself in the empty well of the House, saw the mace reposed in state before the Speaker's chair.

The legislation, entitled The Hardware and Lumber Limited Preference Shares Amendment Act, or words to that effect, was passed that afternoon. The undertaking to protect the H & L minority shareholders was concluded with Ashenheim, and a letter to this effect, addressed to them, appeared in *The Gleaner* of June 12, 1970. I could finally breathe a sigh of relief that the adventure was over. Except for one small detail. It was now my management responsibility to reorganise Hardware and Lumber and to ensure that the Pan-Jam promises made during the take-over campaign were fulfilled.

CHAPTER EIGHTEEN

PUT ON TRIAL

Pan-Jam's offices were on the 6th floor of the first high-rise building it had constructed on Harbour Street, in downtown Kingston, then named the North American Life building in honour of its prime tenant. I was assigned a handsome corner office looking over the harbour and Maurice was ensconced in a larger office in the corner looking over the city of Kingston, the skyline of which it was his ambition to transform into a modern metropolis worthy of being a capital. A commodious boardroom joined the two offices, decorated with impeccable taste by Valerie, Maurice's wife.

The euphoria of the PNP's victory in the general election of 1972 still lingered in the air and the gradual rot of Democratic Socialism had not yet set in. Life, both personal and business, pulsed with new energy and ambition. I welcomed each new business challenge, determined to help Maurice achieve his dream of molding Pan-Jam into a model corporate conglomerate.

On occasion, recognition came to me in my own right. Manley appointed me a member of the Prime Minister's Exploratory Committee on Art and Culture, chaired by Professor Rex Nettleford of the UWI. It soon became obvious to me that this was a thinly disguised ploy to decriminalize the use of ganja and to sacramentalize Obeah as part of the island's religious tradition. But many of the committee members would have none of this and the exercise ended with a tame report drafted by Nettleford with my help which, like so many reports submitted to Prime Ministers, was rusticated to file 13.

On the advice of the Prime Minister, and with the consent of the leader of the Opposition, I was also appointed a member of the Judicial Services Commission under the Chairmanship of the Chief Justice, an appointment generally thought to be one of considerable importance. In practice, decisions were taken in caucus, largely influenced by political considerations, and there was no authentic role for a so-called independent member. At Commission meetings the debate was usually about compensation, rather than competence or corruption. I was obliged to swear the Official Secrets oath and am content to hide behind this thin veil in refusing to comment on the calibre of some of the judges.

During my transition year at Wherry Wharf the company continued to produce outstanding profits and the reorganization of Hardware and Lumber under my supervision, although complicated, was making satisfactory progress. When it was time to take up my position as Group Managing Director of Pan-Jamaican Investment Trust, I recommended that the current chief accountant at Wherry Wharf, an intense black man, with an intense black beard and eyes that were perpetually bloodshot, be promoted from his current position to managing director of Wherry Wharf. This, in the context of the political situation, proved to be a serious error of judgment.

The PNP, now comfortably seated in the ideological saddle, began its campaign of militant Socialism, stressing the rights of workers without any concomitant emphasis on duties. This, combined with the continuing influences from the Black Power movement in America, contributed to a volatile social and business environment in Jamaica, ready to explode at any time. My promoted successor at Wherry Wharf, under the patronage and influence of Tony Spaulding, one of the PNP's most left-wing ministers, began bringing in a cadre of radicals to the Wherry Wharf management team. Concerned by the reports reaching me, I had occasion one day to visit my old stamping ground to investigate the suspicious activities of a department head. Upon my arrival, the entire workforce rioted in his defence. Thugs from Spaulding's constituency mixed with the workers, further inciting them to violence. Phone lines to the main switchboard were cut and I was physically hustled by clusters of workers, led mostly by women, shouting that I was to be tried by a people's court assembled in the cafeteria. This comic parody of scenes from the French Revolution did not seem real to me, yet I sensed that I was in palpable danger. I took refuge in my old office, bolting myself in. Fortunately, the direct phone line there was still working and I managed to get a call through to Maurice Facey. He promised to summon the police and Miss Edith Nelson, a senior officer of the Bustamante Industrial Trade Union, which represented the Wherry Wharf workers.

Before either the cops or Miss Nelson arrived, the phone on the desk rang and a voice asked if I would hold for the Prime Minister. Rescue, I thought, was at hand. Was I hearing the distant beat of a Jamaican Defence Force helicopter come to extract me from the mêlée?

"How are you, Ralph?" Manley asked.

"The situation is pretty tense," I replied.

"It always is," I heard him remark, and he proceeded to reveal the reason for his call.

He wished to commission Wayne Brown, the Trinidadian poet, to write a biography of Edna Manley, his mother, and knowing my interest in the arts, would I head up a small committee of private sector leaders to fund the engagement? He took my sputtering response, I am sure, as acquiescence and when I managed to tell him of my predicament, he said, "Don't hesitate to let me know if there is anything I can do." He hung up.

Miss Nelson arrived shortly after Manley's phone call. She was a woman in her seventies, as thin as she was wise. She appeared to berate me and ordered that I remain confined to my office while the workers briefed her in another part of the building. The briefing took over an hour and then I heard her shout to the crowd, "And now I must hear management's side of the story." At this point she collapsed into a chair in my office and ordered me to rebolt the door.

"Thompson," she admonished, "you get what you deserve. Why you so foolish as to let Wherry Wharf employ all these Communists. The man they supporting is a graduate of one of those ultra liberal universities in California. She then outlined her strategy for saving my life. "It is 1:30 now, past their lunch time. They getting hungry and you know Jamaican man put his belly before anything else. It will take another hour for me to get your side of the story. By then they dying from hunger. Then I will make my move." At the appointed time, she made me walk closely behind her into the restless crowd, the while heading quickly for the front gate of the compound.

"This man is only an employee like you," she shouted. "I am taking Thompson to Mr. Facey and will personally present your grievances to him." By this time we were outside the gate where she hustled me into her car. The Jamaican act of "sucking" one's teeth is, in the entire world, the most unique gesture of defeat, resignation and defiance combined in one slurp of sound. As we drove off, I could hear the workers sucking their collective teeth, drifting off in search of food. Miss Edith Nelson, ghost of famine, had saved my life.

CHAPTER NINETEEN

DEPARTURE

Lionel Trilling of Columbia University defines ideology as "the habit or ritual of showing respect for certain formulas to which, for various reasons having to do with emotional safety, we have very strong ties but of whose full meaning and consequences in actuality we have no clear understanding."

Michael Manley undoubtedly felt the need for emotional safety and he certainly had no clear idea of how the ideology of Democratic Socialism was going to infect Jamaican society and impoverish the island's economy. Central to his pet ideological formula was the concept of "Politics of Participation", which he touted as the best method to oil the process of social engineering.

Accordingly, I was frequently among a group of private sector businessmen invited to Jamaica House after dinner to meet with the Prime Minister and a clutch of his advisors. On one occasion, when the meeting was over, I paused in the foyer to chat with a friend and in the course of conversation rested my papers on the small table on which the visitor's book was displayed. Not until I had walked to my car in the parking lot did I realize that I was missing my notes of the meeting. I hurried back to retrieve them, the lobby deserted except for the soldier on guard. The doors to the Cabinet room were slightly ajar and I could hear laughter as Manley and his colleagues indulged in the badinage of a *post mortem* of the meeting.

"You see how it works, gentlemen," the Prime Minster chortled. "The trick is to let them talk, listen patiently to their tired capitalist theories and then go ahead and do what you have to do anyway."

I grabbed my papers and made a hasty retreat.

On another occasion, Doreen and I were surprised to receive an invitation to an informal dinner in the Manley's quarters above the Cabinet room. There were only two other couples and Beverley, the Prime Minister's then wife, served the meal herself. The atmosphere was decidedly intimate. After the other couples had departed, the evening ended with the playing of parlour games, which provided Manley with the opportunity of showing off his erudition and dexterity. I suggested a game, popular in Japan, in which two persons face each other on their knees. On the count of three they simultaneously throw out one of three possible hand symbols representing paper, scissors and rock. Paper covers rock and a clenched fist. But scissors cuts paper and rock breaks scissors. There is some psychology to the game. Will an opponent who has won a round repeat the successful symbol and if so how many times?

On this particular night it was Doreen who consistently outguessed the PM. Manley put a good face on it, but I could tell that he was not pleased at being vanquished by a woman. The irony was that the game is not one in which a player can try to lose. The image that I took away from the evening was Manley's excessive repetition of the paper symbol, a flat hand vigorously thrown out, his fingers trembling slightly, the knuckles beginning to knot with arthritis. I would have thought that a clenched fist would have come more naturally to him.

★   ★   ★

Pan-Jam built a hotel in New Kingston, strategically located between the Hilton and Sheraton hotels, and Maurice Facey, through his Canadian contacts, concluded a management contract with the Skyline group in Toronto. The facility opened with some amount of fanfare and a resident manager, a Canadian, was duly appointed. But the timing of the venture was not auspicious, for Manley's strident anti-capitalist posturing was beginning adversely to affect the island's tourist industry generally and Kingston hotels in particular. Management attached considerable importance to local patronage and the piano bar at the Skyline hotel was becoming a popular watering hole.

One night Mr. Anthony Spaulding, the Minister of Housing and one of the most radical of the Manley entourage and one of the architects of the political gang warfare that claimed 800 lives in the 1980 general elections, invaded the Skyline bar with a group of his political thugs, all of them wearing Rasta tams. The Canadian manager asked them politely to remove their head gear while in the bar. He was immediately accused of being a racist and, encouraged by the Minister, the posse proceeded to demolish the bar, flinging chairs at mirrors, upending tables and sending overseas visitors scurrying for safety.

Public opinion about the event was mixed, but Maurice and I were chagrined to note that John Hearne, the renowned novelist, in his weekly column in *The Gleaner* made light of the incident, equating it with the raucous but good-natured behaviour of college undergraduates in his day. He obviously had no concept of the damage that had been done, not only to the hotel itself, but to the island's tourist industry. There was danger that Skyline would abandon its management contract and Maurice asked me to contact John Hearne to see if he would modify his position in an attempt to calm the escalating furor that the incident was generating.

I admired Hearne as a writer but did not know him well except that he was a confidant of Manley's and a staunch PNP supporter. I invited him to lunch at Terra Nova and he accepted. A short, wiry man, his face and stubbly hair gave off an orange glow indicating his mixed racial ancestry, a person sometimes affectionately referred to as a "red man". His eyes were slits through which he peered with intimidating intensity, more theatrical than real. He tended to bluster, but as the lunch progressed and I put forward my arguments about Minister Spaulding's dangerous behaviour, I could tell that he was contrite about his column.

Over the months after that meeting we became close friends and in time he totally distanced himself from Manley and the PNP. He was greatly disturbed by the part Manley's henchmen had played in the Orange Street fire, a terrorist attack on a JLP tenement in which old women and little children were shot or allowed to perish in the flames. At considerable personal danger he wrote some brave columns in *The Gleaner* condemning Manley's reckless social experimentation. His was one of the few voices that gave the middle class, those who had not already fled the island, some hope. He became a hero of the anti-socialist faction, rallying support for the Seaga-led opposition. From time to time he billeted at our San San villa to recharge his batteries. His more frequent escape was into a Valhalla of alcohol.

It was during a period of relative tranquillity that Doreen and I journeyed down the Loire valley with Leeta and John Hearne. We had heard stories about a conclave of Jamaican writers living in Paris in 1953, including Roger Mais, Zacky Matalon and Hearne. Leeta was den mother for the group. Hearne, a small man with a strong, muscled body earned a few francs posing nude at one of the art schools. Mais developed cancer and quickly became desperately ill. The mission of the group was to get him back to Jamaica before he died. Travel was in an ancient

John Hearne

London taxi they had been able to buy cheaply in Paris. There were so many tales of humour, faith and courage – I am sorry they were never recorded. The quartet, exhausted physically and emotionally, did manage to get back to Jamaica. Mais's masterpiece *Brother Man* was published in 1954 and he died in 1955.

We rented a Peugeot in Paris and set off to follow the Loire valley as it wound its way down the fertile central plains of France. Leeta had the best French, Doreen able to cope with a few phrases. The two ignoramuses, Hearne and I, sat in the front seat and, as a matter of self-preservation, I did most of the driving. Shortly after departure in the mornings, Hearne would announce that he needed to buy cigarettes or to post a letter. This provided him the opportunity to down a Calvados or two in a local bar, which lifted his spirits until lunch, always accompanied by a bottle of cheap wine.

Leeta and Doreen sat in the back seat, official navigators and savvy interpreters of the *Guide Michelin*. At about four o'clock in the afternoon, designated as the "silly season", the ladies would select a small village a few miles ahead, identify a modest hotel or guest house and a restaurant listed in the *Guide* as acceptable. We were seldom disappointed.

Excursions to and inspections of castles apart, the day trips were a mélange of literary conversations, the froth of humour and incorrigible puns. Hearne told the story of his brief stay in a London hospital when, on seeing an approaching nurse, he hollered at her, "Friend or enema?" His reward was a burst of laughter.

On the return journey to Paris we stopped to view the Roman ruins in Tours and I recalled that this was the home of La Pyramide restaurant, founded by the internationally famous Monsieur Point, now dead but whose reputation remained in the capable hands of his wife and a cohort of ancient waiters, all of whom had served the rich elite of the world.

The restaurant itself was not an imposing structure, rather like a Jamaican Great House with a flight of stone steps on the outside of the building leading to the entrance. When General De Gaulle first made reservations to dine at La Pyramide there was excited speculation as to whether M. Point would dash down the steps to embrace De Gaulle or whether the grand general would mount the steps to be greeted at the entrance by his host. History has it that De Gaulle rushed up the steps, two at a time, to pay his respects to the great chef.

We were greeted by Madame Point, a plump dowager who spoke a little English. The wine list was a massive volume that could give one a hernia to heft it from the table. Details of the food and the rest of the evening are lost in a gentle alcoholic fog. The next day we managed to navigate ourselves back to Paris, where we bid good-bye to the Hearnes and returned to England on our way home.

Back on the island it was obvious that the economic policies of the PNP had begun to take a toll on the standard of living of Jamaicans, but Pan-Jam continued to enjoy a kind of false prosperity and I continued to burn my business and social candles at both ends.

One morning, in the shower, I noticed that one of my testicles was hanging considerably lower than its neighbour and Dr. Emile Khouri, a surgeon at Medical Associates Hospital, diagnosed an inguinal hernia. The operation to repair the problem appeared to go well except that the next day my back was black and blue from neck to buttocks. There was obviously some internal bleeding that Khouri was at a loss to explain.

I was rushed to Columbia Presbyterian hospital in New York for tests by Dr. Nozzle, a renowned South African haematologist. I had previously been operated on at this hospital for a hiatus hernia, a lengthy procedure which had ended with no complications and no excessive bleeding. It transpired on this occasion, however, that a genetic disorder known as disfibrinogenemia had manifested itself, a condition so rare that Dr. Nozzle offered to treat me as a research patient at no charge. I was designated as Kingston 12, only a dozen cases in the world having been then documented. Every day for about two weeks Dr. Nozzle attached me to tubes, drew blood and operated beside my bed a cyclotron machine that made a high pitched whirring sound as it spun.

Then Dr. Nozzle announced that his research grant had dried up so he would be unable to continue his experiments. What he had so far found, however, indicated that the disorder might not affect my normal life span, barring emergencies. Accidents which would require speedy and complicated medical intervention to staunch excessive bleeding would be the greatest danger.

Although I made light of the prognosis, I accepted, subconsciously, that continuing to live in Jamaica would expose me to double jeopardy, the danger of being caught up in the general violence plaguing the island and the lack of medical expertise to deal with my condition, physically or emotionally. I saw myself as a time bomb that could explode at any moment. I tried to adopt a fatalism by refusing even to wear a MedAlert bracelet and convinced myself that I would die like my mother in my fifties. Although in my personal life and in business I continued to perform energetically on a day to day basis, my long term focus remained foggy. My physical condition contributed to an absence of a sense of direction, and this began to merge with doubts about what constituted my true self. Did I really want to be a businessman for the rest of my life? The itch of poetry continued to germinate in my heart.

Political tensions began to poison life. To curry favour with an authoritarian PNP administration, friends were beginning to turn against friends, either revealing to the authorities damaging information that could be substantiated, or inventing accusations which could not. The administration established a Financial Intelligence Unit whose members operated in secret at the airports and in the banks, checking the personal finances of private citizens in a vain effort to prevent the transfer of US dollars abroad. But trying to control foreign exchange was like sand in a clenched fist, the tighter the grip the more the sand oozed out between the fingers.

Jack de Lisser, my friend from college days, was an avid sailor and his yacht *Athena*, which I helped him to build, had won many racing trophies under his captaincy. He was one of the first of my friends to migrate to America, avoiding the Financial Intelligence Unit's scrutiny by an interesting strategy. As a member of the Jamaican Coast Guard reserve he had learned deep sea navigation and one night he stowed his family, his chattels and his cash on board *Athena*, and set course for Miami. After a cruel internship in a hospital there he qualified as an American doctor and retired as chief of the anaesthesiology department of the Miami Veterans' Hospital. Except for brief visits, he has never returned to his homeland.

To qualify for employment in the Jamaican public sector, applicants now had to be passed as good socialists by a special committee headed by the General Secretary of the PNP. It was rumoured that anyone owning a house of more than three bedrooms would be obliged to rent the surplus accommodation to whomsoever applied for it at rates approved by the Rent Restriction Board.

Michael Manley espoused a special friendship with Cuba's Fidel Castro, expressing the desire to climb to the top of the Socialist mountain with him. When members of the private sector objected to policies that they believed were ruining the economy, the Prime Minister, in a public speech, advised that there were five flights a day to Miami. Anybody unhappy with living in Jamaica should take one of them. His advice was heeded, first by the Chinese community, which had come under virulent racial attacks, then by a flood of the middle class, which swirled around the American embassy seeking visas to the US. The most popular bumper sticker read, "Will the last person to leave Jamaica please turn out the lights". The fleeing managerial class caused a brain drain that virtually crippled entrepreneurial activity and investment.

Tensions were beginning to build between Maurice Facey and me about the future of Pan-Jam. He could not abandon the empire he had created in Jamaica but proposed to duplicate it in Canada. He offered me shares in the Canadian corporation he planned setting up, on the basis that I would remain as head of Pan-Jam in Jamaica while he ran the Canadian operation, commuting to Kingston from time to time. I was worried about the future of my four children in a dysfunctional Jamaica and declined the offer. I announced that the Thompson family would shortly be relocating to Florida. This displeased Maurice.

Leaving Jamaica had its complications. We had sold our house in Kingston but had decided *pro tem* to hold onto our San San villa and to keep on the payroll Mary and Joseph, our cook and butler. The lovers in Villier's play *Axel's Castle* contemplate a suicide pact and one of them exclaims, "Living! Our servants will do that for us". We did not quite equate emotional suicide with moving to Florida, but, with Mary and Joseph living in the San San villa, while Doreen cooked in Clearwater and I nightly put out the garbage, the Villier quotation seemed apposite. Two more expert and loyal helpers it would have been hard to find.

Then there was the problem of the paintings. During the early Seventies, as an antidote to the tensions of business, I had been painting seriously on weekends and had accumulated a fairly large inventory – too many pieces to ship to Florida. I culled about six to keep for ourselves and arranged a public exhibition and sale of the rest. This took place at the Victoria Mutual building on Half-Way Tree road and comprised about eighty works. They included self-portrait nudes; these caused a stir and much comment about "holding the mirror up to nature." A large painting of a poui tree was bought by Peter Rousseau and still hangs in his living room. Nearly all the paintings sold.

For several years Maurice had served as Chairman of the Jamaica National Gallery and I as a director. During this period we were also putting together a collection of paintings for Pan-Jam. Valerie, Maurice's wife, and I were delighted when Barrington Watson's *Mother and Child* came on the market, but the Pan-Jam acquisition committee rejected it as being too vulgar for public display, so Valerie and I bought it jointly. It was agreed that each of us would have it for six months a year.

The painting was Watson's masterpiece, a true West Indian Madonna, but with a startlingly different iconography. Traditional Madonnas were vertical or circular compositions, the babe at the seated mother's breast or at her feet. Watson's composition was dramatically horizontal, the black mother stretched out on a bed lying on a white sheet, the infant on the floor beside her, sitting on a chamber pot. The child's head and the mother's face, turned towards each other, were masterfully modelled and the sheet, which occupied two thirds of the canvas, was subtly textured in sepia and an exquisite gradation of greys. The painting was in the Dutch tradition (Watson had studied art in Amsterdam on scholarship), the overall impression being a tender portrait of a West Indian mother and child.

In view of my imminent departure from Jamaica, Valerie wanted us jointly to donate the Watson painting to the National Gallery, but given the priorities of relocation, I was not in a position to extend such largess and requested the gallery to pay me for my half interest. I knew this was considered bad form on my part and I suspect that, to save the situation, Maurice donated funds behind the scenes to conclude the purchase. *Mother and Child* now hangs in the National Gallery and I have had the pleasure of taking my children on a tour of it, proudly confirming that I once owned a half share in the masterpiece.

Another Caribbean artist with whom I established a connection was Erwin deVries from Surinam. He had studied with Watson in Amsterdam and is, in my view, perhaps the strongest, most versatile Caribbean artist. Primarily a sculptor, deVries' ability to switch from abstract expressionism to powerful realism in oil paintings and watercolours was extraordinary. So forcefully did his personality shine through his work no signature was necessary to identify them. He visited Jamaica frequently, and over the years we established a warm friendship with him. He painted portraits of our four children and Doreen.

CHAPTER TWENTY

STARTING OVER IN AMERICA

The decision to leave Jamaica was primarily triggered by concern for Elizabeth, our youngest daughter who, preparing to advance to high school, was at a crucial stage of her education. Jamaican society was becoming uncomfortably tense and violent. On one occasion we turned on the pool lights after midnight, perhaps contemplating a skinny dip, when an army helicopter swooped down, flashed a blinding searchlight into our eyes and issued bullhorn instruction to turn out the pool light. I flicked them once as a kind of greeting and obeyed.

Often on my way to work, a fierce-looking character would rap on the window glass of my car shouting, "White man like you must die!" Business executives learned to vary their routes to work to avoid such threats. Walking one day from a Duke Street law firm to my office, a well-dressed man sidled up to me, a smile on his face as he said softly, "Give me one thousand dollars so I don't have to shoot you." I kept walking but was sure that if I turned into my office he would follow me in. So I passed my destination, turning suddenly into the banking hall of the Bank of Nova Scotia at the corner of Duke and Port Royal Streets. I often kept appointments with the manager there so knew what button to press for entry into the executive office area. I described the man to the manager who discreetly peeked out and there was the extortionist waiting for me. The manager called the police but by the time they arrived the man had disappeared. I was considerably shaken. Now hosts who sent out invitations to house parties were expected to provide a locked drawer or room in which the firearms of the gentlemen could be secured until their departure.

It was difficult to disguise a decision to emigrate for, in order to complete the formalities, applicants were obliged to stand in line for hours in the hot sun outside the American Embassy. Friends driving by would toot their horns and shout their good-byes. Another give-away was a forty-foot container parked outside the residence of a departing family, loading furniture. Criminals were usually correct in their assumption that a family preparing to leave Jamaica would be hoarding and hiding US currency. This was not so in my case, as I had legally transferred the proceeds of the Wherry Wharf sale to a trust company in the Bahamas. We nevertheless experienced a break-in. The house was ransacked, our record collections scattered over the living room floor as the burglars pulled off the record covers, assuming this would be a clever place to hide United States $100 bills. They also cleaned out some of Doreen's best pieces of jewelry.

In retrospect, I now realize that fear of violence in Jamaica was somewhat of a rationalization for satisfying my long pent up desire to study literature, especially poetry, at the graduate level. Courageously, Doreen endorsed my plan, convinced that without some such distraction I would suffer a nervous breakdown.

My poem, "Jamaica Farewell", in *The Denting of a Wave*, gives some clue about what I was feeling. In the last stanza I wrote:

> An indifferent Kingston
> flushed itself into the harbour
> silting up the ocean
> with departures. The road
> curled around the airport
> like a question mark,
> its meagre wrist of land
> as fragile as your embracing hands.

Clearwater, a peaceful American town of about 50,000 souls, located on the west coast of Florida, was Doreen's choice for where we would spend the next nine years. It was far enough north of the hustle and bustle of Miami, now the capital city of Latin America, but not so far north as to expose us to the rigours of winter weather. It also had the advantage of being close to St. Petersburg where Larry, our son, was attending university. Deborah, our second daughter, was still at St. Clare's in Oxford completing her A level studies preparatory to attending Tulane University in New Orleans. Stephanie, our eldest, was soon to be married, so considered herself a temporary guest in the house we rented on the outskirts of the town. Our permanent household consisted of Doreen, me and Elizabeth, our youngest, who was then eleven years old.

Our first cultural conflict in America involved Stephanie's application to the immigration authorities in Tampa for Gary Scott, her Jamaican fiancé, to be permitted entry to the United States for the purpose of settling in America and getting married in Clearwater. Since Stephanie was an American citizen I thought that this would be routine, but the lady with whom we had to deal made it clear that she thought this was a marriage of convenience and refused the application. Gary was "brown" in Jamaican terms, but in the American hierarchy of race he was a black man and therefore suspect. Stephanie had been in love with Gary since she was thirteen, had abandoned her studies at Wellesley to be with him in Canada where he was enrolled at Ryerson Polytechnic Institute. She had graduated from the University of Toronto and at this stage she and Gary thought that their chances of success would be greater in America than in a politically unstable Jamaica.

Fired up with righteous indignation at such overt prejudice, I galloped like Don Quixote to do battle with immigration in Tampa. I vouched for Gary, disclosed our financial resources and threatened to call the press, all my advocacy in ever increasing decibels until I was sure the mayor could hear my ranting in his office. Eventually news of the impasse did reach the mayor and he issued instructions for the entry permission to be granted. Perhaps this inauspicious start was an omen of things to come, for after 28 years of marriage and two sons, Stephanie and Gary separated. In fact they had been together for 38 years, perhaps a courtship that began too early to last.

Fortunately, both separated parents share their pride in two brilliant sons. After Campion College in Jamaica, Nicholas, the eldest, attended Choate Rosemary Hall in Connecticut, and Sean, two years younger than his brother, was enrolled in Andover High School – both top echelon prep schools in America. Nicholas was accepted at Harvard but chose the Wharton School of Finance for his undergraduate degree. Sean, was also accepted at Harvard but seduced by sun and Californian girls, opted for Stanford. Nick went on the obtain a double MBA, one in Public Administration from Harvard's Kennedy Centre, the other an executive MBA from Colombia University in New York. Sean graduated from Stanford and proceeded to earn his MBA at Harvard. After gaining valuable job experience in America, both brothers returned to Jamaica to launch their business careers.

Another cultural conflict was manifested in Deborah's reaction to life in America. She was enrolled at Tulane University, but after Oxford was not enamoured of the quality of life at the college. Her roommate was on drugs and dropped out after her freshman year. Deborah was nervous about driving, a bicycle being the favoured method of transportation in Oxford, and she had never acquired a license. She soon discovered that without this document it was almost impossible to function in America. Fortunately, at the start of her junior year at Tulane, she was offered a year at the University of Aberdeen in Scotland as an exchange student where she earned a Master's in English and Philosophy. Having fallen in love with Scotland, she fell in love with Richard Gordon, a Scotsman. They were married in Edinburgh at the Catholic cathedral and for the reception we rented Borthwick castle. This was where Mary Queen of Scots and her lover, the Earl of Bothwell, spent their last night together before the advancing English forces captured the castle and Bothwell, a cad, rode off into the night leaving Mary to her fate. A single kilted highlander piped Deborah and Richard into the great hall. They now have three children, the eldest daughter a Scottish solicitor, the second daughter a doctor completing her residence at Guys Hospital in London. Oskar, the boy, a graduate of the prestigious Magdalen School for boys in Oxford, is now studying at University College London.

Our new Clearwater home was in a typical Florida subdivision where the houses duplicated themselves in rows, a stone's throw from each other. There were no front fences and at night when we sat out on our handkerchief of lawn we could hear the traffic on Belcher Avenue and the hum of high tension wires overhead.

Looking back, it is clear how little nine years of Florida engaged my creative imagination. There is just one poem "Florida" in *The Denting of a Wave*, which is chiefly a record of alienation from the houses "so anxious to avoid/ the sweat of living, all their dust and draft/ are packed in garbage pans equipped with wheels". I can see behind the poem's images of American hygienic efficiency, pain over the loss of Jamaica's disorderly fertility. In this suburb,

> The doors of the garages lift open on
> command, saying 'aah' for the inspection
> of tools aligned like teeth along the walls.

Liz, however, quickly adjusted to life in Clearwater, learning to code-switch her speech so that no one could guess that she was not American. On graduation from high school, she not only won all major academic honours but received the American Legion's gold medal for embodying all the outstanding qualities of a young patriotic American. This was a source of some ironic amusement in the Thompson family. Liz went on to graduate *cum laude* from Wellesley, her mother's alma mater. This pleased Doreen enormously. Liz then went on to Law school where she earned her Doctor Juris degree and passed the Florida Bar at first try. This pleased me immensely. Eager to find a job, she attended interviews at several law firms. At one, the interviewing partner fell in love with her; they married and have two peerless children. Brian, Liz's husband, is an extrovert who is fascinated by the Jamaican culture and has accepted with good grace the eccentricities of his in-laws.

Larry's career was more checkered. Upon graduating from college, he was hired by Aetna Insurance Company and, after training in Tampa, assigned to their San Francisco office. There he met and married an ambitious Texas girl and they had a son, Matthew. She was not satisfied with her husband's progress in the corporate world and the marriage ended by mutual consent. Larry started his own third party administration firm located in Fresno, married Karen, a divorcee with two sons and found himself spending nearly all his working hours in a plane visiting clients. After some successful and exhausting years, Larry closed down the business and is now employed as senior vice-president in a health insurance company headquartered in Syracuse. He works out of an office in Fresno where he has built himself a gracious house. His son, Matthew, after graduating from University, became an IT specialist and works in Santa Barbara.

The Jamaican Diaspora in the Clearwater area numbered some one hundred families but, without the support of our customary Jamaican helpers, we were all so busy cooking food, washing dishes, ironing shirts, making beds and putting out the garbage that there was little energy left for socializing. Doreen, who had enjoyed a privileged youth and the initial comforts of our marriage, bore the rigours of these American rituals with patience and fortitude. She learned to cook and how to endure solitude. When we invited new American friends to dinner they seldom returned our hospitality, so no lasting relationships were established.

My dream of completing a Master's degree in English was to be fulfilled at the University of South Florida where I was admitted as a graduate student in September of 1976. This was the beginning of a new adventure, pursued with vigour but no particular plan for its conclusion. The University of South Florida campus, undistinguished architecturally but ruthlessly efficient, was a forty minute commute from Clearwater. It had a student body of 12,000, about the same population as London when Chaucer lived over one of the gates of the city, spying on who went in and who went out. Graduate classes were scheduled from 6 pm to 10 pm and the library remained open till midnight.

My fellow students were a mix of recent undergraduates and mature candidates who worked at their regular employment during the day. The semester schedule was hectic and physically challenging, with new courses every quarter. Any type of illness, even a common cold, that resulted in missing one session, was a major setback. There was little personal interaction between classmates.

The course in early American literature was taught by Jack B. Moore, an engaging professor who had studied at Columbia University in New York under Lionel Trilling. Moore had lived for a year in Africa, had written a book on W.E.B. Du Bois and was a local director of the American Civil Liberties Union. Moore took a shine to my essays and invited me to read several of them to the class. We became fast friends, a relationship marked over the years by a spirited exchange of correspondence.

I was subsequently able to arrange for the University of the West Indies to invite him to Jamaica as part of the Distinguished Lecture Series where he delivered a lecture on Margaret Sanger, the American birth-control pioneer and free speech activist. Jack took early retirement from USF to concentrate on his writing and three years later, while driving with his family on the Eastside Highway in New York, he stopped at a red light, slumped over the steering wheel and died of a heart attack. He was just 67.

My first course at USF was on John Milton, who seemed to me to bear some resemblance to my own character. In my term paper I commented on the two aspects of the poet's personality. I argued that Milton's temperament reflected two apparently contradictory aspects, one satisfied with proportion and limitation, the other revelling in the luxuriant and the unrestrained. My view was that these aspects are only apparently contradictory, because it is preferable to think of them not as linear extremes but as dynamic tensions, twisting like the "double helix" discovered by Watson and Crick to be the form of the DNA unit. The backbones of each spiral are constantly changing, and sometimes in exactly opposite juxtapositions to each other, but the "double helix" has its own unity and, hence, its unique personality.

The paper earned me an "A".

The Romantic poets were compressed into one quarter, taught by a professor who was an ordained minister. He was not an inspiring teacher, which was a disappointment, but I am grateful now for the heavy reading assignments that exposed me to new material. I was more fortunate with Professor Bentley who taught Yeats and Eliot. I wrote a paper on Eliot entitled "The Nada and Toda in Eliot", comparing "The Hollow Men" with "Minerva". Bentley gave me my only mark less than an "A". He said that the paper was good but he expected more of me. For a moment, the ghost of my mother was in his office.

The course designated "Continental Drama" covered Shaw, Ibsen and Strindberg. I wrote my final paper on Ibsen, which brought back memories of when I played the "Pen" in the madhouse scene from *Peer Gynt*, produced in my undergraduate days at Fordham.

One of the most impressive features of USF was its library. I was thankful that the graduate program included a compulsory course in "Bibliography" – how to use the many features of a good library. It was my first exposure to research, which allowed for the uncovering of arcane literary references. I spent hours sitting on the floor between the stacks looking up references to Derek Walcott, and my fellow Jamaicans John Hearne and John Figueroa. It was somewhat strange that for the final paper in such a technical course we were offered the choice of submitting a creative work – a short story perhaps. Because I was rushed, I cobbled together some of the poems I had been writing and to my surprise the professor was impressed with the collection, discussed each poem with me and urged me to submit three or four for publication.

After a year at USF, in the middle of learning to speak early English in my course on Chaucer, I had a fearful vision that what capital I had been able to rescue from Jamaica was flowing out of the academic pipeline at a furious rate. The situation was not helped by the fact that at any one time three of our four children were at universities or preparing to attend one. I had made a covenant with them that if they released me from any obligation, real or psychological, to leave them an inheritance, I would pay for their education up to whatever level they wished to progress. This *contract social* had already cost me a fortune, but my determination not to default on my promise made it even more urgent to find gainful employment in America.

CHAPTER TWENTY-ONE

BUSINESS ADVENTURES IN FLORIDA

Wally Walker, one of the American directors of the Wolman Wood Preserving Company in Jamaica, lived in Tampa and Doreen and I renewed our friendship with him when we settled in Clearwater. I indicated to him at one of our get-togethers that I was looking for an investment opportunity and he mentioned the Weekley Lumber Company owned by Johnny Weekley, who was reaching retirement age. The Weekley operation was headquartered in Tampa and had an active branch in Cocoa Beach on the east coast of Florida which serviced the Miami area. The annual lumber throughput for both Weekley locations was 36,000,000 board feet of pine lumber, about the same as Jamaica's total annual imports when I was in the business there, obviously not an insignificant operation. The Weekley Lumber Company, like Wherry Wharf when I owned it, was an Osmose licensee for wood preservative chemicals, another feature of common interest.

Tampa was a half hours' drive across the causeway from Clearwater and although still a rather sleepy Southern town it was obviously poised for dramatic growth, anchored by a new airport that was one of the most modern and efficient in America. Johnny Weekley was an amiable Southern gentleman in manner and speech. In all our preliminary dealings he was entirely straightforward. The Tampa lumber yard occupied about an acre of prime commercial land and the Cocoa Beach site was about two acres with a large frontage on U.S. Highway 1, the main transportation artery to Miami. Both sites operated Osmose pressure treatment plants in addition to wholesaling lumber throughout South Florida.

Based on my preliminary inspection I was concerned that neither site was fenced, an inconceivable imprudence in Jamaica where, to prevent theft, high protective walls topped with razor wire were a necessity. Johnny smiled at my concern. "In America our social security net is so generous no one, not even a nigger," he said, "would trouble to move a piece of lumber from the yard. You have nothing to worry about." On another occasion we were in a lunch queue at a Morrison cafeteria. Johnny was immediately behind a black woman with a little boy on her shoulder. I could hear Johnny playing "kitschy koo" with the child, and when they were out of hearing he turned to me and said, "Is there anything more beautiful in the world than a little nigger child?" I was in no doubt that I had a problem, but no idea of its scope and ramifications.

Even though Johnny was willing to finance up to 75% of the purchase price of the business, I had insufficient capital left to bite off such a large investment. I put out feelers to see if other Jamaicans in the Diaspora might be willing to join a consortium to acquire the Weekley business. I was pleasantly surprised to get positive feedback from, of all people, Deryck Stone, my opponent in the Hardware and Lumber take-over fight. Disillusioned with Michael Manley's handling of the bauxite industry, Stone had departed Jamaica before me and now lived in Richmond, Virginia, serving as legal advisor to Reynolds. Tommy Surridge, who had returned from Jamaica to Canada, was also enthusi-astic, but insisted that we visit Ottawa in person to collect the cheque for his subscription. Jack de Lisser considered it a privilege to be included with the investing group.

In the proposed management structure, Stone would be Chairman, I would be CEO. I was also successful in persuading François Petot, the Osmose vice-president who had sold me the Wherry Wharf Osmose plant, to join the investment group as Senior Vice President of market-ing. Buffalo, where Osmose was headquartered, had the previous winter been inundated with one of the most vicious snowstorms in a decade, and Petot and his family were psychologically ready to move south. Additionally, I offered him a generous amount of promoter's shares, which motivated him to quit his job immediately and join me in the formative period of the Weekley acquisition. Under the terms of the sales agreement, my salary as CEO was limited to $30,000 per annum for three years. This became a particular hardship in its last two years, given the inroads of inflation, but the deal, which was consummated in September of 1977, would have collapsed if I had not agreed to this restriction. Weekley agreed to stay on as purchasing manager, Petot handled the portfolio for domestic and export sales and I concentrated on general administration and finance.

Under my administration the business prospered, receiving each year full, unqualified audits by Touche Ross. Generous dividends were paid annually, and to broaden the shareholding base of the company I persuaded the directors to approve a share option scheme, which allowed key members of staff to acquire a stake in the enterprise.

Control of lumber supplies from Honduras, still generously endowed with first growth pine, the preferred variety in the Caribbean and as far away as the Canary Islands, was critical to the expansion of the Pan-Florida export division. I was convinced that to get the edge we needed a permanent representative based in Honduras, and preferably a family member, such a connection being an important part of the Honduran culture.

I proposed that Gary Scott, Stephanie's husband, should be so appointed. Not only was he fluent in Spanish but, as a man of mixed racial background, his colour reflected the majority of businessmen in Honduras and would be a considerable asset. I wondered if Petot would be upset at the appointment, but he readily endorsed the dynamics of the situation and, in any case, he was having family difficulties and wanted to cut back on foreign travel.

Scott took up his assignment in Honduras, living with his family in a rented house in Tegucigalpa. He did a splendid job of ensuring that export orders were up to standard and supplied on a timely basis. He also expanded the operation to include fencing slats and tomato stakes for the Florida tomato growers.

Petot continued to handle the large international export sales, and on one memorable occasion he and I journeyed to the Canary Islands to check on an important shipment of high grade lumber we had dispatched from Honduras. The Canaries enjoyed a brisk tourist trade with European visitors anxious to sunbathe on the black sand beaches that dotted the islands. One day, after a problem with the shipment had been settled, our local agent took us to see a popular beach on Las Palmas, anxious to show it off. Sand was blowing off the Sahara, stinging our faces, so I was not particularly disposed to a lengthy inspection, even though most of the ladies on the beach were topless.

"How do our beaches compare with yours in Jamaica?" the agent asked.

"Well," I replied, trying to be diplomatic, "we have beautiful white sand beaches…"

Before I could continue the sentence he interrupted me.

"Ah, Senor Thompson," he sighed, "that is the difference. In Jamaica you have white sand beaches for black people. In Las Palmas we have black sand beaches for white people."

★   ★   ★

The Thompson life style in Clearwater was not extravagant but relatively comfortable. We bought a modest house on Yulee Drive which sat on two adjoining lots, at the edge of which was a sizeable creek. There was a swimming pool in the backyard in which, during the summer months, I splashed after work. Doreen had always enjoyed gardening, but the Florida heat and her fear of snakes severely restricted this hobby. With no mountains to provide perspective, the landscape failed to seduce me to record it on canvas, so I abandoned the pleasure of painting. The house comfortably accommodated Doreen, Ermyn, Doreen's mother, Liz, our youngest daughter and me.

Ermyn depended on us for support. She was an agreeable guest although I think Liz might have felt constrained in bringing her current boyfriends to meet us. Ever the grande dame, Ermyn once visited the newspaper stand without her purse. Unable to pay for the carton of Pall Malls she had purchased, she smiled at the owner and proclaimed, "My name is Ermyn Lyons. I forgot my pocketbook at home, but I shall return tomorrow to pay for my purchase." Then she walked out the store. She honoured her promise and thereafter was granted unlimited credit.

★   ★   ★

We believed that travel was an important and continuing process in the education of our children and we had been liberal in trusting them to explore foreign countries on their own. When we lived in Jamaica, Stephanie and a girlfriend, both sixteen, visited Mexico and told amusing tales of how they managed to avoid having their backsides pinched by ardent caballeros.

Larry and a friend joined a group of boys and girls on a trip to France when they were twelve. A highlight of the adventure was canoeing down the Ardeche. We were regaled with details of near catastrophes, but I am sure there were other experiences about which we heard nothing.

On one of our trips to Europe in 1981, Debbie and Liz accompanied us. At this stage Debbie had high school Spanish and Liz had high school French, which mitigated the inevitable crises of travel in France and Spain. This made life more comfortable for Dody and me, but the girls were anxious to set off on their own. We gave our permission. In Greece they enjoyed sunbathing topless, but their choice of accommodation proved to be unfortunate. What they hoped was an inexpensive guest house turned out to be a brothel. Men were trailing them in the corridor and one persistent lothario kept knocking on their door. Liz unpacked her travel knife, opened the door and, tapping the blade against her teeth told the intruder to "Piss off!" The girls then slammed the door shut and barricaded it with the dressing table. At 4 am they sneaked out through the back door and headed for the railroad station.

The opportunity to travel provided a needed break from the controlled boredom, verging on ennui, of life in Clearwater. After my managerial adventures with Maurice Facey and Pan Jamaican Trust, I was running the Weekley Company with one hand. In truth I saw the Weekley investment as a vehicle to provide me with employment and, after the early years of expansion, I became more conservative in taking on new ventures and the risks these would involve. I introduced a generous defined benefits pension scheme which, although approved by the Board, obviously irritated the Chairman, Deryck Stone, who thought I should have consulted him on the details. But Petot was also a beneficiary of the scheme and had thrown his weight behind it.

There were other relatively minor irritations building up for which I was probably to blame. When I was due for a new company car I bought a Lincoln town car, whereas Petot was assigned a Buick station wagon. But my inexcusable sin was reassigning Gary Scott from Honduras to the Tampa office to handle all export sales from headquarters. This put the wind up Petot, who must have thought it a trespass on his chances of promotion. It probably seemed like creeping nepotism to Stone and the move outraged Johnny Weekley and other senior staff members who, although content to have a "black" man run an office in Honduras, instinctively rebelled against having him permanently working with them in Tampa, standing with them in the lunch line at the Morrison's cafeteria.

Seduced by my own success I had become autocratic in running the organisation but I was also imprudently generous in watering down my own shareholding so that key executives could buy into the company. This reached a stage where I no longer owned controlling shares in the parent company and was thus vulnerable, without realizing it, to a leveraged buy-out attempt by a group now aligned against me, led by an ambitious Petot who wanted my job.

At 9 am one Saturday morning, while I was still in my pajamas, the doorbell rang and the mailman presented me with a registered letter. It was a brief communication from Stone terminating my employment with Pan-Florida, effective immediately. Only then did I realize how stupid I had been not to insist on a management contract, believing, in my hubris, that I was indispensable. The termination notice stunned me and traumatized Doreen, a state from which she took a long time to recover.

A series of hostile conferences then took place. The advisor to Petot in the negotiations was a senior partner in a prestigious Tampa law firm, undoubtedly identified and recommended by Stone. I was represented by David Freeman, a young Miami litigator recommended by Packman, Neuwahl and Rosenberg, the legal firm which had set up the pension plan so anathema to the Chairman.

Freeman's general negotiating point was "If it ain't broke, why fix it." My first stance was bellicose, threatening to sue for unjust dismissal. Although Petot was often nasty and petty, it became clear to me that he had been instructed by the directors to negotiate a settlement along the lines of a leveraged buy-out. Stone, I knew, would have been uncomfortable trying to guide the company with a large continuing minority group loyal to me, a group that would have included Gary Scott, Jack de Lisser and my sister, Audrey.

With an after-tax profit base of about one million dollars a year, I proposed that the company be valued for five million US dollars, of which the selling shareholders as a group, representing 35% of the shares, would be entitled to $1,075,000 US. This was eventfully agreed, the terms of payment being 25% in cash, the balance by a series of promissory notes payable over eight years with a final "balloon" payment due in 1991. I insisted that the notes be secured by a first mortgage over the Cocoa Beach property, for which I had received an MAI valuation of a million dollars. There were heavy legal fees on both sides, and most of my 25% cash payment was reinvested in a company which Gary Scott, now without a job, was about to launch as a new business. Doreen and I were to be paid a monthly cheque of ten thousand dollars, covering principal and interest. Audrey's share was about four thousand dollars a month. The final agreement was signed in August of 1983, the day Elizabeth flew to Boston to enroll in Wellesley College.

With no job, but a reasonable monthly income from the buy-out, I was able to persuade myself that I was now formally retired at the age of fifty-four, conveniently blocking from my mind what the situation would be in eight years when the last Pan-Florida installment payment came to an end. I had no sense of direction and little sense of time. I seemed to possess an ability to find rest between possibilities, a kind of Keatsian "negative capability" – which might work in literature but could be fatal in life. Part of the reason for this flaw was my conviction that I would die young, probably as a result of disfibrinogenemia, so why worry about the future. Mother had died at 54. Perhaps I had only a few years left.

CHAPTER TWENTY-TWO

AGRO 21

The political situation in Jamaica had worsened after our departure in 1976. In 1980, Edward Seaga had wrested political power from Michael Manley in a general election fraught with violence and intimidation. The Jamaica Diaspora in Clearwater were overjoyed and waited expectantly to see if Seaga would be able to restore the economy to some semblance of order and growth.

The verdict was still out when our phone rang. It was Prime Minister Seaga on the other end.

"I am told you have retired at a disgracefully young age. I would like you to return to Jamaica to run Agro 21 for me."

He explained that Agro 21 was the name he had given to a programme, the focus of which was to develop non-traditional, value-added agricultural products for export. Agro 21 had got off to a good start under the guidance of Jim Rinella, a USAID funded expatriate, but his contract was about to expire and Seaga wanted somebody with a local image to take over from the American.

"But, Prime Minister," I protested, "I hardly know the difference between a yam and a potato."

He replied, "But you know your way around a balance sheet and it's about time for agriculture to be run as a business. You will have all the technical help you may need. USAID will continue to fund the programme as well as your salary, but, please, be modest in your expectations for I am asking you to take on this assignment in the national interest. Phone me back tomorrow and let me have a figure so I can pass it by USAID." And he hung up.

The Thompson household was in a frenzy of excitement at the prospect of returning to Jamaica and only then did it come home to me how unhappy Doreen must have been during our exile in America. I phoned Seaga to accept the assignment and quoted an annual salary of US$50,000.

But in addition to salary I was to be provided with executive accommodation as well as a car and chauffeur. USAID arranged for a moving company to pack up our household effects and ship them to Jamaica. Pending their arrival, we were put up for two months in a suite at the Pegasus Hotel in Kingston. During this time we were able to rent out our house in Clearwater and to identify an upscale townhouse at the Pines on Millsborough Avenue, around the corner from our former home on Dillsbury Avenue.

The Agro 21 offices were in a modern high-rise building located in the Law of the Sea Conference Centre in downtown Kingston. The corporation was a government owned entity with a board of directors appointed by the Prime Minister. It operated with considerable autonomy, though subject to USAID guidelines for its financing. Its primary objective was to promote private sector investment in non-traditional agriculture and to this end employed a small cadre of agricultural experts who, under Rinella, my predecessor, had identified a range of new crops for each of which feasibility and agronomic studies had been prepared. Agro 21 was mandated to get projects off the ground, but it was not an implementing agency. That role fell to the National Investment Bank of Jamaica, whose chairman was Mayer Matalon, a PNP supporter who nevertheless gave public service under both administrations.

A group of Israeli investors headed by Eli Tissona had started growing winter vegetables at Spring Plains. They had introduced drip irrigation to the island and pioneered breeding tilapia fish in freshwater ponds. I only visited the Spring Plains operation once but was duly impressed by its scope and the enthusiasm of Tissona and his team of Israeli experts.

It was obvious to me that Agro 21 had been set up by Seaga to bypass the bloated bureaucracy of the Ministry of Agriculture. There were large salary scale differences between local staff at the Ministry and local staff recruited for Agro 21. This in itself was cause for tension between the two entities. But so important was the Agro 21 programme to Seaga's overall economic plans for the island that he chaired a monthly meeting at Jamaica House to cut through disagreements between various government departments. As part of a posse of bright young professional women recruited to serve at Jamaica House, Seaga appointed Viv Logan as his agricultural secretary and she was the day-to-day liaison with Agro 21. She was also a director of the corporation and wielded enormous influence with the Prime Minister, as indeed did all those Jamaica House women who had his ear and who could shut out from his appointment calendar almost everyone who fell out of favour with them.

At the time of my taking over from Rinella at Agro 21, lands that had traditionally been in sugar cane at Bernard Lodge, a large abandoned sugar estate on the outskirts of Kingston, had lain idle for some time, its series of irrigation canals and artesian wells dry and in a state of disrepair. I found myself with two immediate priorities: to find a group of private sector investors who would provide an equity base for a company set up to grow winter vegetables at Bernard Lodge and, with USAID funding, to rehabilitate the entire irrigation system there. The private sector's equity investment in the vegetable project would be supported by government loans to Agro 21, on whose board investors would sit.

Because of my past association with the family, my first pitch was made to Richard Issa, and I think I embarrassed him into making a commitment. His letter of intent helped me to secure Grace Kennedy's involvement and, in a rush of blood to the head, I announced to the two investors already committed that I was going to try to inveigle Desmond Blades of Musson (Jamaica) Ltd into taking a one-third stake. Eyes rolled, making it obvious to me that Blades was a mysterious figure, a loner who no one really knew or understood. A hard worker, he ran a tight ship in more ways than one, and seemed to make a point of keeping his distance from politicians, never asking for favours or, for that matter, bestowing any.

I had occasionally seen Desmond and Peggy, his wife, on the beach at San San, but they were not part of our more boisterous crowd and usually kept quietly to themselves. This may have been how they accommodated the grief of losing their 19-year-old son, their only son, killed in a tragic motorcar accident. I cannot conceive how parents overcome such a tragedy and manage to repossess their lives. Any eccentricities they developed or defence mechanisms they adopted to cope with their loss were totally acceptable in my view.

I made a cold call on Blades at his office on Duke Street. He was seated behind a large desk, operating an adding machine as a preliminary to signing cheques. A man of about my age, he was balding, his upper lip defined by a narrow well-trimmed moustache. He had a rather reluctant smile, starting on one side of his face and spreading to the other as if discovering itself. I glanced at a photograph of him in a yachting cap on the wall behind his desk and thought he looked the part of a German U-boat captain in World War II, his eyes small and constricted from constant squinting into a periscope.

I did not remember the Blades' history as I sat in front of him making my twenty minute pitch for the winter vegetable project. At the end of it he said matter-of-factly, "You can collect my cheque as soon as the others have sent in theirs." The interview was over. We shook hands and he went back to adding up his bills.

Having successfully put together a private sector investment group, I found myself facing the challenge of managing a large irrigation scheme, essentially an engineering project on the abandoned Bernard Lodge sugar estate. It soon became obvious that corruption, kick-backs and labour unrest would be the principal dangers I would have to guard against. The labour unrest centered on the division of work between supporters of the political parties. I solved this by assigning one mile of the canal rehabilitation to the JLP workers and the next mile to the PNP workers and so on for its length.

Although the private sector investors regularly attended directors' meetings of Agro 21 and were kept fully informed about problems and progress, they exercised little management control, leaving this to me. A local manager was hired, one of his first jobs to train an army of unemployed women in the area who would be needed to reap winter vegetables for export. This was easier said than done. The market for sweet peppers and cucumbers in America and the UK set strict quality standards. Any bruised or deformed produce might result in an entire shipment being rejected. Even more incomprehensible to the field hands was a specification that mandated that any vegetable which was too large should not be reaped. To them bigger must be better, and they harvested accordingly, which only increased the rejection rate.

The Agro 21 team worked doggedly to get the project going, but we soon encountered major marketing problems at the other end of the distribution chain. We were in the hands of private produce importers in America and Britain, a clique of often marginal operators who, whenever their sales were slow or the weather was bad, rejected shipment after shipment on specious technical grounds. In other cases, although shipments were accepted, payment for them was unreasonably delayed. The Jamaican private sector investors had no better ideas than management did on how to solve these problems. I spent time in Miami, New York and London trying to identify reliable agents who would handle the Jamaican vegetables with some degree of honesty. The limited success I achieved could not solve the fundamental problem. To make the system work, Agro 21 would have to take over the foreign marketing itself. We had neither the expertise nor the funds for such a mammoth task.

In the meantime, the project limped on while Viv Logan grew more and more impatient, irritated at the prospect of failure but unable to propose any solution. Seaga understood the situation, and when the original tranche of government loan funds was exhausted, he agreed, at considerable political risk, to pump more money into the project. The private sector investors came to directors' meetings, already resigned to writing off their investment as a bad debt for tax purposes.

Despite the fact that the Bernard Lodge vegetable project was slowly slipping into bankruptcy, I was not entirely unhappy with the progress Agro 21 was making in carrying out its mandate. Vegetables were only one part of the Agro 21 stew. It was also charged with divesting some 80,000 acres of government-owned agricultural land to small and medium investors. As an implementation instrument for this policy, I created what became known as the "Agro 21 lease", a document that granted the lessee possession of the land for a period of 49 years. By the end of my Agro 21 stint, some 50,000 acres of idle lands had been divested and no accusation of political favouritism was ever levelled at the organisation.

Other Agro 21 tasks involved the establishment of a horticultural park on lands at Caymanas. Roses, anthuriums and other exotic species of flowers were grown in shade houses for export. Despite the constant battle of fighting diseases, the park was a success. Agro 21 also spearheaded the growing of rice and corn, created animal feed formulas for the cattle industry and fostered orchard crops like mangoes and papaya for export. Another outstanding success was the role Agro 21 played in the establishment of acres of freshwater ponds on the outskirts of Kingston for growing tilapia fish. The tonnage of tilapia production increased over a relatively short time from 200,000 lbs. to over 4,000,000 lbs.

In addition to an exhausting schedule at Agro 21, Seaga appointed me as a director on a number of government boards including the National Investment Bank of Jamaica, the Agricultural Credit Bank, Forest Industries Development Company and Eastern Banana Estates.

Doreen and I were on the list of guests invited to all public functions, but the more prominently I was featured nationally as some kind of agricultural guru, the more disgruntled some factions in the Ministry of Agriculture became. They began openly to attack me and the Agro 21 programme and, in truth, both were vulnerable; me because of my lack of specific agricultural experience, which it was all too easy to expose, and Agro 21 because of the failure of the winter vegetable project.

I wrote to Seaga, frankly pointing out that my perceived weaknesses as Executive Chairman of Agro 21 might be hurting him politically. I offered to resign, but if he wished me to stay on, I suggested that he split the roles of Chairman and Managing Director, appointing to the former position a person with impeccable agricultural experience. He accepted this suggestion and in September of 1987 appointed a new Agro 21 board of directors with Dickie Jackson as Chairman under whom I would continue to serve as Managing Director. Jackson had inherited the Bowden coconut farm from his father and had spent most of his career in agriculture. He was also a lawyer who, like me, had no active practice. Handsome and diplomatic, he succeeded in charming Viv Logan into a sort of neutrality and the Agro 21 spirit was restored.

In June, Dody and I were vacationing in London. While she was out shopping, the phone in our room rang. It was the Governor General's private secretary calling from Jamaica to advise that on the recommendation of the Prime Minister I was to be awarded the national honour of the Order of Distinction with the rank of Commander. Pending an official announcement later in the year I was allowed to tell my wife but no one else. When the appointments were made public I was delighted to see that a similar honour had been granted to Dickie Jackson. The medals were bestowed on us at Kings House by Sir Florizel Glasspole, the then Governor General. There was a garden party atmosphere to the occasion as Dody and I strolled among the congratulating crowd.

I was subsequently awarded another honour of which I am particularly proud. I was among the first graduates of St George's College to be inducted into that institution's Hall of Fame, a fitting reminder of how much I owe to my Jesuit education in both Jamaica and America.

★   ★   ★

1988 was a tumultuous year in more ways than one. In September a hurricane named Gilbert galloped like a mad stallion over the spine of the island, from east to west with winds of 140 miles per hour. Much of the island's infrastructure was destroyed and agricultural production decimated. The day after the blow, Seaga contacted me by radio to advise that a Jamaica Defence Force helicopter was standing by at Up Park Camp to take a technical advisor and me on a surveillance flight over the island. I was to report to him on damage the next day, which I did. The efficiency with which Seaga handled the aftermath of the hurricane was widely acknowledged.

National Award

CHAPTER TWENTY-THREE

FINANCIAL CRISIS

I suppose it is a cliché of the life cycle that periods of accomplishment and success suddenly plunge into disaster, not necessarily due to hubris or complacency, but to some unexpected external force. This was the case in September of 1988, just after the hurricane, when without explanation, payment of the Pan-Florida promissory notes ceased. A hiatus of disbelief and confusion soon gave way to the sorry realization that Pan-Florida had closed its doors and had abandoned its operational sites in Tampa and Cocoa Beach. Petot had sold his Florida home and departed the state with no forwarding address. He had bankrupted in five years the Pan-Florida enterprise it had taken me six years to bring to peak profitability.

The outstanding balance on the promissory notes was just under a million US dollars, protected by a first mortgage on the Cocoa property. My decision to foreclose this mortgage turned out to be an error of judgment, but at the time it seemed the logical next step to take. There was also an element of cultural ignorance. I could not conceive of any circumstances in which the rights of a mortgagee could be expunged and I totally underestimated how costly legal fees could be for enforcing the security. After long delays, title to the holding passed to me and I proceeded to put it up for sale.

Although a sizeable chunk of my income had disappeared with the default of the Pan-Florida notes, I was not unduly concerned about procedural delays because USAID was paying me a reasonable salary for my services as Managing Director of Agro 21. But having regained title to the Cocoa property my attempts to sell it involved further expenses and legal fees. One prospective local purchaser raised the spectre of environmental problems and when I refused his suggestion that the asking price be reduced by half, he reported the matter to the State Environmental Protection Agency. Thus began my nightmare encounter with the American legal system, a final irony since as a member of the New York Bar I was still an officer of the courts.

In 1979 the tragedy of Love Canal had shocked the American nation. A middle-class residential complex had been built on land polluted by dangerous chemicals from a nearby plant. Families living in the subdivision discovered that a disproportionate number of their children were being stricken with cancer, resulting in suffering and death. The site was condemned and new draconian environmental legislation was passed. The legislative reaction to the Love Canal disaster was analogous to the Patriot Act that became law following the terrorist attack on the World Trade Centre and the destruction of its twin towers on September 11, 2001. Both responses were cases of the ends justifying the means, always a suspect moral position.

No one's health had ever been damaged as the result of the lumber treating process at the Weekley sites. These were run scrupulously in conformity with guidelines set out by the suppliers of the chemicals involved.

At the slightest hint of a problem, the EPA law made it the obligation of the property owner to commission and pay for an environmental study to prove compliance. This gave rise to a new cohort of private sector engineering companies and consultants who, for astronomical fees, were the only entities licensed to carry out studies acceptable to the EPA.

Florida State officials were now threatening to impose civil fines for EPA breaches at the Cocoa property and I was obliged to pay out additional legal fees to stave off this attack. But worse was to come. The State turned the files over to the Federal EPA office that shared jurisdiction with it, the added menace being that, at the Federal level, EPA violations were a criminal offense for which I could be sentenced to a long prison term. A summons for my arrest was issued by a U.S. District Attorney whose office was in Titusville. My dilemma was whether to surrender myself to American jurisdiction or continue to take refuge in Jamaica. To resolve this dilemma entailed retaining a criminal lawyer at yet more additional fees. He advised surrender.

I found it legally offensive that criminal responsibility for EPA violations could attach to someone who had acquired the property as a mortgagee, especially since the breaches were alleged to have occurred some thirteen years prior to my retaking title by virtue of foreclosing the mortgage. But such was the law.

The final decision was that I would appear before the U.S. District Attorney under the terms of a "limited immunity" negotiated by my lawyer. On arrival in Cocoa Beach, Doreen and I checked into a cheap motel. Uncertain as to whether I would be sent to prison pending bail, Dody remained cloistered there while I attended the interview. My lawyer drove me to the U.S. District Attorney's office where the atmosphere was intimidating. A uniformed State trooper with a gun on his hip guarded the door. I was finger-printed and the attorney, a small, thin man named Harland, read me my rights and plugged in a long-playing tape recorder.

My testimony inevitably involved Petot's role in the scheme of things. Harland was particularly interested in the leveraged buy-out of Pan-Florida and the factors which had caused the split. This meant trying to explain the reaction of Petot and Weekley to Gary, a "black" man in American terms, occasioned by his reassignment from Honduras to head office in Tampa. Harland was himself a southerner so I assumed he understood the dynamics involved.

My grilling lasted some six hours, but eventually I was allowed to leave and the State trooper unlocked the door. The criminal lawyer thought I had performed well, but confirmed that there would be no final determination in the matter. It might simply remain in limbo. Emotionally exhausted and near collapse I returned to Dody in the motel and thence back to Jamaica.

As 1988 drew to an end there was talk that Seaga would call a general election for early the following year. There was consensus that he had handled recovery from hurricane Gilbert with extraordinary administrative skill. This was probably a factor in his going to the public in February of 1989. Under coercion from the I.M.F. to reform the civil service, Seaga had made hundreds of government workers redundant and there were those who thought he would pay a political price for this. I had remained convinced that he would be returned to office; they proved to be right.

The PNP scored a resounding victory, winning 44 of 60 Parliamentary seats. Seaga's loss was a personal calamity for the Thompsons. In accordance with the Westminster tradition, I immediately tendered my resignation as MD of Agro 21 to the new Minister of Agriculture, as did Dickie Jackson in his capacity as Chairman. Both resignations were accepted with alacrity. By noon the next day, two members of a PNP "transition" team invaded the Agro 21 offices and demanded to be shown certain files. They announced that they expected such files to be produced within an hour to ensure that they could not be doctored. Much to their chagrin, my secretary was able to retrieve the files in fifteen minutes.

Within a week the extent of the Thompson devastation became apparent. Pan-Florida had defaulted on its promissory notes, and legal fees to deal with the EPA problems in America had exhausted all our savings. Once again I found myself unemployed and with no source of income.

It was urgent, therefore, for me to find a job. This, at the age of sixty-two would not be easy. One prospect might be Desmond Blades who, although I had caused him to lose a considerable amount of money in the winter vegetable adventure, had some regard for my managerial talents.

The negotiations with Blades dragged on till July. Eventually I was obliged to accept a remuneration package totalling J$300,000 per annum. At the then rate of exchange of J$6.5 to US$1.0 this worked out to US$ 46,154.00 per annum, just less than the amount I was being paid at Agro 21, but without the supplemental income from the Pan-Florida notes. However, the package also included a fully maintained company car. Desmond was always generous with company cars and I was presented with a new Mazda 929.

As had been the case when I went to work for Abe Issa, Desmond had no clear idea of what my duties would be. I was assigned a small office adjacent to his at Musson headquarters on Duke Street and my business card read, "Dr. Ralph C. Thompson. Finance and Corporate Administration". My ad hoc assignments included trying to control theft at three supermarkets as well as supervising the manufacture of license plates and furniture pulls. I also advised on the purchase of real estate, which Desmond used as a land bank for "dealing profits" when these were needed to improve cash flow. But what I began to do best for Desmond was to bolster his public relations image. I greatly admired his business perspicacity, so there was no artifice in this. When friends who knew my professional and managerial background asked if I found it difficult working for Desmond, my defence of his honour was spontaneous and heartfelt.

During the years of my long business association with Desmond Blades my admiration for him continued to grow, and Doreen and I became good personal friends with him and Peggy, his wife. We often spent weekends with them at their San San villa, either as their sole guests or with another couple. He was a generous host, punctilious in serving wine with dinner and an expensive cognac after. At first we did not know how seriously he suffered from diabetes. He would excuse himself after a meal and retire to give himself an insulin injection, but showed no inclination to control his diet.

Desmond never objected to talking shop on week-ends and since Peggy was *au fait* with the business, major decisions were often taken while treading water in the ocean channel that fronted the villa. A man of courage, he refused to be faced down and this contributed to his survival during the upheavals of the Seventies. As Peggy once put it, "the only time Desmond takes off his glasses is to fight or make love."

On one occasion, Peggy claimed that Roman Catholics prayed to the Virgin Mary but Protestants prayed to Jesus. In trying to convince her that such a dichotomy does not really exist, that both religions do both, the talk turned to prayer in general. I was surprised when Desmond nominated the Serenity prayer by the theologian Reinhold Niebuhr, which he proceeded to recite from memory:

> Lord grant me the serenity to accept the things I cannot change, the courage to change the things I can, and the wisdom to know the difference.

He asked me what my favourite prayer was and I confessed: "Pray as if everything depends on God, but work as if everything depends on you."

One weekend I asked Desmond what his thoughts were on succession when he had to retire or died. Without hesitation he replied "My grandson, P.B., will take over." I knew Desmond well enough to demur. "But surely you are taking a big gamble. P.B's father is English, his son is the product of an elite English public school and there are plans for him to attend an English university. He only comes to Jamaica on short school vacations. How can you be sure that he will adjust to Jamaican culture, learn to speak patois?"

"It's a gamble," he admitted, "but P.B. is enthusiastic about taking over the helm from me. He is very bright and an aggressive entrepreneur. I will have to break him in slowly."

★ ★ ★

Unquestionably, the hiatus between Seaga losing the general election and my employment with Musson marked the nadir of my life. Yet I seemed to thrive on the stress and challenge of survival. Spendthrift when money was plentiful, I seemed to have the ability cheerfully to accept poverty when the roll of the dice so ordained. Was this the roller-coaster existence Doreen committed to accept at our wedding when she promised to take me for richer or for poorer? But she never complained. As soon as the deal with Desmond had been struck she found for us an enchanting three bedroom townhouse on Bracknell Avenue, at a rent we could afford, and where we lived for twenty-two years.

Sitting on our verandah at night, cocktails in hand, the townhouse provided a magnificent middle-distance view of the city of Kingston, its shimmering lights and the harbour beyond, embraced by the cantle of the Palisadoes road which curled around the harbour's edge to the airport. The view and the social implications of its vantage point fed into a number of my later poems, which reflect on the comforts of privilege and the unease that came from knowledge of the turbulent city that lay below. In "Vigil", in *Moving On*, I wrote:

> At the end of a hard day
> dusk lurks in the shadows
> on a verandah overlooking Kingston,
> an awning pulled up like a lid
> of an eye afraid to blink.
>
> The lights below flicker
> like torches held by warriors
> waiting to reclaim lost territory,
> ready to creep forward
> if the eyelid lowers...

Portraits of the children painted by Erwin deVries adorned the staircase wall and in the living room we hung an Albert Huie nude, a primitive Kapo, a Nakama (my Japanese tutor), a Montoya, the Mexican master, and two of my own paintings. There was a brick back patio where we were able to entertain small groups for cocktails and our round mahogany dining table could seat eight, the guest limit for dinner parties. Doreen now had an opportunity to show off our silver and crystal collection, some pieces inherited from her family, some acquired by us over the years.

To house our library, bookcases were everywhere, in the den, the guest room, our bedroom, the dining room and even on the verandah. For research or pleasure I was usually able to find a book to the purpose.

Under Doreen's supervision and our helper Lurline's eccentric but willing attention, the townhouse became a refuge from the cares of the working day. St Thomas Aquinas defines peace as "the tranquillity of order" and this insight was celebrated in every room of the house.

Desmond Blades was a major shareholder in Seprod Limited, Jamaica's largest food and agricultural supplies manufacturer, a company that had played an important part in my Wherry Wharf adventure. During the Seventies, the socialist Manley regime had imposed price controls on all Seprod products and cynically blamed all shortages of essential food items on the company. Since, under socialist doctrine, the Seprod

Kingston North

investors were automatically entitled to a 16% return on equity, management had no incentive to be efficient. There was no foreign currency with which to renew plant and equipment, so the gradual deterioration of the Seprod facilities was inevitable. When Seaga removed price controls, Seprod began a slow return to profitability. But Harrison, the General Manager, was determined to integrate backward into the chicken business, and for this purpose set up a company called Goldcrest Farms Limited, in which Seprod and other investors, including Blades in his personal capacity, subscribed for shares. Harrison, who tended to treat the Seprod board of directors with disdain, assured it that financing for the venture would be made available by the National Commercial Bank, then under the direction of Don Banks.

British consultants with expertise in the chicken industry were commissioned to undertake a feasibility study on the project. Desmond asked me to critique it. I did so and warned him that, even if the promised loan funds were forthcoming from NCB, there would be an insufficient equity base to support the loan structure. To try to save the situation, Desmond arranged for Dickie Jackson to be appointed Chairman of Seprod in the hope that, unlike his predecessor, he would be able to rein in Harrison. Desmond also appointed me to the Goldcrest board of directors, so in effect the old Agro 21 team was back on the playing field. Shortly after my arrival on the Goldcrest board, the word spread that Harrison was dying of cancer and had only a few months to live.

This was crisis time. Dickie Jackson was appointed executive chairman of Seprod and in April of 1991 I was "seconded" from Musson to Seprod as Budget Officer. My salary was increased from $300,000 to $450,000 p.a. Salary apart, I was caught up in the excitement of Seprod's battle for survival.

No sooner had these new arrangements been put in place than NCB advised that its board of directors had turned down the Goldcrest loan application. I was not surprised, because Seprod already owed NCB a sizeable overdraft, which Don Banks, National Commercial Bank's Managing Director, was convinced would never be repaid. By this time I had been able to use the "cover" of my position as Budget Officer to dig into every corner of the Seprod/Goldcrest operation. What I found was frightening. Harrison, his judgment probably impaired by his disease, had proceeded without board approval to place orders for the Goldcrest equipment with US suppliers in the name of Seprod to the tune of millions of dollars. Improvident contracts had also been entered into between Goldcrest and Jamaican farmers for chicken houses and the supply of chicken feeds by Seprod. It was clear that Goldcrest would have to be placed in liquidation, but would this also be the fate of the once mighty Seprod?

CHAPTER TWENTY-FOUR

SEPROD

I was now a member of the main Seprod board and at the first meeting I attended I recommended that Jackson and I leave the island two days hence to try to negotiate out of the equipment supply contracts Goldcrest had entered into with various American manufacturers. If the contracts were enforced, this would in effect bankrupt Seprod. We picked the six main suppliers located across the US from Atlanta, Salt Lake City, to a Texas town called Nacogdoches. My approach in the negotiations was to confirm that the project was in trouble, that we were not asking for the return of deposits, but that Seprod had to be released from any further payments if the company was to avoid bankruptcy. They thought my reference to bankruptcy meant Seprod, with whom they had contracted, but I meant Goldcrest. As I had learned from personal experience, Americans are paranoid about legal expenses. This ploy worked, especially when I mentioned that I was an American attorney and a member of the New York Bar. I did not want the suppliers to have the opportunity of checking with their lawyers, so on returning to the hotel I stayed up half the night drafting the appropriate "releases". All of the suppliers signed the releases and we returned exhausted to Jamaica. One bullet had been dodged.

Over the next several months, Jackson and I worked as a team to reorganise the Seprod management structure and to see Goldcrest through the liquidation procedure. Then, during a Seprod board meeting that he was chairing, Jackson excused himself and left the room. We thought this was a call of nature and he was headed for the bathroom. But a few moments later a hysterical junior clerk burst in, screaming, "Come quickly, the Chairman has collapsed."

He was prostrate on the carpet outside his office, pink vomit gushing from his mouth. There is always an ambulance on standby at Seprod and we rushed him to the hospital where an emergency operation was performed to stop internal bleeding. But his condition worsened and I urged him to go by air ambulance to Miami for specialist treatment there. Even with the best care in Miami it was touch and go; he was suffering from some rare form of leukemia. He recovered sufficiently to return to Jamaica, but it was obvious that his days of running Seprod were over.

Once more fate had rearranged the billiard balls on the table of my life. I was appointed Group Managing Director of Seprod, with Byron Thompson, my namesake, as deputy managing director. I knew nothing about manufacturing and relied on Byron Thompson's expertise in this area, while devoting my energies to general administration, finance and reorganizing the Seprod management structure.

I soon discovered that Seprod was a corporate creature of inherited tensions and contradictions. Originally a subsidiary of the Jamaica Coconut Board, itself an ill-defined legal entity, Seprod became a public company quoted on the Jamaica Stock exchange when the Coconut Board, in desperate need of cash, issued a prospectus inviting Jamaican investors to subscribe for shares. Major players in the food distribution trade invested heavily in the enterprise, anxious to protect their source of locally manufactured products. Firms like Musson (Jamaica) Ltd and Grace Kennedy and Company acquired about 35% of the ownership, balanced by the 35% retained by the Coconut Board. The remaining 30% was spread among the general public.

Psychologically, the Coconut Board representatives on the Seprod board of directors still believed that the company belonged to them. This attitude was reinforced by certain legislative privileges afforded the Coconut Board, privileges incompatible with Seprod's status as a public company. No one in Jamaica, including Seprod, could import cooking oil without a license from the Coconut Board, and paying a "cess" thereon. This cess was a misguided effort by the government to protect the coconut industry, despite the fact that for health reasons the market for cooking oil had switched from coconut oil to soya oil.

At the operational level, Seprod employed a labour force that over the years had been militantly represented by the Bustamante Industrial Trade Union, headed by Hugh Shearer, a former Prime Minister, in whose constituency the Seprod head office and some of its manufacturing plants were located. The attitude of previous managements was to surrender to union demands, no matter how outrageous, and to pass on to customers the increased production coasts. Annual wage claims of 40% were not uncommon. This line-of-least resistance strategy was possible because many Seprod divisions enjoyed a monopoly position in the market, protected by high duties on competing imported products, products that in some instances were totally banned. I suspected that continued reliance on this state of affairs would be imprudent because the PNP government had changed its ideological stripes and was now espousing a private sector, market-driven economy. With globalization beginning to gather momentum, I knew it was only a matter of time before high tariff protections would be abolished.

Corruption at Seprod was actively practiced by some and abetted by others who refused to snitch on their fellow employees from the conviction, established in the Seventies, that worker solidarity was the eleventh commandment of socialist doctrine. Kick-backs at lower management levels were common and product theft was rife, especially of the expensive perfumes used in the manufacture of soaps. Whilst individual employees worked energetically on the production lines, understood the machinery and performed their various tasks with considerable skill and expertise, it was management that had failed to provide proper leadership, abdicating its responsibility to control events rather than settling for the status quo.

In implementing the necessary restructuring, Byron Thompson, my deputy, was loyal and knowledgeable, even though he probably resented me having been appointed as MD over him. But we became friends and I encouraged him to study for his executive MBA in order to broaden his background. The major changes in administration and corporate strategy I was able to implement could not have been effective without Byron's unstinting cooperation.

I had played a significant role in saving Seprod from bankruptcy by negotiating us out of the Goldcrest contracts. It was now my ongoing task to change Seprod's corporate culture, to bring it back to full profitability as a professionally run organisation. Years ago Seprod had played an important role in the rehabilitation and prosperity of Wherry Wharf by providing a steady stream of wharfage income from the discharge of corn. Fate, it seemed, had ordained my reconnection with Seprod, and I was eager to accept the challenges of my appointment as C.E.O. I found in an old minute book the original contract between Seprod and Wherry Wharf, signed in my youthful scrawl. Now I occupied a corner office in the executive headquarters building and out of my window I could see the corn boats unloading at Wherry Wharf.

As CEO I began to implement much needed changes. Following the American model, I established a treasury department as distinct from the accounting functions. This change was necessary because the Jamaican foreign exchange market was in a state of chaos and it called for a special talent to play the market and negotiate the best rates in a crazily see-sawing movement of supply and demand. Seprod required about US$2 million a month for the purchase of raw materials to keep the factories open. The one-man treasury department, headed by Sushil Jain, per-formed splendidly in avoiding any disruptions. An Indian who made his home in Jamaica, Sushil had an acute analytical mind and made a significant contribution to the management team.

Dealing with the Bustamante Trade Union, which represented some 1200 Seprod workers, presented a daunting challenge. Inflation was rife in the economy and this triggered ridiculously high wage claims by the union, claims that I was determined to resist. Desmond Blades was now chairman of the Seprod board and he agreed with me. A confrontation was inevitable. The workers went on strike and when I arrived at work on its first day, I found the driveway from the main road to the Seprod front gate sprinkled from curb to curb with broken glass bottles. At the entrance, workers on either side of my car were brandishing their fists and hurling racial insults. The gate was padlocked with a hefty chain and when I tried to reverse down the gauntlet, the workers started rocking the car preparatory to turning it over. Miraculously my tyres withstood the assault of the bottle shards and I managed to escape.

The strike lasted four weeks and cost the company $40 million. The workers slowly returned to their jobs, finally convinced that there was a new management ethos at Seprod and a new Managing Director who was not going to be a pushover. To improve the overall industrial relations climate, Byron and I met weekly with small groups of Seprod workers, trying to get across to them the realities of an economy that was about to abandon protectionism and open up the local market to foreign compe-tition. This was an exhausting exercise, but it eventually succeeded.

Despite all these difficulties, Seprod, like a heavily loaded cargo vessel, was slowly changing course towards profitability. I was con-scious, however, that the original lease that I had negotiated with Harrison for unloading corn at Wherry Wharf had only a few years left to run. The most dramatic solution was to have Seprod buy back Wherry Wharf from Maurice Facey, who had acquired it when I sold the business to Pan-Jamaican Investment Trust.

Negotiating the repurchase of Wherry Wharf with Maurice marked a new chapter in our relationship. Maurice's asking price was somewhat high, but I proposed that most of the purchase price be satisfied by Seprod shares at the closing mid-market price. Maurice wanted a firm figure and nominated $27.50 per share. I agreed and Pan-Jam was duly issued 1,065,454 Seprod Shares. Much to my disappointment, Maurice insisted on maintaining ownership of the Wherry Wharf name. This cut all ties with my family connection. I renamed the complex "Seprod Wharf and Storage". The Jamaica Stock Market never afforded Seprod a share price as high as $27.50 and eventually Pan-Jamaican, after several years, quietly liquidated its holding by selling its shares on the stock market.

Meantime, Caribbean Broilers, owned by the Hendrickson family, was making solid inroads in the animal feed market and was anxious to acquire a private wharf at which to land its raw materials. On a "return on assets" basis, Seprod Wharf and Storage was no longer a dynamic profit centre so, with the approval of the board, I sold it to Caribbean Broilers for a price substantially higher than I had paid Maurice for it.

The soap and detergent division was also a problem. When detergents showed a profit, soaps incurred a loss. When soaps managed to be profitable, this was negated with a vengeance by detergents. Cheap soaps were being imported from Mexico and India at prices with which we could not compete. My decision to close down the soap and detergent division was strongly opposed by the old guard who had started the division and were emotionally attached to it. I believe I was one of the first Jamaican managing directors of a large corporation with the will to "downsize" in preparation for globalization.

CHAPTER TWENTY-FIVE

SELLING BRANDS

The old Seprod management had been vigilant in protecting the brands that it had promoted over the years. Brands like Chlorox bleach, Castile soap, Sudsil detergent, Chef cooking oil and Chiffon margarine were household words in Jamaica. Soon after closing down the soap and detergent division, word reached me that Colgate, the giant US corporation, might be interested in buying the Chlorox bleach brand. I do not think that anyone in Jamaica knew on what basis brands were sold. I worked out a stand-alone profit-and-loss account for our bleach, soap and detergent brands, arriving at a profit before tax to which I applied a price-earnings ratio of six. Fortunately I kept these rustic calculations to myself. Colgate sent a representative to Jamaica to pursue buying the Chlorox bleach brand and in the course of conversation he let slip that the usual Colgate purchase price formula for buying brands was based on one year's sales. This was electrifying news to me. I made it clear that we would only consider selling all our bleach, soap and detergent brands as a "package", not any individual brand. The representative was not optimistic that Colgate would entertain this.

It was at this stage that I consulted with Desmond Blades as Seprod chairman and advised him that I was planning to go to New York to continue negotiations there with my counterpart in Colgate's American division. I had only one request, that Doreen accompany me as my secretary. Desmond readily agreed. "I never travel anywhere without Peggy," he pointed out. The matter of legal representation was discussed and I was able to convince Desmond that as a member of the New York Bar I would be able to practice in that city and deal with any legal niceties on my own. This would save mammoth legal fees and from a tax perspective it would be preferable for the contract to be concluded off shore.

At Colgate headquarters I was greeted cordially by John Williamson who had started his career at Price Waterhouse and was now number three in the overall Colgate hierarchy. He was an Irishman, probably a Catholic, and one of his sons was attending Fordham University, my *alma mater*. This was an auspicious start, but he insisted that he wanted only the Chlorox bleach brand and put on the table a purchase price for it that did indeed correspond to one year's sales. As a finesse he reiterated that he really did not want the other brands, but if the price was sufficiently attractive he might consider a package. My finesse was that if I could not conclude a deal with Colgate, I would be on my way to London to offer the package to Lever Brothers. Since the market was split 50% to Seprod, 25% to Colgate and 25% to Lever, whoever bought Seprod's market share would control 75% of the lucrative Jamaican market. I felt I was in the stronger bargaining position, but Williamson was still demanding audited accounts. "Thompson," he said, "Colgate in its entire history has never made an acquisition without audited accounts. It would cost me my job. You Jamaicans have some balls to present me with such a 'blue sky' proposition."

There comes a delicate time in every negotiation when a bluff is necessary without totally foreclosing any future move by the other party. I began to pack up my papers, shrugged on my overcoat and said, "Anyway Williamson, on my next visit to the Big Apple I'll bring you a bottle of twenty-year-old Jamaican rum." We shook hands and I left. Had Doreen not been waiting for me at the hotel for a post mortem, I would have needed a psychiatrist.

It was a month before I heard from Williamson again, suggesting that the negotiations be resumed. At the next session in New York in January 1996 I delivered the bottle of rum. On this occasion Williamson was supported by a battery of lawyers from the Colgate legal department, various brand specialists and the representative who had first approached me in Jamaica. I was decidedly outnumbered, but the session was useful for coming to grips with technical matters. Were the brands properly registered and copyrighted in Jamaican and the other Caribbean islands? Would Seprod sign a non-competition agreement as part of the package? Would I be prepared to grant Colgate an option to buy some of the soap-making machinery, now idle after the shutdown of that division?

A final figure for the overall package was arrived at after I agreed to reduce the selling price from 12 to 7 months sales of the brands, a price far above my initial expectation. The Colgate legal department agreed to prepare all the contracts overnight. In anticipation of this I had arranged with Citibank Jamaica to open an account with Citibank New York into which the Colgate cheque could be deposited and which would start earning interest immediately.

At 4:30 pm on a Thursday, the contract, non-competition and option agreements were signed and I was handed a Colgate cheque in the amount of $224,000,000. Williamson and I parted as good friends and respected adversaries. Shortly after the sale of the brands, Colgate exercised its option to buy the machinery and this provided an additional $25,000,0000 to the Seprod coffers. I had closed down the soap and detergent division to staunch losses. To be able to sell the brands had never been a part of my motivation. The money paid by Colgate was truly manna from heaven.

I jubilantly walked up Park Avenue; the windows of the Citibank tower were glazed amber by the setting winter sun. I ascended by the same elevator I had used when I had persuaded the fat Citibank lady to sing one more time by upping the loan needed for the Hardware and Lumber takeover. I then returned to the hotel to celebrate with Doreen.

When the Chairman reported the sale of the brands at the next Seprod board meeting it was duly noted, but there was not a word of congratulation or appreciation. I was hurt. After the meeting I drove home to share my disappointment with Doreen, repeating Mr. Shakespeare's words about wintry winds not being as cold as man's ingratitude – even in the tropics.

At this junction Seprod had repaid all its bank loans and the surplus funds from the sale of the brands were transferred to an investment account. The portfolio doubled itself in a few years. Don Banks, Manager of National Commercial Bank phoned me. "I never thought," he said, "that Seprod would survive. You have worked a miracle."

CHAPTER TWENTY-SIX

GOODBYE SEPROD

In 1999, I was being paid a salary of J$4 million per annum plus a percent of Seprod's pre-tax profits. With all the children out of school and supporting themselves, this allowed me to continue the slow process of rebuilding savings and net worth. When my Seprod contract came up for review I fully expected it to be renewed. It was not. Desmond Blades said that he put up a fierce fight on my behalf and I believe him. But the Seprod Board, understandably in retrospect, felt that a publicly traded company could be criticized for retaining a CEO in his seventies. It was time to give Byron Thompson his chance at the helm and I was happy for him. Nothing succeeds like a successor and Byron has run the company brilliantly after taking over the management reins from me. I was paid six months' salary, half of what I thought would have been appropriate, given what I had accomplished in reorganizing Seprod and negotiating the sale of the brands. Again, there was no Board resolution thanking me for my services, no farewell dinner.

But the press was kind. The *Jamaica Observer* newspaper, upon my retirement in 1999, lauded my achievements at Seprod:

> Dr. Ralph Thompson, the hard-nosed CEO who transformed the Seprod group from a lumbering labour-intensive manufacturer, into a nimble, profitable company, has announced his retirement at 71. Under Thompson's guidance, Seprod became a metaphor for all that was good about company rightsizing. Indeed Seprod became the symbol of what the possibilities were for local companies with visionary leadership.

Desmond Blades had his own subtle way of adjusting his moral balance sheet to accommodate a change of circumstances. Perhaps in light of the less than generous terms of my departure from Seprod, he offered me the managing directorship of the C. D. Alexander Realty Company, a minor Musson subsidiary that was floundering. He also arranged for me to remain a director of the Musson parent company and a number of its subsidiaries, including T. Geddes Grant and General Accident Insurance.

My flexible work schedule at C.D. Alexander allowed me to accept an invitation from *The Gleaner* newspaper to become a member of its editorial panel, a group of writers unknown to each other, whose anonymous daily editorials constituted them as official spokespersons for the paper. This was a challenging experience. I would read *The Gleaner* every morning and select from the news a topic I thought worthy of editorial comment. The submission, not more than 800 words, had to be sent to the editor by FAX no later than 11 am. I then had to wait for the following morning's paper to see if the editorial had been accepted. Its rejection could be because the topic was not suitable, because the writing was not thought to be up to standard or because another member of the editorial panel had made his or her submission before mine. My acceptance rate averaged about two editorials a week, and over the period about one hundred of my editorials were published. They were never edited, but either accepted or rejected as is. The procedure with its inexorable deadline placed me under intense strain. But this was more than offset by the excitement of my secret, behind-the-scenes influence on public opinion. One of my editorials might set the agenda of the radio "call in" programmes, hosts like Wilmot (Motty) Perkins sometimes endorsing my views, sometimes trashing them. On occasion Stephanie my daughter would telephone to say, "Dad, I know you wrote today's editorials. Only you would quote Aristotle to make a point."

Over time the tension of being on the editorial panel took its toll. My psoriasis, a skin condition that affects highly strung personalities, began to worsen, a clear signal that I should quit. I regretfully tendered my resignation to the Editor-in-Chief.

The Thompson Clan

BR, LR: Liz, Stephanie, Larry, Debbie
FR: Doreen and Ralph

CHAPTER TWENTY-SEVEN

EDUCATION IN JAMAICA

In retrospect I can identify my areas of interest, other than paid work, to be painting, poetry, public speaking, broadcasting, writing on current affairs – especially education, and attempts to deepen the religious insights of my Catholic faith. Despite long hours in the service of others, it has been the time spent exploring these interests and trying to define myself in relation to them that has given me the greatest personal satisfaction and vivified my existence.

I have been for a long time absorbed in analyzing the weaknesses of the Jamaican education system and making recommendations for its improvement. Based on data supplied by my sister, Audrey, who was trained as a psychiatric social worker, I drew to public attention that a child in its first year of existence will learn more than it will for the rest of its life. The brain of the newborn is pulsing with millions of synapses, potential knowledge centres that, if emotionally supported and intellectually stimulated, have the potential to develop exponentially and to burst into a crescendo of creativity. Sadly, though, these synapses cannot be stored in inventory for future actualization. They begin to deplete rapidly and become dysfunctional if not used.

My investigations revealed that early childhood education in Jamaica, from the ages of one to six, was left largely to community-supported basic schools run by private sector entrepreneurs. Miss "Matilda", with little or no training, would open a basic school on her verandah for which she charged whatever fees the traffic could bear. In most cases, teaching staff had no formal pedagogic training and were paid little more than a domestic helper. Teaching was by rote, the "C.A.T- spells-cat-method". There was no common curriculum and classes were conducted mainly in patois. There were no standards of sanitation or space, no insurance, no protection against covert child abuse.

Why, I asked, did the government not take over early childhood education, incorporate it into the public education system and use it to help sustain family values? Many readers of my press articles cringed at the picture I painted of life in the ghetto and rural areas where sometimes eight adults lived in one small room, sharing a mattress on the floor, children exposed to early sexual stimulation where their mothers sometimes hosted different men, where there were frequent verbal clashes and disputes were sometimes settled with the chop of a machete.

Even in the public education system there were problems. The 20,000 strong Jamaica Teachers Association was a militant trade union and it was virtually impossible to rid the system of inept or dysfunctional teachers. This was denied by the Ministry of Education and the Jamaica Teachers Association, of course, but by now I had been sufficiently exposed to the system to know that the dismissal of unproductive teachers was a rare occurrence.

Alex, an influential *Gleaner* columnist, with tongue in cheek, wrote an article in 2001 setting out his selections for a "kitchen cabinet" of private sector individuals who, he proposed, could run the country better than the present crop of politicians. I was nominated as minister of education. Perhaps to silence me, the elected Minister of Education arranged my appointment, by the Governor General, as a member of the National Council on Education. Since I firmly believed that Jamaican children were as bright as children anywhere else in the world, I thought it useful to check what results were being achieved in English and Mathematics at the end of the secondary education cycle. The Caribbean Examination Council, headquartered in Barbados, administered the CSEC examinations in these two foundation subjects, common to all the West Indies territories. Official results announced annually by the Ministry of Education lumped all Jamaican secondary schools together, the pass rate averaging about 50% in English and 35% in Mathematics. As unsatisfactory as these results might be considered, I was suspicious that some masking was taking place, that the situation was worse than officialdom wished to reveal.

I was able to "disaggregate" the performance of individual secondary schools and the results of this exercise were shocking. It was bad enough that the Ministry of Education, by lumping all the secondary schools together, was using the high-performing schools to pull up the overall average, but the manner in which pass rates were calculated was shamefully misleading. The principal of each high school, at his or her sole discretion, was allowed to decide *a priori* which students would be selected to take the exams. Principals exercised this discretion differently, some with the courage of their convictions and teaching skills,

Cartoon from *The Gleaner*

sending up the entire enrolled cohort to sit the exam; others, anticipating disaster, culled those they thought would fail. The Ministry of Education, which calculated pass rates as a percent of those actually sitting the exams rather than as a percent of the total cohort, was an accomplice in the deception. On this basis, no "like for like" comparisons could logically be made, but even when I publicly exposed the manipulation, this statistically senseless method of comparing pass rates continued to be used. With the disaggregated figures now at my disposal, I was able, by way of example, to find one school with an enrolled cohort of 77 youngsters that permitted only one student to sit the CXC exam in Mathematics. Had he passed, the officially announced pass rate for this school would have been a misleading 100%. In the event, he failed and the pass rate plunged to zero.

The refusal of the Ministry of Education to change its method of calculating pass rates raised my ire. Parents who, at considerable financial sacrifice, entrusted their children for five years to a secondary school had the right to expect that, in ordinary circumstances, the teaching skills of the institution would ensure that most of its charges graduated with some form of formal qualification for entering the Jamaican work force. Calculated correctly, the overall pass rate in English would be 30% and in Mathematics 18%. But there was more depressing news.

Disaggregation showed that there were 63 traditional high schools whose enrollment reflected about 30% of the total secondary school population. Another category comprised 80 non-traditional high schools attended by about 70% of the secondary school population, mostly children of the poor, who flowed into the system from government primary schools, children who scored badly on the GSAT placement exam. Correctly calculated, the failure rates for the non-traditional secondary schools were catastrophic – an average of 90% in English and 96% in Mathematics. These percentages hardly changed over the six years that I examined CXC results.

Considering the repercussions for national development of these failure rates, I felt an obligation to draw this sorry state of affairs to public attention, and the media gave full coverage to my analysis. The ultimate government finesse to the pressure I was generating was to form an Early Childhood Commission, chaired by Dr. Maureen Samms-Vaughan, a medical doctor and a respected researcher and professor at the University of the West Indies. I was appointed a member. Samms-Vaughan and I circled each other at some distance in the early days, but I came to admire her professionalism. In time, I think she began to see me as an ally, someone with private sector experience who could help her cut through bureaucratic red tape. The Commission has drafted standards and regulations for the running of Basic schools, but whether these can be enforced without closing down the entire system remains to be seen. With time, the strain of public advocacy on behalf of education, both as a member of the Commission and in the media, became too much for an octogenarian and obliged me to resign from the Commission.

One day in the parking lot of Sovereign Centre, an old Rasta, shabby and unkempt, sidled up to me and asked, "Why you not writing about education anymore?"

"Because nobody listens to me."

He smiled. "I tell you in ten years most of your recommendations will be implemented. Look at me, no man is a prophet in his own country."

What I wrote in a poem called "Roots", in *Taking Words for a Walk* sums up my feelings about how painfully Jamaica will pay, and is paying, for the way it treats some of its children:

> The switch of choice
> is thin and supple,
> welts festering in the boy's black skin,
> one for each year of his defiance,
> fingers practicing in secret to curl
> around the barrel of an AK-47.
> The teachers cut their switches
> from the tamarind tree which spreads
> a fine shade across the school yard.
> Under his bare feet
> he can feel the roots growing
> wide as the branches,
> plotting underground to crack
> the foundations of the school house walls,
> to burst the pediments,
> to snap the roof's spine.

CHAPTER TWENTY-EIGHT

THE CONSOLATIONS OF POETRY

Poetry has always been the ordering passion of my life, a spiritual and aesthetic balance to the tensions of the workplace. I dispatched poems to the international literary journals and received in exchange rejection slips that accumulated with humiliating speed. But sometime in 1991 the *Jamaica Journal* accepted four of my poems and they caught the eye of Ian McDonald, the Guyanese poet and editor. McDonald wrote to his friend Edward Baugh in Jamaica asking, "Who is this Thompson? I have never heard of him. His poems are so starkly beautiful."

Eddie Baugh, one of Jamaica's leading poets, was a professor at the University of the West Indies and its public orator. A slight man physically, he exerted a giant influence on students who signed up to take his courses. Endowed with a magnificent speaking voice, which he can control like a musical instrument, his portrayal of Claudius in Shakespeare's *Hamlet* is part of theatre folklore in Jamaica. He recorded a CD of some of his poems and asked me to write the liner notes. In praising his voice I wrote: "A Baugh poem poised on the page is one thing, but a Baugh poem interpreted, modulated and projected by the Baugh voice is a unique experience. His rich baritone is an instrument finely tuned from his days as an actor."

Baugh passed McDonald's comment to me and I wrote a formal letter to him thanking him for his interest. This was the beginning of a fruitful correspondence and a cherished friendship.

McDonald, a white West Indian, had read history at Cambridge and had earned his "blue" in tennis. Stocky and with an unruly shock of hair, he broke easily into a smile, but was a deeply thoughtful individual committed to social justice and the Arts. He edited the Guyanese literary journal *Kyk-Over-Al* and, when we became acquainted, Peepal Tree Press, an English publishing house run by Jeremy Poynting and devoted to promoting Caribbean writing, had just published a collection of his poems entitled *Jaffo The Calypsonian*.

McDonald wrote a letter of introduction to Poynting who asked me to submit a manuscript. To my delight it was accepted and in 1992 Peepal Tree press published my first poetry collection entitled *The Denting of a Wave*. In the acknowledgment section, credit was given to publications in which my poems had appeared. These included *The Gleaner, Carib 5, Jamaica Journal, Kyk-Over-Al, The Caribbean Writer* and *London Magazine*.

Poynting flew to Jamaica for the launch of the book at which Eddie Baugh presided. It was held at the Creative Arts Centre of the University and was attended by a curious gaggle of friends and literary types still uncertain whether or not to take me seriously as a poet. Fortunately, the collection received some favourable international reviews, which helped to dispel any lingering doubts.

I had visited Peepal Tree Press in Leeds and discovered that it was then literally a one man operation driven by Poynting's fierce ambition to make a serious contribution to the publishing of Caribbean literature. He taught in further education in Leeds, and used his salary to support the press. He had completed a Ph.D on the literary representation of the Indian presence in the Caribbean and had named the press for the peepal tree brought from India to Trinidad and Guyana by the first wave of indentured workers for the sugar plantations. He worked 18 hours a day, teaching, reading scripts, editing them, designing covers, physically manning the presses and trying to collect his accounts receivable from bookshops in the various islands.

Jeremy had never learned to drive an automobile, but it was easy to forgive his peccadilloes in light of the fervour with which he pursued his publishing dreams. Eventually all the hard work and long hours paid off and currently Peepal Tree Press boasts a distinguished list of Caribbean and Black British writers, the largest in the world – an extraordinary accomplishment. For his work he has been awarded an Honorary Doctor of Letters degree from the University of the West Indies at Mona. In due course I hope that he receives a knighthood, an ironic reward for an erstwhile Communist.

In 1997, Peepal Tree Press published my second collection entitled *Moving On*. The cover featured one of my paintings and the acknowledgments of previously published poems included *Ariel* (Canada), *The Mississippi Review* (USA), *The Caribbean Writer, London Magazine* and *The Dulwich Poetry Festival Anthology* (UK). Altogether I have had four poems published in *London Magazine* – and five times that number rejected. Alan Ross, a leading literary figure in England, was an adventurous editor of the reincarnated *London Magazine*. Dissolute in appearance and dishevelled in dress, he had an unfailing instinct for spotting new talent and being able to persuade the famous to favour *London Magazine* with their work. Ross's early publication of a Walcott poem helped to establish Derek's reputation in England and in gratitude he often granted Ross first refusal on some new work. Louis Simpson was another West Indian poet whom Ross was eager to feature in *London Magazine*.

One day I had just received a cheque from *London Magazine* in the amount of ten guineas for a poem entitled "Good-Bye Picasso" when the news broke that Ross had died suddenly. I could not bring myself to cash the cheque.

★   ★   ★

Louis Simpson must have been in his late sixties when I first met him. I knew his work including a poem about his father with the famous opening line:

> "My father in the night commanding no
> has work to do…"

A rival of Norman Manley, Simpson's father had been a leading Jamaican lawyer whose marriage to a Russian actress produced two sons, Louis and his elder brother Herbert. Their mother had caught the eye of the lawyer when she came to Jamaica with a Hollywood crew to make a Grade B movie in which she was to play a minor part. Instructed to fall off a bridge into a river and pretend to be drowning, her performance had a ring of authenticity to it because she did not know how to swim, and nearly drowned while the cameras were turning. Louis' father helped to rescue her and made her his bride.

Louis was sent off to Munro, a Jamaican boarding school modelled on the cruellest institutions of that type in England. He survived and graduated at seventeen, by which time his father had divorced his Russian wife and married his secretary. Louis was desperately unhappy, impatient to leave Jamaica and join his mother in New York. World War II was raging and he signed up as a private in the American army, and saw action in some of the fiercest European battles, including the fighting at Bastogne.

After the war, Simpson earned a Ph.D. degree at Columbia University and lived for several years in France where he self-published his first collection of poems. His talent was too incandescent to be hidden under a bushel and he eventually became one of the most important narrative poets of the 20th century, winning the Pulitzer Prize for poetry in 1963. He had never returned to his island home. During the course of our friendship I discovered that he was a cousin of Douglas Fletcher, a prominent lawyer and retired Jamaica ambassador to Washington. Douglas explained that Simpson had such uncomfortable memories of his father and stepmother that, although they were now both dead, he could not bring himself to revisit the site of his unhappiness. Douglas and I took on the challenge of getting him to change his mind. We conspired to extract from UWI a formal invitation for him to participate in the Distinguished Lecture series, for which air fares for himself and his wife and a small honorarium would be paid.

From the moment we met in Jamaica, Simpson and I became close friends. He was Poetry Professor Emeritus at New York University and because of his years of teaching was not reluctant to praise or criticise poems that I sent him for comment. I was privileged to be asked to write the entry on Simpson in two editions of the Routledge Encyclopedia of Post-Colonial Literatures. The first entry about me in that publication was written by John Figueroa, the second by Eddie Baugh. Simpson and I developed a rich correspondence and I consider myself blessed to have had such a mentor.

My third collection was a verse novel with the title *View From Mount Diablo*, the devil's mountain being the ancient designation given to the tortuous road linking Kingston to the North Coast. It dealt with the passage of Jamaica from relative colonial innocence to the disturbing turbulence of the post-independence experience, touching on the subjects of narco-crime, political corruption and police violence, amongst much else. The poem, submitted under a sobriquet according to the competition rules, so the judges would not know who the author was, won first prize in the Jamaican National Literary competition for 2001. Peepal Tree Press agreed to publish it and Simpson generously wrote a blurb for the back cover that read:

> *View From Mount Diablo* is a remarkable achievement. Its knowledge of the island, the entwining of private lives and politics, lifts Jamaican poetry to a level that has not been attempted before. The poetry is strong, imaginative, fascinating in detail. It describes terrible things with understatement, yet with compassion. This is narrative poetry at its best.

View From Mount Diablo was launched by Valerie Facey, and Wayne Brown (who had arranged the publication of sections of the poem in the *Jamaica Observer*, which did much to promote sales) delivered a graceful and perspicacious introduction. The book had a second life when John

Cycling: the cover image for *Moving On*

Lennard, recruited from the UK as Professor of English and American literature at the University of the West Indies, taught a seminar course on *View*, for which he prepared a set of scholarly annotations. We became friends and he is the first, live polymath that I have ever encountered. The verse novel caused quite a stir and Peepal Tree Press agreed to issue a second, annotated edition in 2009.

It was also Louis Simpson who was kind enough to give me letter of introduction to Dennis O'Driscoll, an Irish poet and critic, when he learnt that Doreen and I were planning a vacation in Ireland. I confess that I knew nothing about O'Driscoll at the time. I presented my introduction in Dublin and Dennis and his wife Julie, herself a poet, invited us to lunch. Dennis, I learned, could only spare an hour and a half because he had to get back to his substantive job as an executive with the Irish Customs department. We were both businessmen who wrote poetry and this became a special bond. On my return to Jamaica I sent O'Driscoll some of my poems and, like Simpson, he seemed happy to comment on them.

★   ★   ★

During my tenure as Managing Director of Seprod I was invited to become a member of the Breakfast Club, an influential morning radio talk show hosted by Anthony Abrahams, ex-JLP Minister of Tourism, and Beverley Manley, ex-wife of former Prime Minister Michael Manley. At this time I was also writing editorials for *The Gleaner* newspaper, so considered myself reasonably resourced to comment on current affairs. But over the years of my participation in the Breakfast Club programme I found myself frequently quoting a few lines of poetry, which may or may not have been *a propos* to the subject under discussion. Eventually the programme, on Wednesdays, when I was in attendance, opened with my reading a short poem, seldom one of mine, which the night before I had written out on an index card. Beverley Manley took the cue and would ritually ask, "What have you got for us in your pocket this morning?" I was astonished that long after my pontifications on the state of the Jamaican economy were forgotten, friends and strangers would approach me and ask what poem I was hiding in my pocket. Such is the power of the muse!

I proffer no profound *ars poetica* for my poetry. In the *Caribbean Review of Books*, Louis Simpson singled out for comment my poem "Harbour View", which he praised as "one of the perfectly realized poems in the book – perfect because the poem refrains from trying to make anything grander or more significant of the view than it is". Bowing to this caution I have always tried to write within my range, whether lyric or narrative. I love the sound of poems – the crackling of consonants, the lilt of labials, the echo one vowel confers on its neighbour up or down the scale. I look for relationships and ironies that I can capture in a unique way for my readers, always hoping to discover a small truth in metaphor and mood.

All art is an attempt to encode in a more permanent form the transience of the world – whether its beauties or its sorrows, its epiphanies or its tragedies but always with the compulsion to share with others the joy of the creative process. All artists are exhibitionists, which is why painters exhibit and poets publish.

Being a white man in a black country imposes its own burden. It is understandable that the more nationalistic commentators might dismiss me as a cultural intruder and ignore me as "socially irrelevant". But I have been moved by the magnanimity with which senior Jamaican poets and writers have accepted me into their ranks, such as John Hearne, John Figueroa, Edward Baugh, Mervyn Morris and Wayne Brown. As a West Indian writer I can claim friendship with Derek Walcott and Ian McDonald and a wide "brotherhood" of poets published by Peepal Tree Press. Writing poetry is a private and lonely occupation, which for long hours and over long periods can cut one off from family and friends. I am very conscious of having neglected Doreen and the children in pursuit of the Muse. Poetry has also reinforced my state of self-absorption, which I try to justify as a means of living the "examined" life recommended in the Gospels. This has often resulted in my being anti-social and in this regard writing a memoir or autobiography can be tricky terrain. Almost by definition the genre can be self-serving and easily abused. After much thought, however, I decided to trust my conscience and write on.

★   ★   ★

I met Derek Walcott at the wedding of one of the Figueroa daughters. Dressed in a white sharkskin suit, he was sprawled in a lounge chair under a mango tree surrounded by admirers. I remarked that Figueroa, always the editor, had even rewritten one of the psalms printed in the wedding programme. This tickled Walcott's wry sense of humour and he exploded into one of those fits of laughter for which he was famous, sometimes falling to the ground on his knees in a crescendo of giggles.

"Thompson say Figs rewriting the psalms... his next book to be "The Song of Songs Revised and Updated."

John Figueroa, near-white, bald and with a flowing rabbinical beard, was used to Derek's teasing and took it in his stride. To Walcott's generation of West Indian writers, Figueroa was an important figure, sometimes as inspiration, often as critic, always in the thick of the literary action both at home and abroad. He was an important anthologist and had been a catalyst for Walcott's "Ruins of a Great House" and Walcott had dedicated to him his moving poem, "Nearing Forty".

Moody at the best of times, Walcott, when I first met him was a heavy drinker and an aggressive drunk. One night on our patio he nearly came to blows with Figueroa over an assessment of Naipaul. Figs thought that Naipaul's *The Mimic Men* summed up the West Indian psyche with considerable perspicacity. Walcott would have none of that. Naipaul, he thought, was a cynical nihilist, an exemplary prose writer but a shrivelled soul. I had to intervene and separate the protagonists.

We often hosted visiting literary luminaries on the patio at our Dillsbury Avenue residence. Martin Carter, the remarkable Guyanese poet, was one such. He arrived for lunch, already drunk, refused to eat and kept drinking at a steady pace. Doreen, always a gracious hostess, was worried about him, urged him to try some hot soup. Of a sudden he jumped to his feet, this gesture silencing our other guests, and he recited an extempore poem dedicated to Doreen. "I speak in your honour, Ma'am. You are so beautiful". He sat down and the drinking and conversation resumed only to be interrupted by another Carter tribute to my wife. When the spirit moved him, he jumped to his feet a third time, repeating the performance.

A few years later we told this story to Mervyn Morris, a true friend and now Jamaica's Poet Laureate. It became the inspiration for one of his poems entitled "Toasting the Muse", the last verse of which envisions that he was a guest at the lunch in honour of Carter. It is a lovely tribute to Doreen:

> I been there, sort of.
> For in that ambience I too
> was smitten, by what seemed
> to me unusual radiance,
> beauty of spirit lighting up the place,
> but I kept quiet about it, made small talk
> stayed sober and enjoyed the food.

I Been There, Sort Of became the title of Mervyn's *New and Selected Poems* published by Carcanet in the UK. I was honoured when he asked me to launch it at the UWI Creative Arts Centre. He reciprocated in 2013 by launching my *Taking Words for a Walk, New and Selected Poems*, ending his speech with a reference to me as "one of Jamaica's very finest poets".

Walcott, who had been a prodigious drinker, suddenly and irrevocably gave up drinking. He was diabetic and his doctor made it clear that unless he cut down on his drinking his life expectancy would be considerably shortened. Confronted with the prospect of death before perfection of his gift, he found the will-power to give up the booze entirely. Thereafter he remained moody but was a stimulating and sympathetic friend.

CHAPTER TWENTY-NINE

WALCOTT

My friendship with Walcott ripened during three tours to Jamaica of the Trinidad Theatre Workshop, of which he was founder in 1959, and director until 1976 when he resigned. The tours took place between 1971 and 1973. The first tour featured two of Walcott's plays, *Ti Jean and his Brothers* and *Dream on Monkey Mountain*; the second tour *The Charlatan* and *Franklin* and the third tour *The Joker of Seville*. Each was a resounding success.

This was during my managing directorship of Pan-Jamaican Investment Trust, and Maurice Facey left to me all the organising and financing details of the tours. Doreen and Fay Barovier, my secretary, pitched in to help with the myriad details of organising a troupe of some thirty persons. They were indispensable in dealing with the inevitable temperamental outbursts and mini crises which are an integral part of the theatrical experience all over the world.

Walcott was a demanding director who tried to control every artistic aspect of the productions from costumes to music. The Trinidad cast of the Theatre Workshop loved Jamaica and with each tour the overall standards of presentation became more professional. With the staging of *The Joker of Seville*, I persuaded Walcott to allow Pan-Jam to hire Richard Montgomery, a visiting theatre designer from England, to create the costumes and stage sets for the work. Rather than dressing the Spanish nobles in traditional hose and crimson capes, Montgomery proposed, preposterously some thought, that they be dressed as Japanese Samurai warriors, an effect to be achieved by strapping straw shin guards and straw breast plates onto the actors. At first, the cast refused to be part of such a spectacle, but Walcott, himself in awe of Montgomery's imaginative suggestion, persuaded them to think "outside the costume box". Judging by audience reaction, the brilliance of the concept was confirmed. *The Joker of Seville*, published by Farrar, Straus and Giroux in 1978, was generously dedicated by Walcott "For Ralph and Dody

Derek Walcott and Ralph Thompson on Reduit Beach, St Lucia

Thompson". The Trinidad Theatre Workshop season of plays was performed at the Creative Arts Centre in the grounds of the University of the West Indies, Mona, from which institution Walcott had graduated some years previously with a mediocre degree. Utterly bored with the second-class colonial approach to education adopted by the university in those days, Walcott refused to study for his final exams. In a paper for his Diploma of Education exam, one question asked "What are the characteristics of a good ruler?" Walcott scrawled on his paper, "Twelve inches" and slouched from the room.

We hosted a Sunday party for the Trinidad Theatre Workshop cast around the pool at our Dillsbury Avenue home. The Trinidad penchant for joviality was everywhere in evidence, but I spotted Walcott by himself leaning on a verandah post, surveying the bacchanal with a strange detachment.

In an effort to read his mood and to provoke him into some meaningful conversation, I asked him if he was afraid of death.

"I am obsessed with death," he replied. "Terrified that I might die before I can bring my gift to perfection."

To reassure him, I prophetically replied, "Don't worry. One day you will win the Nobel prize for poetry."

As our friendship with Walcott ripened, on one occasion he extended to me, Dody and our daughter Liz the hospitality of his house in Brookline, Massachusetts, a *pied a terre* purchased with the proceeds of his MacArthur grant. Walcott had recently married Norlene Metivier, one of the dancers in the Trinidad Theatre Workshop group, and his Lizzie (herself now a published novelist with Peepal Tree Press), a daughter by Margaret, his second wife, was spending time with her father. We accepted the Walcott invitation even though space in the flat was cramped. The two Lizes slept on the pull-out couch in the living room cuddled together, one black and one white.

Doreen and I were planning a trip to England and Walcott offered to write a letter of introduction for me to Alan Ross, the editor of *London Magazine*, which in a previous dispensation had published poems by Keats and De Quincey. Walcott's manual Olivetti typewriter was set up in a bay window alcove of the living room and on it he tapped out this eccentric introduction:

Sir Alan of Ross,
This missive delivered by herald sennets in my dear ami of ancient standing, a poet, a painter, scholar, gentleman and white Jamaican who, or is it whom, make that about whom I have... wait. I have spoken of you to him beau coup de fon, so tell him hello and don't try to show him London

because he knows it. His name is Ralph, his wife's name is Dody, my name is Derek, your name is Alan and so on, and thank you for the lovely evening at your place, even if Figs trailed his beard through the soup. Derek

On another occasion, Derek and Norlene spent a week with us in Clearwater and he gave a memorable reading at the University of South Florida where I was working on my master's degree. Rather than recite individual poems, he read (in some cases chanted) the first act of *Dream on Monkey Mountain*. He acted all the parts with emotional intensity.

Norlene, the child bride, wished to visit Disney World, a two hour drive from Clearwater, but this did not appeal to Derek. Doreen sided with Norlene and eventually Derek was persuaded. We spent a day at the "Kingdom", Walcott, the future Laureate, bringing up the rear carrying a teddy bear that Norlene had won.

In 1981, Walcott was inducted as an honorary member of the American Academy and Institute of Arts and Letters. At his invitation, Doreen and I flew to New York for the main function, but each honoree was allowed only one guest for the formal luncheon, so the honour of sitting at Walcott's table fell to me. Gathered around the table were Ralph Ellison, William Jay Smith, who had nominated Walcott, Mrs. Smith and Joseph Brodsky, a Laureate to be. It was rather difficult to hear or understand the various conversations taking place at the same time. Brodsky had a thick Russian accent and at the best of times Walcott tends to mumble. I felt decidedly out of place. Being in the lumber trade hardly seemed an appropriate qualification for hobnobbing with such exalted literary types.

In the main reception hall, before lunch, I had met some iconic personalities – John Updike, Robert Penn Warren and John Cheever. I.M. Pei, the architect, greeted Walcott, full of good humour and energy. Stanley Kunitz and Richard Wilbur introduced themselves. Kunitz was short, old and crotchety. He confessed to not having read Walcott's latest book because "You have a stingy publisher. They don't send out enough free copies." Wilbur looked like a retired football player or tennis buff, much too athletic to produce the delicate formalist verse for which he is renowned.

On the stage for the presentation, Walcott was seated in the front row between Isaac Bashevis Singer, the Nobel novelist, and C. P. Snow. Across the aisle were Eudora Welty and Susan Sontag. Archibald McLeish won the gold medal for poetry and was introduced by Wilbur.

Walcott suggested to me that Wilbur, a far superior poet, must have found this a difficult task. Robert Motherwell introduced I.M. Pei and he was the only speaker to refresh his remarks with a *soupçon* of humour. This almost total absence of wit and style on the part of the luminaries puzzled and disillusioned me.

At a subsequent meeting of the Academy, Walcott invited Doreen to be his luncheon guest and among the luminaries seated at his table on this occasion was Mr. George F. Kennan, the American diplomat and historian, whose textbook on foreign policy she had studied at Wellesley.

At this stage in our friendship with Walcott, I was beginning to understand how difficult it must have been for a West Indian poet and playwright to support himself on his writings. On one occasion, desperate to meet some personal obligations, Walcott swallowed his pride and asked me to lend him US$400. I was happy to accommodate him and had the sense not to suggest that he accept the money as a gift. For three or four years we never spoke about the transaction. Then one day, when Walcott was staying with us in Jamaica, I found, after his departure, an envelope on my desk with my name in his handwriting containing four one hundred dollar bills. There was no thank you note, but I could feel the embarrassment with which he had lived for so long lift and fade away. This re-established his independence in the dynamics of our relationship and ratcheted our friendship to a higher, more intimate level.

Joseph Papp, the New York theatre guru, had pioneered a summer programme of Shakespeare plays performed in Central Park. At the end of the season he agreed to stage Walcott's *Ti Jean and his Brothers* as part of the series, a signal honour. Doreen and I flew to New York for the opening and after a matinee, as it was getting dark, I remember walking across Central Park with Derek and Margaret, his second wife. When there was talk about the safety of such a stroll, Margaret exclaimed, "We will have to keep our eyes out for the mugger fuckers."

I had first met Margaret in Trinidad at the Walcott's Diego Martin home. A few friends and much booze. Margaret was a haughty beauty with flashing eyes and an inspired intelligence. Derek, who had little time for reading novels, commissioned her to prepare a short list of the two or three most significant publications each month and trusted her judgment implicitly. Even after their divorce Derek confided to me, "Margaret and I had interludes during our marriage of indescribable angelic joy and insatiable passion. If she was a nymphomaniac, I was a satyr." Whenever I remember Margaret, God rest her soul, I think of Walcott's lines:

When have I ever not loved
The pain of love but this has moved
From love to mania

Derek had a son, Peter, by his first wife and two daughters, Elizabeth and Anna, by Margaret. The daughters were vivacious and talented, but his son had emotional and physical problems that Derek bore with hope and fortitude. A skilful draftsman and painter, Peter was handicapped with rheumatoid arthritis that became worse with the passing years. Derek seldom spoke about this cross in his life and never gave up trying to find some appropriate accommodation to ensure a degree of happiness in Peter's life.

Doreen and I visited New York frequently and tried to be there whenever one of Derek's plays was being performed. We were in the audience for the Off-Broadway production of *Remembrance*. Backstage we met the late Roscoe Lee Brown who starred in it. Our favourite caravanserai was the Stanhope Hotel on 5th Avenue, almost opposite the Metropolitan Museum. Management always assigned us the same suite, which became the venue for after-theatre parties for Derek and his friends. One of these was Derek's editor at Farrar, Straus and Giraux, Pat Strachan, who not only possessed a finely tuned literary sensibility but showed remarkable skill and patience in putting up with Walcott's moodiness. After leaving Farrar, Straus and Giraux she moved to Harcourt Brace, where she became one of Harold Bloom's editors.

Our get-togethers in New York often included Joseph Brodsky, a genius, who after his escape from the Russian Gulag burst upon the international literary scene like a meteor, too bright to last for very long. Already when we met him he had undergone open-heart surgery. He wore white shirts, open to the waist, as if to show off his scar. Balding and with pale grey eyes, he was already ethereal, pure energy and spirit, who greeted his friends, old and new, with the salutation, "Kisses, Kisses." He inscribed a collection of his poems for me with the mandate "Read 'em and weep."

On one occasion, Brodsky and Walcott wished to attend the premiere of Francis Ford Coppola's film *Apocalypse Now*, scheduled for high noon in Manhattan. Dody and I were commissioned to stand in line from 10 a.m to secure four tickets. We were all to meet in the lobby of the theatre, Walcott arriving just as the lights were being dimmed, but no sign of Brodsky. By this time there was no hope of us all being able to sit together, so Dody and I found two seats and left Walcott with two tickets to await his friend. After the movie, we had lunch at the Sheraton Hotel coffee shop across the street. It was a toss-up which the poets despised more: the hospital ambience of the eatery or the pretensions of the film. Marlon Brando, trying to mouth Eliot's famous lines from "The Hollow Men" was collectively regarded as a disaster.

On another occasion Dody and I hosted a dinner at a famous Indian restaurant in New York at the top of the Essex House Hotel. Brodsky possessed, I am sure, an encyclopedic memory, knew all the Indian dishes, their ingredients and spices. He did the ordering, much to the amazement of the young Indian waiter. During the course of the meal Brodsky and Walcott argued about the merits of Robert Frost. Brodsky ranked him as the leading American poet and intellectual. Walcott disagreed and I allowed my curry to get cold while listening to their debate. At dessert, they were challenging each other about which poems/poets they would include in an ideal anthology. I remember consensus being reached on only four – Christina Rossetti, Emily Dickinson, Wallace Stevens and Gerard Manley Hopkins.

Walcott was devastated by Brodsky's sudden death. His widow was trying to obtain permission for him to be buried in his beloved Venice, but there was hardly any room left in the St Michael cemetery and the chances of getting permission for the entombment there of a Jewish atheist seemed remote, though from his poetry I had concluded that, atheist or no atheist, Brodsky had the deepest religious sensibility of any modern poet, Walcott included. I was pleased to learn that permission for the interment was eventually granted.

CHAPTER THIRTY

A READING WITH THE LAUREATES

I had long expressed an unshakeable conviction that Walcott would one day win the Nobel Prize for literature. When in October 1992 the news broke on the BBC of his award, I immediately telephoned him at his Boston apartment. A sleepy voice answered, and it turned out that it was only fifteen minutes before my call that the representative of the Nobel committee had contacted Derek to tell him of the honour. He was in shock and kept repeating the date of the presentation in Stockholm, assuming that Doreen and I would be there to celebrate with him. It was one of the great disappointments of my life that at this time our financial resources were such that we could not afford the trip.

An old man by any reckoning, I was completing my tenth year working for Desmond Blades, anxious to avoid "the ruthless self-absorption of old age", as one writer puts it. One day, my ruminations were interrupted by a telephone call from Walcott. He mumbled in my ear that St Lucia would be organizing a Nobel Laureate week during which his 75th birthday was to be honoured. Eddie Baugh had been invited to deliver the 2005 Derek Walcott Lecture and there was to be a public poetry reading in which Walcott wished me to take part. I was stunned, even as I heard him mumble, "But just because you white, don't think you can hog the microphone. Only four poems, hear."

The Baughs and I had adjoining rooms at the hotel overlooking Castries harbour. Our official escort advised that she would pick us up the following morning for rehearsal at the Gaiety on Rodney Bay. The Gaiety, a combination community centre and theatre, was a large air-conditioned hall inside a vaguely art deco shell. Walcott and some friends were gathered in the forecourt. I watched him lope towards me and we embraced.

"Let me introduce Seamus Heaney and Marie, his wife," he said. Another shock. I would be reading not with one, but two Nobel Laureates.

I mentioned to Heaney that perhaps we had a mutual friend in the Irish poet Dennis O'Driscoll. Seamus took a step back in disbelief at the coincidence. "And how do you know Dennis?" he asked. I told him about my visit to Ireland and my letter of introduction by Louis Simpson. Literary associations began to fall in place. Heaney was a close friend of O'Driscoll, and considered him to be one of Ireland's outstanding poets, gifted also with an astute critical sense.

I found Heaney's wife to be briskly intelligent, a careful monitor of any repartee involving her husband. On hearing of my friendship with Dennis she interjected, "Oh that O'Driscoll, he knows more about poetry than anyone else in the world, including my husband." During a break, I rushed to a Castries bookstore to buy one of Heaney's books for him to inscribe for me. I selected *Finders Keepers*. It was dedicated to O'Driscoll. More bonding.

Seamus has fine lips enclosed between two heavy apostrophes of cheek. The nose is nondescript, not quite *retrousse*, "granny" glasses perched on the tip. The eyes seldom open to the full round of their circumference, narrow slits in the strong St. Lucia light, giving him a penetrating, insightful gaze. The forehead is almost completely curtained behind a fringe of frizzy hair, worn as a skull cap. This makes him look something like a cross between a leprechaun and a middle-aged Hamlet. Kavanagh, I think it was, wrote about "the wink and elbow jab" of Irish conversation. When you say something that hits the mark with Heaney he points an index finger at you, waist high, thrusts it forward and retracts it quickly into a chuckle.

I was almost incapacitatingly nervous for the public reading. The theatre was full to capacity, the audience headed by the Governor General, who is a woman. The readers were aligned in the front row and I found myself between Baugh and Walcott, Heaney at the end of the row. It had been decided that there would be no individual introductions; each poet would follow his predecessor to the podium, Eddie Baugh to be the first. He finished his reading with a brilliant new poem entitled "Black Sand" and returned to his seat in a fusillade of applause. My turn was next. As I mounted the steps to Olympus it occurred to me that whatever my rank in order of merit, I was ontologically the senior to all the others. I might not have been wiser, but I was indisputably older than all the other poets of the conclave. It was this truth, fragile though it may be, that helped to calm my trepidation.

I shared with the audience my conviction down the years that Walcott would one day win the Nobel Prize for literature. Unable to make the trip to Stockholm, I had to settle for writing a poem about the occasion, which we were only able to watch on a black and white television set in Kingston. I referred to this as "poetry of consolation", a theme that I used to link the four poems I delivered. "Watching Walcott Receive his Nobel Prize" is a slight work, fashioned around the conceit that there was a numbing sameness about the Nobel ceremony, the Laureates all men, all in formal wear, all sitting on identical chairs thinking the same Laureate thoughts. The verse ends:

> Four of the five wore patent leather shoes
> as is the custom but one,
> when he crossed his legs, displayed
> a pair of mid-calf boots zippered on the left
> wrinkled but fortunately black.
> And that was another way
> We could distinguish Walcott from the rest.

Applause mixed with laughter. The next poem was about sexual awakening and I pointed out that its title was "Ablution", not "Absolution". Being a poor boy having to shower under an outside stand-pipe does not foreclose the joys of sexual fantasies – another aspect of poetry as consolation. The poem ends:

> ... could what they say about
> cold showers still be true if this poem
> only tingles into life
> at the remembered shock of early morning water

More applause, enthusiastic, louder laughter.

The third poem was a fantasy of another sort – an imagined boating accident in which my family is thrown into the sea where "the coral claims its right of encrustation/secreting new monuments for another generation." But even in recording such a disaster there is poetry of consolation.

> My right hand, wrist manacled in sand,
> groping for the log book and a pen.

In the final poem, I am the old man the audience sees at the podium, "all other lusts but looking leached away". Like Cezanne, who compulsively painted Sainte-Victoire, plumbing the horizon with the handle of the brush,

> I have learned to measure grandeur with a squint,
> Moiety of all those mountains even faith can't move.

More applause, enthusiastic, louder laughter.

Then it was Walcott's turn, the highlight of his reading a poem entitled "Sainte Lucie", much of it in Creole, which ends simply:

C'est la moi sorti;
Is there that I born

I remembered that when it was first published and we read it in Jamaica, Doreen had tears in her eyes.

Seamus read his four poems in a clear but restrained voice. He ended with the poem about the sudden, unexpected death of his little brother, buried in a four-foot coffin, one foot for each year of the infant's life. The audience response was stunned silence, then prolonged applause.

The following evening, Eddie Baugh delivered the Walcott lecture, a brilliant presentation entitled "Travelling with Walcott". But as usually happens in the West Indies, questions thrown at Baugh from the audience after the lecture implied that Walcott was not sufficiently "Black" in his poetic priorities. Baugh tried to deal diplomatically with the heckling, but Seamus, sensing that perhaps the discussion was getting off track, stood up beside Walcott in the front row and quoted Gerard Manley Hopkins that it is love, not ideology, that ultimately defines a poet's greatness.

Another epiphany awaited me. We were a group, Eddie and Sheila Baugh, Seamus and Marie Heaney, Derek Walcott and Sigrid, Gerd Stern and me. Sigrid, a white European, has lived with Walcott for many years. Imposingly tall and with the echo of a foreign accent on her tongue, she has faithfully endured Walcott's moods and eccentricities. In turn, I have the feeling that Walcott's career would have unravelled without her loyalty, strength and astonishing ability to sustain his "highs" and comfort his "lows". Like one of his poems, it seemed that craft and inspiration worked together as the bedrock of their love.

Gerd Stern, a gaunt, elderly, gentle Jew wore his yarmulke with pride. In his youth he had been a member of the "beat" generation, a personal friend of Kerouac and many of his tribe. Artistic and at home with the avant garde, he had travelled the world as a participant in performance presentations, his own and others, which he videoed for his personal archives. Perhaps taken at first as a "hanger on", it soon became clear to Eddie Baugh and me that his range of friendships were two-way encounters. His conversation was enlightening. In any company his cultural and literary *bona fides* easily established themselves, and I count him as a good friend. A man of independent means, he is generous with his hospitality and through his "Intermedia Foundation" he sponsored and financed CDs of poetry readings by Eddie Baugh and myself.

On the morning after the public poetry reading, our group at Walcott's made a pilgrimage to the church in Roseau where, behind the altar, Dunstan St Omer, Gregorias in Walcott's *Another Life*, had painted his famous mural, celebrated by Walcott in his poem "Altarpiece of the Roseau Valley Church". The mural looked as fresh as the day it was painted, brought to life with commercial emulsion paint, full of action and compassion, African in feeling, influenced by Fernand Léger in style and execution.

We were the only people in the church, a privileged congregation clustered in one pew. Derek, who must have planned it, announced that he would read his famous tribute. He had brought with him a copy of his *Collected Poems* but was not able to find the poem. Eddie Baugh located it for him while we sat in silence to witness the mystical union of paint and poetry. It was a transcendental experience for me, cloistered with two Nobel Laureates, trying to preserve in memory every detail of the encounter.

We were invited to Derek's house for lunch, but he insisted on the ritual of his daily swim. My psoriasis was acting up, too much artistic stress, so I begged off. I was given the freedom of the Walcott complex and after the group's departure I trespassed into the empty studio where Derek paints and writes his poetry.

In the middle of the room there was a wooden refectory table, large enough to seat perhaps thirty monks. Around the periphery of the table Sigrid, I assume, had arranged neat piles of Derek's working materials, note pads, pens, pencils, paint brushes, novels, poetry collections and reference books. Some of his paintings decorated the walls, and in a bay window overlooking the sea, his faithful manual Olivetti typewriter kept solitary vigil. I felt that my trespass violated Derek's hospitality, so I retreated to the main house to await the return of the swimming party. Then came the farewells, a towering kiss from Sigrid, a peck on the cheek from Marie, the embrace of Seamus and Derek still warm on my shoulder.

Sleep came slowly on the last night in the hotel. The St Lucia experience was at one and the same time a highlight and culmination of my life. How many more years might I have to live? I am not perhaps as obsessed with death as Walcott, but it would be unnatural for a man of my age not to speculate. St Paul avers that no man can be sure of his own salvation – a terrifying insight. On the other hand, my confessor tells me that God not only forgives sins but forgets them. This may be a persuasive reason not to write a memoir lest it jog His memory. But I believe in the unconditional love of a divine creator (all artists love what they have made) and take comfort from Heine's conclusion that "the business of God is mercy".

The foundation of the happiness that Doreen and I now share in the evening of our lives is that we are free of most of the contingencies that ownership breeds. Exposed to the radiation of Scholastic philosophy, I believe firmly in the Aristotelian wisdom that life is a process of moving from potency to act, a constant striving to maximize all our God-given gifts, not to exercise one talent only, but to advance on a broad and balanced front, encompassing a range of explorations and epiphanies. This is what I understand an examined life to be. I have also believed in the ideal of the well rounded man, paunch and all. My sister saw me as a Renaissance man, who has paid for his capitalist sins with public service.

The plane took off for the return trip to Jamaica and I prayed for a safe flight. I closed my eyes, caught a whiff of Kellogg's asthma remedy in the cabin and knew that my mother was near, no longer too distracted to listen to my version of how, once upon a time, I read my poetry in public with two Nobel laureates.

CHAPTER 31

THE WEANING AND THE WINNOWING

Memories of childhood from the vantage point of age are probably no
more accurate than pronouncements about age by the young. Parent or
child – we are prisoners of the present. For this reason I have as little faith
in history as I have in prophecy. But how we choose to remember is a
present fact that can be recorded and what we remember becomes
significant both by virtue of what we include and what we exclude.

At the age of 85 I officially retired from the business world and we
relocated from our hilltop townhouse to a small apartment on the plain.
This involved disposing of many of our cherished possessions, most
painfully my library of books of and about poetry. The collection
comprised some 350 volumes that I donated to the University of the
West Indies Library. The books were graciously received by the Librar-
ian but never officially acknowledged as a gift, though they can now be
found listed on the internet as the Ralph Thompson collection.

Then began the "Weaning" – God's way of gradually diminishing the
pleasures of the world in order to excite in us a greater desire for the
rewards of heaven. No one can outclass Shakespeare's description of this
process in *As You Like It* with the awful conclusion: "Sans teeth, sans
eyes, sans taste, sans everything". Thankfully, none of this has yet
afflicted me, but I am saddened by the passing of so many friends and
associates younger than me. The list is daunting: Audrey my beloved
younger sister who had no business dying before me; David Lyons,
Doreen's brother; John Figueroa, John Hearne, Wayne Brown, Jack
Moore, my tutor at USF, Alan Ross of *London Magazine*, Louis Simpson,
Seamus Heaney, Joseph Brodsky, Dennis O'Driscoll; and business
associates whose destinies have been closely entwined with mine, most
shockingly Desmond Blades and Maurice Facey.

There will come a time when the weaning and the winnowing
amalgamate themselves into one heavy sack of sorrow, under whose
weight, slung over one shoulder, we trudge the road of old age. I am

aware that in the existential order, the man Jesus never experienced old
age, so I make bold to dedicate the following poem to him.

> At Eighty-five I have outlived my penis
> and by your Grace there is now a peace of sorts.
> But how to cope with memory, its walls
> scrawled with the graffiti of recall, itch
> lingering still, dreaming the ecstasy of scratch.
> But I have learned from Job how to bargain
> with you, Lord, that after my death you will contra
> the tribulations of my journey against
> the penances assigned for sin,
> by your grace the divine books balanced.

There has been one further award, when the Institute of Jamaica
notified me that in October 2015 they would be awarding me the Silver
Musgrave medal for distinguished eminence in the field of Literature.

If I die before Doreen I request that my funeral service be held at SS
Peter and Paul church, the pedestal with the urn containing my ashes in
almost the exact spot where, at our wedding, I stood watching Doreen
floating down the aisle. How radiant she was and is!

I recall the Scholastic definition of a habit as "a tendency added to
nature", and its surprising, romantic corollary that "beauty is a habit".
What this means is that even if Doreen's waist is no longer as small as it
once was, no matter that gravity is beginning to pull on her breasts, this
is all irrelevant for she has established for herself a habit of beauty, an
inbuilt tendency that over the years has become an integral part of her
total being. Even in death she will be beautiful.

THE END

INDEX

11ᵗʰ engineers (WWI First US regiment to see action in France), 19

133 Hope Road, 86

A Midsummer Night's Dream, 34, 35

Abeng, revolutionary broadsheet, 114

Abrahams Anthony (ex JLP Minister of Tourism), 196

Adams, Charles, 117, 128

Adams, Major Ralph, 64, 77, 79, 80, 81

Aetna Insurance Company p150

Agricultural Credit Bank, 163

Agro 21, 159, 160, 161, 162, 163, 164, 168, 173

Allerdyce Avenue, 87, 110

Alpha Academy High School, 16, 28

American Academy and Institute of Arts and Letters, 203

American Civil Liberties Union, 151

American Embassy, 146

American Polish Society, 46

Andover High School, 148

Andress, Ursula, 91

Anthony (Tony) Spaulding, left wing PNP minister, 135, 138, 139

Antigua, 97, 99

Antoinette (mother's sister, "Aunt Nettie"), 10, 21, 23, 95; Desmond (son), 21

Aquinas, Thomas, 12, 42, 171

Arawak Hotel, St. Ann's Bay, 100, 103

Ardeche, France, 156

Ariel (Canada), 192

As You Like It, 213

Ashenheim, Darryl, 117

Ashenheim, Leslie, 129, 132, 133

Ashenheim, Richard, 94

Ashenheim, Sir Neville, 91, 94

Astaire, Fred and Ginger Rogers, 46

Asthma, 10, 29, 50, 212

Aston (worker at Wherry Wharf), 16, 17

Atlanta, 175

Aunt Bella, 15, 18, 19, 25, 27, 29, 39, 45, 56, 86

Aunt Val (an Isaacs' cousin), 123

Austen, Jane, 88

Axel's Castle (play, Villier), 144

Babu, the gardener, 13

Bahamas, 147

Baker, Captain, 68, 70

Bangkok, Thailand, 73, 74, 75

Bank of Nova Scotia, 96, 146

Barbara, daughter of Uncle Tony, 16

Barovier, Fay (secretary), 200

Barrow, Frank, 121

Baugh, Edward, 8, 191, 192, 194, 197, 207, 208, 210, 211; poem, "Travelling with Walcott", 210

Baugh, Sheila, 210

Belcher Avenue, Florida (Thompson residence on), 149

Bentley, Professor, 151

Bernard Lodge (Kingston), 161, 162, 163

Bird, V.C. (Chief Minister of Antigua), 99

Bishop Emmet (Uncle Bishop), 9, 19, 25, 29, 34, 49, 50

Bishop McEleney, 86

Black Power, 84, 114, 135

Black Sand (Edward Baugh), 208

Blades, Desmond, 124, 169, 161, 170, 171, 173, 176, 177, 180, 183, 207, 213

Blades, P.B., 170

Blades, Peggy, 161, 169, 170, 180

Blaise, Herbert (Chief Minister of Grenada), 99

Blake, Evon, 90

Blake, Viv, 121

Bloom, Harold, 205

Blue Hole, 124

Blue Mountain Inn, 33, 108

Blue Sisters, The (nuns), 11

Boston, 25, 60, 207

Bournemouth bathing complex, 18

Bracknell Avenue (Thompson residence on), 170

Brando, Marlon, 206

Brandon, Mr, 34

Breakfast Club (radio show), 196

Breen, Tommy, 51, 52 and family, 50, 51, 52

British Overseas Stores, 98

Brodsky, Joseph, 203, 205, 206, 213

Brookline, Massachusetts, 202

Brooklyn Navy Yard, 57

Brother Man (Roger Mais), 141

Brother Mark, 42

Brotherhood of Railway Engineers &
Conductors, 47

Brown (Issa family chauffeur), 103

Brown, Arthur (Governor of Central
Bank), 132

Brown, Roscoe Lee, 205

Brown, Wayne (Trinidadian poet), 136,
194, 197, 213

Brown's Town, 86

Buddhism, 75

Buffalo, 111, 154

Bustamante Industrial Trade Union,
176, 177

Bustamante, Alexander, 22

C.D. Alexander Realty Company, 183

Calcutta, 73, 75

Calvary Cemetery, Kingston, 78, 123

Camaguey, 45

Cambridge (University), 10, 191

Camp Lejeune, North Carolina, 19

Camperdown, 11, 13, 18, 20, 27

Campion College, Jamaica, 148

Canada, 144, 154

Canadian Air Force, 31

Canary Islands, 155; Las Palmas, 155

Cargill, Morris, 35

Carib 5, 192

Caribbean Broilers, 179

Caribbean Review of Books, 196

Caribeach Hotels Limited, 99, 116

Carman and Bruce, later Price
Waterhouse, 93, 116, 180

Carter, Martin (Guyanese poet), 198

Carter, Reggie, 90

Castries, 208; harbour, St. Lucia, 207

Castro, Fidel, 143

Catholic Church, 19, 25, 26

Catholicism, 10, 12, 28, 31, 42, 46, 50,
64, 69, 74, 78, 82, 86, 95, 114, 149,
170, 180, 186

Cavaliers Great House, 9

Caymanas, 78, 94, 163

Central Park, NY, 204

Chaplin, Adrian ("Mr Chaps"), 31

Chaucer, 150, 152

Cheever, John, 203

China, Chinese, 130, 143

Choate Rosemary Hall, Connecticut,
148

Clark Air Force Base, Manila, 74

Clayton (Alabama), 79, 80, 81

Clearwater, Florida, 144, 147, 149, 150,
153, 156, 157, 160, 202

Cocoa Beach, Florida, 153, 158, 165,
167

Colgate, 180, 181, 182

Colonial Development Corporation
(CDC), 97, 99, 101

Columbia Presbyterian Hospital, New
York, 142

Columbia University, 66, 137, 151, 193

Commonwealth Development Corporation (CDC), 116

Commonwealth Development Finance
Corporation (CDFC), 116

Communism, 115, 136, 192

Compton, John (Minister of Trade and
Industry St Lucia), 99

Connery, Sean, 91

Constant Spring Hotel, 38

Coore, David, 121

Coppola, Francis Ford, *Apocalypse Now*,
205

Coral Gardens uprising, 114

Coward, Noel, 17

Cowell, Richard p96

Cross Roads, 20, 35, 41

Cuba, 114

Cugat, Xavier, 38

D. Henderson and Company, 98, 103

Dante, Alighieri, 105

de Gaulle, General, 141

de Lisser, Dick, 89

de Lisser, Jack, 43, 44, 45, 46, 55, 82,
86, 143, 154, 158

de Lisser, Joan p91

de Lisser, Normadelle, 55

De Quincey, Thomas, 202

de Vries, Erwin, 145, 171
deCordova, Leonard, 98, 103, 106, 129, 132
Democratic Socialism, 134
Devon House, 108
Dhahran, Saudi Arabia, 73, 74, 76
Dickinson, Emily, 206
diDonna, Lou, 56, 57
Dillsbury Avenue (Thompson residence), p123, 132, 160, 198, 202
Disfibrogenemia, 142
Disney World, Florida, 203
Dominion Trader and *Dominion Pine* (ships), 113
Donlevy, Brian, 51
Dorsey, Tommy, 38
Dr No (film), 91
Duke Street, 93, 110, 146, 161, 169
Dundy, Elaine, 55
Dunn, Oswald, 124
Early Childhood Commission, 189, 190
Eastern Banana Estates, 163
Eastern Caribbean, 96, 97, 98
Edinburgh, 149; Borthwick Castle, 149; Mary Queen of Scots, 149; Earl of Bothwell, 149
Edna (Lyons' housekeeper), 84
Edward McNally, Fr, 53, 54
Elks Club, 47
Elliot, T.S., 151; "The Hollow Men", 206
Ellison, Ralph, 203
Essex House Hotel, 206
Exeter College, 10
Facey, Maurice, 105, 106, 113, 116, 117, 124, 125, 128, 129, 130, 131, 134, 135, 136, 138, 139, 144, 157, 178, 179, 200, 213
Facey, Valerie, 132, 134, 144, 194
Farrar, Straus and Giraux (Walcott's publishers), 200, 205
Federal Environmental Protection Agency (EPA, USA), 167
Federal Republic of Germany, 107
Feltner, Captain Robert, 59, 60, 63
Ferry Irrigation Scheme, 11

Fielding, Clem (Grandma's brother), 31
Fielding, Hannah (Grandma), 9, 18, 20, 21, 27, 28, 31
Figueroa, John, 152, 194, 197, 198, 213
Financial Intelligence Unit, 143
Finders Keepers (Seamus Heaney), 208
Finzi, Mr, 35
First National City Bank (now Citibank), 129, 130, 131, 181, 182
Fletcher, Douglas, 194
Foot, Sir Hugh (Governor), 56
Fordham Drama Club, 46
Fordham Hospital, 44
Fordham Law School, 53, 54
Fordham University p.10, 38, 41, 42, 43, 44, 45, 46, 47, 49, 53, 56, 152, 180
Forest Industries Development Co., 163
Fr Ballou, 32
Fr Welsh, 31
Fr William Hannas, "Wild Bill", 32
Frankfurter, Judge Felix, 62
Harris, Fred (H&L board), 128
Freeman, David, 158
Fresno, 150
Frost, Robert, 206
Gaiety on Rodney Bay, 207
Ganja, 134
Gayson, Colonel, 124
Geddes Grant, T., 183
General Accident Insurance, 183
George, Emil, 121
Georgia Pacific Corporation, 106
Germany, 113
Glasspole, Sir Florizel (Governor General), 164
Gleaner, The, 9, 28, 94, 100, 103, 129, 131, 133, 139, 184, 187, (photo 188), 192, 196
Glick, Dennis, 29
Goldcrest Farms Ltd, 173, 174, 175, 177
Gordon House, 133
Gordon Town, 33
Gordon, "Whiskey", 98

Gordon, Richard (son-in-law), 149
Grace Kennedy, 161, 176
Grand Central, 59
Grand Concourse Paradise Theatre,
    44
Graves, Robert, "White Goddess", 38,
    39
Greene, Adrian, 68, 69, 71, 72
Grenada, 97, 99
Guam, 73
Guys Hospital, London, 149
Half-Way Tree Road, 144
Hall, Mr ("Napoleon"), 99, 101
Hamburg, 95; Vier Jahreszeiten hotel,
    95
Hamilton, Alex, 94
Hamilton, Nurse, 120
Hamlet, 32
Haneda Air Force Base, Tokyo, 62, 63,
    64, 66, 73, 79
Hanover Street, 110
Harbour Street, 134
Hardware and Lumber Limited (H &
    L), 128, 129, 130, 131, 132, 133, 135,
    154
Harland (attorney), 168
Harris, Harry, 46
Harrison, John (Seprod) 106, 107, 109,
    173, 178
Harry, Caswell, 93
Harvard, 148
Hazel Johnston Ballet School, 35
Heaney, Seamus, 207, 208, 210, 211,
    213; Marie Heaney, 207, 211
Hearne, John, 139 (picture, 140), 141,
    142, 152, 197, 213
Hearne, Leeta, 139, 141, 142
Heine, Heinrich, 212
Henriques, Dossie, 129, 132
Heroin (opium), 68, 71, 75
Hickham Air Base, Honolulu, 77
Hill, Ken, 121
Hofus Hardware Company, Honduras,
    103
Holy Childhood Convent, 34
Holy Cross College, Massachusetts,
    88

Honduras, 103, 128, 155, 157, 168
Hopefield Avenue, 86
Hopkins, Gerard Manley, 206, 210
Hostettler, Major, 69
Huie, Albert (artist), 171
Hunter College, 45
Hurricane Gilbert, 164, 168
Hyatt, Charles, 90
Ibsen, Hendrik, 151, 152; *Peer Gynt*,
    152
IMF, 168
Immaculate Conception High School,
    38
Imperial Palace, Japan, 65
Imperial Riding Academy of Japan, 65
Impressionists, 7
Institute of Jamaica, 214
Intermedia Foundation (Gerd Stern),
    210
Irma La Douce (play), 97
Isaacs, Henry (great grandfather), 110
Isaacs, Michael (Uncle Mike) 10, 11,
    13, 14, 16, 17, 19, 24, 25, 26, 31,
    38, 50, 53, 56, 86, 105, 109
Isaacs, Ralph Henry (grandfather,
    "Julian"), 9, p.15, 21, 85
Israel, 74
Issa Joe (Abe's younger brother), 88,
    96, 98
Issa, Abe, 86, 88, 89, 90, 91, 92, 93,
    94, 95, 96, 97, 98, 100, 102, 103,
    104, 105, 107, 169
Issa, Elias (Abe's father), 88
Issa, Richard, 161
Iwo Jima, 73
Jackson, Dickie, 164, 168, 173, 175
Jaffo The Calypsonian (Ian McDonald),
    191
Jain, Sushil, 178
Jamaica Central Bank, 18
Jamaica Coconut Board, 176
Jamaica Defence Force, 164
Jamaica House, 137, 160
Jamaica Journal, 191, 192
Jamaica Labour Party (JLP), 108, 114,
    115, 139, 162
Jamaica National Gallery, 144

Jamaica Observer, 183, 194
Jamaica Stock Exchange, 128, 129, 176, 179
Jamaica Teachers Association, 187
Jamaica Tourist Association, 89
Jamaica, 10, 11, 15, 17, 18, 19, 20, 21, 22, 25, 26, 28, 29, 33, 34, 36, 39, 41, 42, 43, 44, 45, 50, 52, 53, 54, 56, 57, 58, 74, 77, 79, 81, 82, 84, 85, 88, 89, 90, 91, 92, 95, 96, 97, 98, 100, 102, 103, 104, 105, 106, 107, 111, 112, 114, 115, 117, 121, 122, 123, 124, 129, 130, 131, 132, 135, 139, 141, 142, 144, 145, 146, 147, 148, 149, 151, 152, 153, 154, 159, 160, 164, 167, 168, 170, 171, 175, 176, 180, 181, 186, 192, 193, 194, 204, 210, 212
Jamaican Defence Force, 136
Jamaican Georgian Society, 122
Jamaican Historical Society, 122
Jamaican National Literary competition, 194
Japan, 62, 66, 76, 77, 78, 79, 82, 122, 138
Jesuits, 9, p.12, 31, 41, 42, 43, 86, 91, 92
Jewish background, 74, 78, 82, 129
Jewish regiment, 10
Jobson, Mr (land surveyor), 94
Johnson, President L.B.J., 81
Johnson, Pat Mar, 121
Jubilee Hospital, Kingston, 120
Judah, Douglas, 86, 125
Judge Advocate Generals (JAG), 62, 63, 64, 68
Judicial Services Commission, 134
Kapo (artist), 171
Karachi, 76
Kavanagh, P.J., 208
Keats, John, 202; Keatsian "negative capability", 158
Keeling, Sir John (Head of London and Yorkshire Trust), 101, 102
Kennan, George F., 204
Kent, Mr (balance-sheet expert), 96
Kerouac, Jack, 210

Khouri, Dr Emile, 142
Kido, Colonel, 65
King John (Shakespeare) 34
King Jr., Martin Luther, 81
King's House, 82
Kings House, 164
Kingston and St Andrew Corporation, The, 9
Kingston Cricket Club, 110
Kingston Public Hospital p92
Kingston Stock Exchange p128
Kingston Waterfront Development, 109
Kingston, 11, 15, 16, 17, 20, 22, 23, 24, 26, 27, 33, 45, 56, 78, 87, 89, 90, 108, 115, 124, 125, 130, 134, 144, 160, 161, 171 (photo) 172, 194
Knutsford Park, 82, 92, 93, 94
Kokfeld, Albert, Brigadier General, USAF, 72
Korean War, 57, 58, 60, 69
Koven, Murray, 96, 100, 102
Kunitz, Stanley, 203
Kyk-Over-Al, 191, 192
Lagos, Nigeria, 99
Lake, Robert, 128
Lanin, Lester, 38
Lapidus, Ted, 100
Law of the Sea Conference Centre, 160
Leeds (U.K.), 192
Leger, Fernand, 211
Lennard, John, 194
Leprosy (Hansen's disease), 17
Lever Brothers, 181
Levy, Horace, 114
Liberation theology, 114
Liberty – its Use and Abuse, 53
Lightbourne, Robert, 114, 115
Liguanea Plaza, 103
Lindo, Archie, 29
Logan, Viv, 160, 163, 164
Loire Valley, 139, 141
London and Yorkshire Trust, 101, 102
London Magazine, 192, 193
London, 95, 141, 162, 164
Lord, Jim, 116

Lorna (domestic servant), 12
Love Canal tragedy 1979, 167
Lucea, 113
Lurline (housekeeper), 84, 171
Lyons, Ann, (David Lyon's second wife), 87
Lyons, David (Doreen's brother), 82 (photo, 83), 86, 87, 92, 110, 213
Lyons, Emmanuel (Frank's grandfather), 110
Lyons, Ermyn, née Ellis (Doreen's mother), 82 (photo, 83), 95, 110, 156
Lyons, Francis Emmanuel (Mr Frankie, Doreen's father), 82, (photo, 83), 86, 87, 106, 110, 122
MacArthur, General, 65
Magdalen School for boys, Oxford, 149
Maiden Hotel, New Delhi, 76
Mais, Roger, 139, 141
Major Twigger, 26
Malcolm (caretaker at Shadowbrook cabin), 24
Mandela Highway, 128
Manila, 73, 74
Manley, Beverley, 137, 196,
Manley, Edna, 33, 136
Manley, Michael, Prime Minister, 84, 88, 89, 108, 115, 116, 134, 135, 136, 137, 138, 139, 143, 154, 159, 171, 196; "Politics of Participation", 137
Manley, Norman (Chief Minister of Jamaica), 94, 193
Marcuse, Herbert, 114
Mary Burnham (US prep school), 84
Matalon Group, 117
Matalon, Mayer, 117, 160
Matalon, Moses, (Kingston Waterfront Development Company), 109
Matalon, Zacky, 139
Maxwell, John, 89
Mayfair, Lyons' mansion, 82, 86, 87, 110
McCullan, Tom, 69, 70
McDonald, Ian (Guyanese poet & editor), 191, 197

McLeish, Archibald, 203
McMillan, Dudley, 35
Medical Associates Hospital, 123, 142
Merrill's Raiders, 51
Metivier, Norlene, 202, 203
Metropolitan Museum, New York, 205
Mexico, 112; Mexico City, 112
Miami Veterans' Hospital, 143
Miami, 41, 45, 81, 87, 100, 106, 147, 153, 162, 175
Milton, John, 151
Minetzhagen, Mr, 97
Ministry of Agriculture, 160, 163, 168
Ministry of Education, 187, 189
Miss Steadman's Riding Academy, 38, 65
Mona Rehabilitation Centre, 121
Montego Bay, 89, 113, 114
Montgomery, Richard, 200
Montoya (Mexican artist), 171
Moody, Dr Ludlow, 28, 29, 35, 78
Moore, Jack B. (University of South Florida), 151, 213
Morais Audley, 92, 93
Morning Magazine, 121
Morris, Mervyn, 8, 197, 198; "Toasting the Muse", 198; "*I Been There, Sort Of*" *New and Selected Poems* ,198
Morte D'Arthur (Tennyson), 28
Motherwell, Robert, 204
Mt Saint Vincent Academy, 19, 28, 45
Moving On, poetry collection, 14, 49, 171, 192 (photo, 195)
Mr Coombs, 24
Munro (Jamaican boarding school), 193
Myers, Arthur, 86
Myers, Fletcher and Gordon, 98
Myrtle Bank Hotel, 89, 90, 91, 92, 93, 94
Nacogdoches, 175
Naipaul, V S, *The Mimic Men*, 198
Nakama (Master painter) 66, 171
Nama, Sigrid (Walcott's companion), 210, 211
Nassau, 96
Nathan's, 91, 105

Nathaniel (boyhood friend), 25, 26, 29, 78
National Commercial Bank (Jamaica), 173, 182; Don Banks, director , 173, 182
National Gallery of Jamaica, 125
National Investment Bank of Jamaica, 160, 163
National Volunteers Association (NVO), 107, 108
Native Americans, 50
Nelson, Edith (senior officer of Bustamante Industrial Trade Union) 135, 136
Nethersole, "Crab," 18
Nettleford, Professor Rex, (chair of Prime Minister's Exploratory Committee on Art and Culture) 34
New Delhi, 76
New Kingston, 92, 94, 138
New York University, 194
New York, 19, 28, 41, 42, 47, 52, 55, 57, 62, 73, 77, 95, 101, 123, 129, 130, 142, 151, 162, 181, 193, 204, 205, 206
New York's Presbyterian Medical Centre, 52
Newport East, 109, 113
Niagara Falls, 59, 60
Niebuhr, Reinhold, "Serenity Prayer", 170
Nobel Prize for literature, 202, 207, 208
North American Life building, 134
North Korea, North Koreans, 68
North Street, 31, 110
Northeastern University, Massachusetts, 84
Nozzle, Dr, 142
O'Driscoll, Dennis (Irish poet and critic) 196, 208, 213
Obeah, 134
Ocho Rios, 89
Orange Street fire, 139
Ornstein, Mr, 100
Osmose, 110, 111, 153, 154
Ottawa, 154

Oxford (University), 10, 148
Oxford Road, 87
Packman, Neuwahl & Rosenberg, 158
Painting, 125; "Lovers" (photo), 127; "Port Antonio" (photo), 127; "Pavilion", 125, (photo, 126); "San San Beach" (photo), 126
Pam (first girlfriend), 36, 38, 39, 45, 46, 66
Pan Jamaican (Pan-Jam), 116, 117, 118, 125, 128, 129, 130, 131, 132, 133, 134, 135, 138, 142, 144, 157, 178, 179, 200
Pan-Florida, 166, 168, 157, 158, 169
Papp, Joseph (theatre guru), 204
Parboosingh, Dr Ivan, 120, 121
Paris, 55, 139, 141, 142
Parkinson's Disease, 123
Parks Air Force Base, California, 79
Parsons, Ted, 101, 102, 103, 107
Patois (Jamaican), 16, 113
Patriot Act, 167
Patterson, Robert, 28
Pearl (nanny), 121
Pearl, Dennis p116
Peepal Tree Press, 8, 191, 192, 194, 196, 197, 202
Peer Gynt (Ibsen), 46
Pegasus Hotel (Kingston), 160
Pei, I M. (architect), 203, 204
Penn Warren, Robert, 203
People's National Party (PNP), 108, 134, 135, 139, 142, 143, 162, 168, 177
Perkins, Wilmot (Motty), 184
Petot, François, 111, 112, 154, 155, 157, 158, 165, 168
Pilocarpine case, 68, 69, 71
Pines, Millsborough Avenue (Thompson residence), 160
Poems by Ralph Thopmson quoted: "Goodbye Aristotle, So Long America" from Moving On, 49; "Jamaica Farewell", The Denting of a Wave, 147; "Watching Walcott Receive his Nobel Prize", 209; "Ablution", 209; "Straight from the

Horse's Mouth", 40; "Florida", *The Denting of a Wave*, 149; "Good-Bye Picasso", 193; "Harbour View", 196; "Roots", from *Taking Words for a Walk*, 190; "The Colour of Conscience", 17, 29, 85; "Vigil", in *Moving On*, 171; "Carpenters", 24; "Cycling", 34; "He Knows What Height Is", 24; "Uncle Seymour", 14
Port Antonio, 125
Poughkeepsie Elks Club, 123
Poynting, Jeremy, 8, 191, 192
Prendergast, Tessa , 55
Previn, Andre, 51
Prime Minister's Badge of Honour, 122
Princess Margaret, 33
Pringle, John, 91, 108
Protestants, 66, 74
Proust, Marcel, 111
Psoriasis, 184
Pulitzer Prize, 193
Randall, Judah and Harry (lawyers), 93, 94, 96, 98. 125
Rastafarian, Rastafarianism, 114
Reading University (UK), 16
Reduit Beach, St Lucia (photo, 201)
Rendell, Lord, 99
Rent Restriction Board, 143
Reserve Officers Training Corps (ROTC), 44, 49, 57
Retreat House, 19
Rhodes, William (Citibank president), 129, 130
Richards, Governor (of Jamaica) 22, 23, 26
Richmond, Virginia, 154
Rinella, Jim, 159, 160, 161
Rivera, Diego, 112
Rodney, Dr Walter, 115
Romero, Cesar, 51
Rose Hill Campus, 42, 45, 53, 54
Ross, Alan (editor of *London Magazine)*, 192, 193, 202, 213
Rossetti, Christina, 206
Rousseau, Peter, 144
Routledge Encyclopaedia of Post-

Colonial Literatures, 194
Royal Commonwealth Society, 122
Ryerson Polytechnic Institute, Canada, 148
Saigon, 75
Salt Lake City, 175
Sam Isaacs funeral parlour, 110
Samms-Vaughan, Dr Maureen, 189
San Francisco, 62, 150
San San, 124, 161, 169; San San Bay, 124; San San villa, Gremlin Hill, 124, 125, 139, 144
Sanger, Margaret, 151
Santa Barbara, 150
Sarju (salesman), 112, 113
Saturday Evening Post, 33
Schnoor, Hans (Uncle Hans, Antoinette's husband), 21, 22, 86, 95, 106, 113
Scotland, 17
Scott, Gary (son-in-law), 147, 148, 155, 157, 158, 168
Seaga, Edward (PM), 106, 107, 108, 109, 139, 159, 160, 163, 164, 168, 170, 173
Selma-Montgomery civil rights march, 81
Senior Cambridge Entrance exam, 31, 32
Seprod Limited, 106, 107, 108, 109, 171, 173, 174, 175, 176, 177, 178, 179, 180, 181, 182, 183, 196
Shadowbrook, 23, 24, 25, 26, 33, 86
Shakespeare, William, 204, 213
Shaw, Artie, 38
Shaw, G.B, 151
Shearer, Hugh (former PM), 114, 115, 176
Sheen, Bishop Fulton, 92
Sheraton Hotel, NY, 206
Sherry Netherland Hotel, Manhattan, 46
Silver Musgrave medal, 214
Simpson, Herbert, 193
Simpson, Louis (Jamaican poet), 193, 194, 196, 208, 213
Singer Sewing machines, 16

Singer, Isaac Bashevis, 203
Sister Legurie, 28
Sister Rita, 11
Slipe Road, 98
Smith, William Jay, 203
Smith-Bingham, Denis, 124, 125
Snow, C P., 203
Sontag, Susan, 203
South Camp Road, 20, 23, 24, 25, 27,
    28, 29, 33, 34, 38, 39, 56, 63, 65,
    88
Sovereign Centre, 190
Spring Plains, 160
Springfield, 18, 20
SS Peter and Paul Roman Catholic
    Church, 86, 214
St Andrew, 17, 23, 82, 87
St George's College, 28, 31, 32, 34,
    36, 164
St Lucia, 97, 99, 207, 211; Governor
    General, 208
St Michael Cemetery, Venice, 206
St Omer, Dunstan, mural in Roseau
    church, 211
St Paul, 211
St Clare's, Oxford, 147
St George's College, 9
St Joseph's Hospital,16, 35, 120
St Petersburg USA, 147
Stanford, 148
Stanhope Hotel, New York, 205
State Environmental Protection
    Agency (EPA), 166, 167, 169
Stern, Gerd, 210
Stern, Philip, 13
Stevens, Wallace, 206
Stockholm, 207
Stone, Deryck (lawyer), 100, 124, 154,
    157
Strachan, Pat (editor at Farrar, Straus
    & Giraux), 205
Strindberg, Auguste, 152
Sunnymorn, Lyons' winning horse,
    82
Surridge, Tommy, 154
Syracuse, 150
Taking Words for a Walk (Thompson), 85

Tampa, 148, 150, 153, 157, 165, 168
Taylor, Elizabeth, 52
Tegucigalpa, 155
Terra Nova Hotel, Kingston, 103, 139
The Barretts of Wimpole Street, 34
The Carib Theatre, 35
The Caribbean Examination Council,
    187; CSEC examinations, 187; CXC
    exams, 189
The Caribbean Writer, 192
The Denka, crown prince, 65
The Denting of a Wave (Thompson),
    24, 34, 80, 147, 149, 192
The Dulwich Poetry Festival Anthology
    (UK), 192
The Gold Bug (E.A. Poe), 25
The Mississippi Review (USA), 192
"The Movies" Theatre, 35, 36
The River (Jean Renoir), 52
The Scottish Chiefs (Jane Porter), 25
The Verdict is Yours, 121
Thompson, Audrey (sister), 10, 11,
    12, 14, 18, 19, 21, 22, 23, 25, 26,
    27, 28, 29, 35, 36, 38, 45, 49, 50,
    51, 53, 55, 56, 67, 77, 78, 86, 106,
    158, 186, 213
Thompson, Ralph, family: Doreen
    (Dody, wife), 8, 82 (photo, 83), 85,
    86, 87, 91, 92, 95, 99, 104, 108, 109,
    110, 111, 114, 115, 120, 121, 122,
    124, 125, 137, 138, 139, 141, 144,
    145, 147, 149, 150, 153, 156, 157,
    158, 159, 164, 167, 168, 169, 170,
    171, 180, 181, 182, (photo, 185),
    196, 197, 198, 200, 202, 203, 204,
    205, 206, 210, 212, 214; Deborah,
    Debbie (daughter), 110, 120, 147,
    148, 156, (photo, 185); Elizabeth,
    Liz, (daughter), 109, 121, 146, 147,
    149,156, 158, (photo, 185), 202;
    Stephanie (daughter), 120, 147, 148,
    156, 184, (photo, 185); Larry (son),
    94, 95, 120, 121, 147, 149, 156,
    (photo, 185); Karen (daughter-in-
    law),150; grandchildren: Nicholas,
    148; Sean, 148; Oskar, 149;
    Matthew, 150; Uncle Seymour; 14,

20, 29, 92; Tony (uncle), 10, 11, 13, 16, 20, 27; Vincent (uncle), 10, 11, 19, 41, 55, 62; publications: *View from Mount Diablo, The,* 12, 22, 25, 194, 196; *"Taking Words for a Walk",* *New and Selected Poems,* 198
Thompson, Byron, 176, 177, 178, 183
Thompson, Lawrence (father), 18, 19, 34, 41, 47 (photograph, 48) 49, 50, 59, 62, 86
Thompson, Stephanie, née Isaacs (mother), 9, 12, 13, 14, 15, p.16, p17, 18, 19, 20, 21, 22, 24, 25, 26, 27, 28, 29, 31, 33, 35, 36, 38, 39, 41, 44, 49, 50, 51, 53, 55, 56, 57, 62, 66, 67, 77, 78, 85, 92, 105, 107, 122, 123, 142, 151, 158, 212
Thorbourn, Carol, 28
Tissona, Eli, 160
Titusville, 167
Tokyo General Hospital, 69
Tokyo, 62, 64, 65, 68, 73, 76
Toronto, 93, 96, 100
Torrington Bridge, 115
Touche Ross auditing firm, 28
Touche Ross, 154
Tours, 141; La Pyramide restaurant, 141
Tower Isle Hotel (now Couples), 89
Trabb, Captain, 63, 64, 77
Treasure Island, (R.L. Stevenson), 25
Trilling, Lionel, 137, 150
Trinidad Theatre Workshop, 200, 202
Tropical Plaza, 103
Troy State University, 81
Truman, Harry S, 49
Tulane University, New Orleans, 147, 148
US Supreme Court, 62
Ulysses (Joyce), 32
United States Air Force, 57, (photo, 61), 72, 79, 107
University College London, 149
University Hospital of the West Indies, 121
University of Aberdeen, Scotland, 149
University of South Florida (USF), 150, 151, 152, 203, 213
University of the West Indies, 115, 151, 191, 192, 194, 196, 202, 212; library, 213
University of Toronto, 148
Up Park Camp (WWII enemy alien internment camp) ,21, 22, 38, 164
Updike, John, 203
USA, 19, 41, 43, 44, 45, 124, 130, 148, 149, 152, 153, 162, 164, 169
USAID, 159, 160, 161
UWI Creative Arts Centre, 198, 202
Vaz, Noel, 34
Victoria Mutual building, 144
Victory Gardens, 20
Viet Nam, 74, 75
W E B Du Bois, 151
Walcott, *Another Life,* 211
Walcott, Derek,
Walcott, Derek, 152, 193, 197, 198, 199, 200, (photo, 201), 202, 203, 204, 205, 206, 207, 208, 209, 210, 211; Nobel Laureate, 207, 211, 212; family: Margaret (DW's second wife), 202, 204, 205; Peter (son by first wife), 205; Elizabeth, Lizzie, 202, 205 (daughter); Anna (daughter), 205; plays: *Ti Jean and his Brothers,* 200, 204; *Dream on Monkey Mountain,* 200, 203; *The Charlatan,* 200; *Franklin,* 200; *The Joker of Seville,* 200; *Remembrance,* 205; poems: "Sainte Lucie", 210; "Ruins of a Great House", 198; "Nearing Forty", 198
Waldorf Astoria, Park Avenue, 130
Walker, Wally, 153
Wallace, George (Major Adams' partner), 80, 81
Ward Theatre, 34; Foundation, 122
Washington, 194
Watson and Crick's DNA "double-helix", 151
Watson, Barrington, "Mother and Child", 144, 145
WEE CARE, 121
Weekley Lumber Company, 153, 157,

167; Johnny Weekley, 153, 154, 157, 168

Wellesley College, 84, 148, 149, 158, 204

Welty, Eudora, 203

West Indies and Caribbean Developments Ltd (WIC), 96, 97, 98, 99, 100, 101, 102, 103, 104, 106, 109

West Point, 46, 49

Wharton School of Finance, 148

Wherry Wharf, 15, 16, 17, 22, 35, 36, 44, 45, 55, 72, 78, 105, 106, 107, 108, 109, 110, 112, 113, 114, 115, 116, 117, 128, 131, 135, 136, 147, 153, 154, 171, 177, 178, 179

Wilbur, Richard, 203

Williams Pharmacology, 70

Williams, Esme (cook), 84

Williams, Israel, 113

Williamson, John, 180, 181, 182

Wilson, Major, 60

Wolman Wood Preserving Company, 153

Wolmer's Girls School, 13, 84

Women's Club, The, 122

Wong, Dr, 110

Wood, John and wife, 33; "Jamaica Palette", 33

World Trade Centre attack, 167

World War I, 21, 55

World War II, 20, 21, 43, 60, 86, 193

Yasuko (Japanese lover), 66, 67, 69, 79, 80

Yeats, W.B., 151

Yulee Drive (Thompson residence on), 156

Zaplisky family, 46

Ziadie, Millard, 82

ZQI (Jamaica's 1st broadcasting station), 29

The Denting of a Wave
ISBN: 9780948833625; pp. 88; pub. 1993; price £7.99

Rich in image, sonority and wit, Ralph Thompson's poems are the fruits of a maturity which has learned to confront the facts of life and death with both exuberance and dread. Humane and finely crafted, his poems are firmly rooted in Caribbean particularity, but are universal in their concerns. He has the story-teller's gift which grips, then leaves the reader pondering on the subtleties beneath the surface. This collection will establish him as a serious voice in West Indian poetry.

"First rate poetry... intelligent and gifted with a sense of humour" – Louis Simpson, *The Caribbean Review of Books*.

Moving On
ISBN 9781900715171; pp. 104; pub. 1998; price £8.99

The poems in *Moving On* recreate moments of change, loss and epiphany. There are vivid glimpses of a prewar Jamaican childhood – of sexual discovery under a billiard table and of the rude ingratitude of a goat saved from dissection in the school biology lab. The long sequence, "Goodbye Aristotle, So Long America", explores the years of study at a Jesuit university in America and the making both of a lifetime's values and of the sense of irony which has made it possible to live with them. Other poems reflect on the experience of ageing, of increasing vulnerability, but also of an increased appreciation for what sustains human relationships through time. Jamaica is present in these poems as a place of aching natural beauty, but whose violent human energies can only be viewed with an ambivalent love and fear, where: "In the city's bursting funeral parlours/ the corpses glow at night, nimbus of blue/ acetylene burning the darkness under the roof,/ lighting the windows – crunch of bone and sinew/ as a foot curls into a cloven hoof."

Thomas Reiter writes in *The Caribbean Writer*: "One of the many strengths of *Moving On* is its intricate and intelligent organization, overall and within each of the three units: 'Moving On', 'Crossings', and 'This New Light'. The first poem in the book, 'Looking Back', is a tuning fork to which texts resonate in their search for meaning through memory, that precious faculty that is forever 'trailing behind / like a cut anchor rope.' No doubt the poet concurs with Derek Walcott's statement in his Nobel lecture that 'all of the Antilles every island, is an effort of memory.' The focus of the initial grouping is 'Goodbye Aristotle, So Long America', an ambitious poem in eighteen sections. Topically wide-ranging and set in a variety of forms, the materials are variously political, theological, sexual, familial, and aesthetic. Moreover, those concerns appear in other poems in *Moving On*. Especially interesting are 'Mister Son', a persona poem done in patois, and 'Uncle Seymour', an illustration of Thompson's gift for storytelling, for piecing history together..."

Sheila Garcia-Bisnott writes in *The Weekly Gleaner*: "It is exquisite poetry throughout. Images of 'the sun turning cynical', 'the ocean, washing colonial guilt/like seaweed from an unrepentant beach', of 'an awning pulled up like the lid/of an eye afraid to blink' and of 'the lip of the sea and the lip of the sky/zip-locked the horizon' are pure art. *Moving On* is a feast."

The View from Mount Diablo
ISBN: 9781845231446; pp. 160; pub. 2003, 2009; price £12.99

View from Mount Diablo won the 2001 Jamaican National Literary Award.

A crime-novel in verse, *View from Mount Diablo* explores the transformation of Jamaica from a sleepy colonial society to a post-colonial nation where political corruption, drug wars, and avenging authorities have made life hell. The resentments class and racial privilege provoke underscore both the turmoil in society and the relationships at the heart of the narrative, between Adam Cole, a dreamy white boy driven by personal tragedy to crusading journalism, squint-eyed Nellie Simpson, once a servant, then a political enforcer, and stuttering Nathan, gardener and groom turned cocaine baron. Beyond this trio is a dazzling array of real and fictitious characters including Bustamante, coke-trade middleman Tony Blake, the informer Blaka, who finds religion, a corrupt plantation owner, and a murderous police officer.

In a time when 'Blood / cheaper than drugs', *View from Mount Diablo* asserts the power of art to tell the truth, to use form and selection of incident to shape unmanageable circumstance into meaningful narrative, and touch the heart to stir the citizen to action. Rich with religious implication, this is a prophetic work of exasperated love, abandoning the softening light of "an old romantic view" for a "harsh, uncompromising glare" and blending lyrical narrative with wrenching tragedy.

The 2009 annotated edition, edited by John Lennard, offers a full introduction situating Thompson's verse-novel in its formal, Caribbean, and global contexts, and provides detailed notes explicating background history, real events transposed into fiction, and the skilled foreshortening that maps an individual life onto a national calamity.

Louis Simpson, the Jamaican-American Pulitzer Prize-winning poet writes: "*View from Mount Diablo* is a remarkable achievement. Its knowledge of the island, the entwining of private lives and politics, lifts Jamaican poetry to a level that has not been attempted before. The poetry is strong, imaginative, fascinating in detail. It describes terrible things with understatement, yet with compassion. I don't think anything could be more harrowing than the rape of Chantal, or the boy begging Alexander to spare his life... This is narrative poetry at its best. Not only Jamaicans, but I think readers in England and the USA, will appreciate this book. It is something new."

Taking Words for a Walk: New and Selected Poems
ISBN: 9781845231958; pp. 144; pub. 2012; price £9.99

The selected poems in this collection, some significantly revised, both retain their original lustre and enter into a rewarding dialogue with a collection's worth of new poems. These display a remarkable octogenarian energy which sparks Thompson's range from narrative to lyric: ambition, rebellion, loss of innocence, memory, love, death and spiritual yearning are just some of the themes the poems explore. There is a tough honesty to Thompson's work, not confessional in a Lowell sense, but with insights rooted in experience and undiluted by any sense of "political correctness". As in previous collections there is an underlying seriousness leavened by wit and a self-deprecating humour. His world is an intensely Jamaican one, but his poems very consciously engage in a dialogue that is universal. Hailed as a "superb craftsman" by the *Routledge Encyclopaedia of Post Colonial Literature in English*, Thompson is at home in many forms: free verse, rhymed quatrains, haiku and villanelles – in patois or standard English. The centrepiece of the new work of *Taking Words for a Walk* is a long poem, "The Colour of Conscience", which explores the dynamics, personal and social, of being a white poet in a black country. The collection overflows with love of the beauty of Jamaica and its people, the dynamic that brings life to all his poems.

All available online from www.peepaltreepress.com,
or email sales@peepaltreepress.com
or write: Peepal Tree Press, 17 King's Avenue, Leeds LS6 1QS, UK
or phone +44 (0)133 2451703